AFTER
EMERSON

AMERICAN PHILOSOPHY
John J. Stuhr, *editor*

EDITORIAL BOARD
Susan Bordo
Vincent Colapietro
John Lachs
Noëlle McAfee
José Medina
Cheyney Ryan
Richard Shusterman

AFTER EMERSON

John T. Lysaker

INDIANA UNIVERSITY PRESS

This book is a publication of

Indiana University Press
Office of Scholarly Publishing
Herman B Wells Library 350
1320 East 10th Street
Bloomington, Indiana 47405 USA

iupress.indiana.edu

© 2017 by John T. Lysaker

All rights reserved

No part of this book may be reproduced or utilized in any form or by any means, electronic or mechanical, including photocopying and recording, or by any information storage and retrieval system, without permission in writing from the publisher. The Association of American University Presses' Resolution on Permissions constitutes the only exception to this prohibition.

♾ The paper used in this publication meets the minimum requirements of the American National Standard for Information Sciences—Permanence of Paper for Printed Library Materials, ANSI Z39.48-1992.

Manufactured in the United States of America

Library of Congress Cataloging-in-Publication Data

Names: Lysaker, John T., author.
Title: After Emerson / John T. Lysaker.
Description: Bloomington : Indiana University Press, 2017. | Series: American philosophy | Includes bibliographical references and index.
Identifiers: LCCN 2017017967 (print) | LCCN 2016048147 (ebook) | ISBN 9780253026033 (eb) | ISBN 9780253025982 (cl : alk. paper) | ISBN 9780253026002 (pb : alk. paper)
Subjects: LCSH: Philosophy, American—21st century. | Emerson, Ralph Waldo, 1803–1882.
Classification: LCC B946 (print) | LCC B946 .L97 2017 (ebook) | DDC 814/.3—dc23
LC record available at https://lccn.loc.gov/2017017967

1 2 3 4 5 22 21 20 19 18 17

For John Stuhr

Against Remorse.—A thinker sees his own deeds as experiments and questions—as the kind of things that bring about disclosures. Above all, success and failure are for him *answers*. To be annoyed or feel remorse because something goes wrong—that he leaves to those who act because they have received orders and have to reckon with a beating when his lordship is not satisfied with the result.

—*Friedrich Nietzsche*

CONTENTS

Acknowledgments   *xi*

   Where Do We Find Ourselves?   1
   Not with Syllables but Men   19
   Essaying America   40
   Living Multiplicity: A Matter of Course   61
   Emerson, Race, and the Conduct of Life   88
   Reforming Ethical Life   109
   Emerson and the Case of Philosophy   132

Abbreviations for Emerson's Works   *173*
Bibliography   *175*
Index   *181*

ACKNOWLEDGMENTS

This book, like all books, like all lives, appears with help. Some of that help has been institutional. Four of these essays were published previously, although those versions have been reworked in the context of the whole now assembled, hence new titles for most. "Where Do We Find Ourselves" appeared as "Finding My Way through Moral Space" in *Epoche: A Journal for the History of Philosophy* (vol. 17, no. 1, 2012); "Not with Syllables but Men" appeared as "Not with Syllables but Men: Emerson's Poetics of the Whole" in *Pragmatism Today* (Winter, 2011); "Essaying America" appeared in *Journal of Speculative Philosophy* (vol. 26, no. 3, 2012) as did "Reforming Ethical Life" under the title "Praxis and Form: Thirty Notes for an Ethics of the Future" (vol. 25, no. 2, 2011). My thanks go to those publications for their support and permission to rework and publish these pieces in the context of a book.

A year's leave at Emory's Fox Center for Humanistic Inquiry allowed me to finish the old and complete the new in a wonderful group of humanists. I will always remember 2015–2016 as one of the most productive I ever had.

Emory University is generous with its support for research. Funds from the office of Dean Robin Forman allowed me to hire Tony Leyh, who ably corralled several references and helped assemble the bibliography, and Rebekah Spera, who proofread and compiled the index. The Sire Program in undergraduate research also sponsored Vincent Xu, who ably helped me work through Emerson's texts in pursuit of terms such as race, slavery,

Negro, etc. That work was integral to what became "Emerson, Race, and the Conduct of Life."

My ongoing participation in the American Philosophies Forum has enabled me to be more ambitious as a writer, and one essay in particular, "Reforming Ethical Life," began there.

The Society for the Advancement of American Philosophy heard versions of "Not with Syllables but Men" and "Emerson, Race, and the Conduct of Life," and presenting them in that context helped make them better than they otherwise would be. (My first time through the issue of Emerson and race found me in the company of Melvin Rogers, whose deep smarts and learning were an ongoing benefit, particularly when we disagreed.) I am also just grateful that there is a society that welcomes forays into American romanticism.

Erik Vogt invited me to present the Blanchard W. Means Memorial Lecture at Trinity College in 2015. After discussing several topics, we settled on Emerson and race, which led the essay close to its present state. I was and remain grateful for the opportunity to share that work in such a receptive and engaging community.

When "Not with Syllables but Men" appeared in press, I dedicated it to two poets, Garrett Hongo and Terry Hummer. Both have deepened my ability to work with poetry (and thus with philosophy as well), and that persists, like my gratitude, across this volume. Thanks also to Garrett for inviting me to contribute to a phenomenal festschrift for Charles Wright published by *Northwest Review* (vol. 49, no. 2, 2011). My contribution has found its way into and enriched "Not with Syllables but Men."

"Essaying America" also had a first run at the Society for the Advancement of American Philosophy conference alongside papers by Cindy Willett and Shannon Sullivan, both of whom I continue to admire. It was its second run, however, at the Summer Institute of American Philosophy that led me to push it toward the character it now has. Scott Pratt and Erin McKenna were particularly engaged interlocutors, for which I am grateful. And even though we still hear the word "America" differently, I share the tradition of resistance that they exemplify and have documented, though more as a passive anarchist settling and unsettling a *terra infirma* than a philosophical citizen of something like "America."

"Living Multiplicity" grew out of what is now fifteen years of work with Paul Lysaker on the nature of schizophrenia and its impact on the course of a life, work that has also impacted, for the better, the course of my own. Thinking in clinical contexts and in the face of profound suffering brought me back to thoughts through which most of this volume flows. This essay significantly revises but remains continuous with what we presented together in chapter 3 of *Schizophrenia and the Fate of the Self* and earlier essays.

"Living Multiplicity" also reflects a decade of dialogues with Mark Johnson, who exemplifies genuine collegiality and friendship, which is often asymmetrical in its benefits, as in this case—I learned a good deal more than I was able to give.

"Where Do We Find Ourselves?" began as a paper on the work of my dissertation director, Charles Scott, which I gave at a conference in his honor. I would like that honor to carry over into this version.

I am not risk averse. The pages that follow make this plain. But being so is only possible in a larger context of support. One can go it alone for a spell because in general one is not. On many levels, Indiana University Press has supported my work in and now after Emerson. Dee Mortensen in particular has not only received and reviewed that work, improved it, but, in conversation, prodded it down more exciting lines of thought. At a DC meeting of the American Philosophical Association, she threw out the idea of a volume of essays and here we are. I am thankful to have had the opportunity to grow as a thinker and writer in her company. I would have had even less to offer if I had not.

Outside of any conceivable obligation, John Stuhr has always supported me without a glimmer of anticipation for some favor in return. This has allowed me to develop my thought outside the usual modes of specialization expected of those working in contemporary research universities, and with a degree of rhetorical ambition not always sought or rewarded in professional philosophy. This gift—which has given me to myself, and in a manner I find becoming—exceeds measure. I can only receive it in the abandon of an unqualified gratitude, which rises even as I type. As I dedicate this book to him, I hope these deeper currents crest the wave of that gesture.

Several publishers and literary agents have facilitated the reproduction of poems or portions of poems. Excerpts from "Shirt" from SELECTED POEMS by Robert Pinsky. Copyright © 2011 by Robert Pinsky. Reprinted by permission of Farrar, Straus and Giroux, LLC. "Star Turn" from NEGATIVE BLUE: SELECTED LATER POEMS by Charles Wright. Copyright © 2000 by Charles Wright. Reprinted by permission of Farrar, Straus and Giroux, LLC. "The Heavens" [9 l.] and excerpt of 12 l. from "the Flames" from THE THRONE OF THE THIRD HEAVEN OF THE NATIONS MILLENNIUM GENERAL ASSEMBLY: POEMS COLLECTED AND NEW by DENIS JOHNSON. Copyright (c) 1969, 1976, 1982, 1987, 1995 by

Denis Johnson. Reprinted by permission of HarperCollins Publishers. Excerpt of fifteen lines from "Santa Barbara road" from HUMAN WISHES by ROBERT HASS. Copyright (c) 1989 by Robert Hass. Reprinted by permission of HarperCollins Publishers. *Flow Chart* by John Ashbery. Copyright © 1991 by John Ashbery. Reprinted by permission of Georges Borchardt, Inc., on behalf of the author. All rights reserved. Lines from John Ashbery's FLOW CHART, Carcanet Press Limited, Manchester, 1991, also are reprinted by permission of Carcanet Press Limited. "The System" from *Three Poems* by John Ashbery. Copyright © 1970, 1971, 1972 by John Ashbery. Reprinted by permission of Georges Borchardt, Inc., on behalf of the author. All rights reserved.

AFTER
EMERSON

WHERE DO WE FIND OURSELVES?

Our being is descending into us from we know not whence.
—*Ralph Waldo Emerson*

—I. How do you inhabit the world? When you stretch, caress and kiss, when you read and write, *how* are you? If you were to give a descriptively rich and convincing account of yourself on this score, what terms would you use? Would you speak of muscles contracting and expanding, of circulatory systems, synapses, and the careful maintenance of body temperature? Would you speak of experiences you've had, of smells and sounds, of recurring thoughts and feelings, perhaps even commitments? Would you speak of the company you keep, of your parents or your country, of friends, enemies, colleagues? Would you speak of gender, race, sexuality, or some socioeconomic status? What of your culture, subculture, or generational demographic? Would you speak of a mentor, a hero, possibly a god, and the mark their presence (or absence) has left on your bearings?

How do you inhabit the world? If you were to give a descriptively rich and convincing account of yourself on this score, one you would comfortably offer as self-knowledge, what grammar would you use? Would you speak of those events and things that have made and continue to shape you, most without your say-so? Would you also speak of how you've undergone and engaged those events and things, submitted to some, resisted others, and conspired with those that seemed to open a path worth pursuing? Would you speak of the ones to whom you speak (including some future you), or of the very fact that you often address others without knowing it?

Are you of that address, say when responding to queries or speaking in the hope that you might be heard?

So much to say and so many ways to say it—events, experiences, I's and you's, we's and me's, handshakes, kisses, blinking eyes, words of hate and a cluster of toxins by a power plant that no one wants in their backyard but most are happy to have in yours. As you try to tell it, tell yourself, which voice will you use? When is it appropriate to speak in the passive? After all, it's hard to strut about as if we authored most of the ways we inhabit the world, despite the self-proclaimed lies of self-made men. Would you save the active voice for the influence of what-you-are-not upon what-you-are? Or is it push and pull, everything active and colliding? Or would you venture an account in the middle voice, one neither active nor passive? Do we need a distinct voice to say our part in how a human life does its thing in events like understanding, wanting, not feeling like it, just finding our way?

However you reply, and I hope you have, do you simultaneously address how well you inhabit the world, how it goes it for you? Do you simultaneously (which is not to say equally) consider what your bearing does for, perhaps even to, others? Is some sense of success, goodness, pleasure, mediocrity, justice, virtue, duty, happiness, or flourishing woven through your sense of how you inhabit the world? Can you reply without evaluating the ways you inhabit the world? Or is an evaluation of such ways itself a way?

"How do you inhabit the world?" A certain kind of philosophy is woven into this question, though not in any professional sense. Questions concerning our place in nature, our character, our continuities and discontinuities with one another, other animals, with things are as much a part of our bearing as questions about dinner, the affections of another, or where the sun goes after dusk. We are constantly giving voice to what seems constant, to what recurs. I say this because human cultures mark rites of passage surrounding birth, procreation, and death, and they do so with images and stories that situate us in some larger drama, say of ancestors, mountains, gods, final battles, heaven and earth. From a sense of balance to an anticipation for summer, from the thought, "if only they could see me now" to our feel for what this might mean in the big scheme of things, humans continually orient themselves and I take each to count as a reply to a question like "how do you inhabit the world," a reply that might say, like a bear, as the rational animal, if only like a rose.

"How do you inhabit the world?" A certain kind of philosophy is woven into this question, and if it is quick on its feet, it becomes apparent that the question has already replied to its own query. In pausing to ask and formulate the question, one already inhabits the world in a determinate manner. As Heidegger made evident in *Sein und Zeit*, not only is philosophy a way of inhabiting the world, but also, questions, any question, only arise out of determinate inhabitations. No reflective act marks the point at which we begin to inhabit the world. Not just the Owl of Minerva flies at dusk. Reflection itself is retrospective, a response to how we have already responded to a world in which we are prereflectively enmeshed.

How do you inhabit the world? Emerson titled his sixth collection of essays *The Conduct of Life*. Published in 1860, the collection was rendered into German in 1862 as *Die Führung des Lebens*. As Heikki Kovalainen reports, the volume so struck the young Nietzsche that he recounted the collision in two very early essays, "Fatum und Geschichte" and "Willensfreiheit und Fatum," both of which quote Emerson at length (Kovalainen 2010). But that is not why I recall *The Conduct of Life*. The title, like this earlier line from "The American Scholar" of 1837, is instructive: "I do not see how any man can afford, for the sake of his nerves and his nap, to spare any action in which he can partake. It is pearls and rubies to his discourse. Drudgery, calamity, exasperation, want, are instructors in eloquence and wisdom. The true scholar grudges every opportunity of action past by, as a loss of power" (CW1, 59). Actions instruct, particularly when marked by friction, when the world insists, which it always does at some level or other. There, where we find the world in our way, the character of our life becomes salient. Habits are thrown into relief, and as habits, and so too moods, even temperament—fluctuating, affective orientations that Emerson finds whenever he finds objects. But more than our bearings prove salient in action. The world, in its continuities with and differences from our bearings, also makes itself known in our doing, whether in experimental conditions or daily pursuits, though also in our arrivals and relations. Think of a lover's unexpected hesitation—a familiar hand suddenly trembles with something other than desire, and we tremble as we sense what is beginning to arrive. Or think of the history that resides, unsettled in words like Chappaqua, Umpqua, or Chattahoochee. How does one name it? "Genocide" leaps to mind but shatters against all it gathers, though the clamor bears some witness to horror. Undone by a different horror, Celan nevertheless offers an instructive thought.

> Before your late face,
> a lone-
> wandering between
> nights that change me too,
> something came to stand,

which was already with us once, un-
touched by thoughts. (Celan 1995—translation modified)

Untouched by thoughts? Every day these words—Chappaqua, Umpqua, or Chattahoochee—are said and read. And the dead buried therein persist only in the further indignity heaped on them. But if we catch the insult, and mark it, a bit of the world makes itself known.

And then there is this for those who labor to find themselves. To the degree you can, work your mind into the pull of genes on what has become your hand, your tooth, the stirrup, anvil, and hammer, taste buds, and synaptic gates. Think of your cells regenerating, some possibly going rogue. What is your breakfast doing now? Its sugars, its fats, its fiber? How long have you've been sitting there?

A kind of eloquence accompanies our thoughts and deeds; they say a good deal about how we inhabit the world and the world we inhabit. We thus need to hear Emerson's 1860 collection in two registers. In the conduct of life, life is conducted. (Again and again we will labor with what is possibly a third sense.) But this is perhaps too easy, as if one might read from deeds the truth of one's inhabitation, as if actions not only were louder than words, but clearer, more distinct. But suppose that the conduct of life does not simply express some substantial nature lurking and coursing through us. Push past the figure-ground gestalt and accept the pull and push that is the world and your rolls therein. Because conduct conducts, how we inhabit the world is in part a function of how we have inhabited the world, and a material variable in the world we inhabit. Following Wordsworth, and independent of any natural piety, the child fathers the man—although these cycles of birth and rebirth are, as you know, more than a matter of fathers and sons.

In finding the conduct of life generative, I also find myself recalled to the opening phrase of Emerson's "Experience," where he asks: "Where do we find ourselves?" (CW3, 29) On a first reading, "ourselves" seems to be his principal concern. But as the essay proceeds, a different focus comes into view, one illumined by Stanley Cavell (1989) in "Finding as Founding." Across "Experience," Emerson repeatedly returns to the task of finding his footing in life's buck and sway, in the "evanescence and lubricity of all objects," which he terms the "most unhandsome part of our condition" (CW3, 29). In fact, by the essay's close, finding the where of our lives, locating the evolving limits at which we find ourselves (which Emerson figures as the "lords of life"), finding becomes the focal concern of an Emersonian account of how we inhabit the world. More elaborately, I would say that our conductivity runs along a coil. We find ourselves conducting life and that finding both adds to the current we later find and opens that current to intensifications, redirections, and displacements.

——II. I asked, "how do we inhabit the world" and I found determinate ways of inhabiting already in the asking. I asked again and found that should I turn in any direction, even inward, the world meets me as I go. I asked again and found that modes of inhabiting the world also conduct life, opening and closing futures for me, for you, but also for so much more than either. The question, "how do you inhabit the world" is thus also a question of "how do you conduct the world." But not just that; we are not simply wires, or so I want to say, having found finding. Said otherwise, the conduct of life, at least in our case, is tied to self-finding, to how we locate ourselves and respond to that location.

But all these plays with "conduct" and "finding," with "currents" and "location" suggest another facet of what I am now terming our conductivity. Where do we find ourselves? In language, though I hasten to add, *as we work at finding*. Words and phrases, grammars and genres, they mark another lord of life, one that, as Emerson has it, "we find in our way." Our way runs through language, and along that way, we quote its long histories, follow its suggestiveness, embrace its grammars, fuss with its nuances, and try to say things just-so: "black hole," "being-in-the-world," "I can't tell you how sorry I am," "Bah-bah-bahbah, bah-bah-bahbah, I wanna be sedated." To find oneself within language is thus to find the task of finding oneself thickened. Cavell, again on point: "Emerson will say, or show, that words demand conversion or transfiguration or reattachment" (1989, 82).

By way of Emerson, I've been retracing thoughts one might find elsewhere, most notably in *Sein und Zeit*, though also, with important differences, in *Experience and Nature*, and then with other differences in thinkers such as William James, Simone de Beauvoir, and Merleau-Ponty, and behind them all, with more differences still, in Hegel. I see no necessity in proceeding as I did. It may be that I find myself still in the current of Emerson's texts, and certain phrases in particular, but that does not establish Emerson as the obvious author to essay in the context of self-knowledge. Numerous others have engaged the question. The sheer plurality of perspectives and styles that constitute *Souls of Black Folk* continues to astonish and instruct. But I will not spend the day in explanation, as Emerson himself says in "Self-Reliance" following a startling conversion of two scriptural covenants: "I shun father and mother and wife and brother, when my genius calls me.

I would write on the lintels of the doorpost Whim. I hope it is somewhat better than whim at last, but we cannot spend the day in explanation" (CW2, 30). Instead, this thought, the conduct of life in and as self-finding, is one I would bring into conversation with two contemporaries.

In *Sources of the Self*, Charles Taylor tries to establish a range of transcendental conditions circumscribing what I have been calling the conduct of life in and as self-finding. According to Taylor, we find ourselves as selves always already within moral spaces (or frameworks) that locate our lives relative to some sense of the good. In fact, Taylor believes that questions such as "how do you inhabit the world" and "where do we find ourselves" only make sense in a moral space organized by a framework, hence his invocation of the transcendental. If we cannot answer the question "to what end?," such questions, qua actions, are senseless, wind in dry grass, sound without fury, bah-bah-bahbah, bah-bah-bahbah, no need for sedation. In other words, we ask such questions because they enable us to "know where we stand," which is to say: (1) to know what we stand for, and (2) to know how well we are doing. And only that kind of knowledge, or rather its pursuit, gives life meaning. "Not to have a framework," Taylor concludes, "is to fall into a life which is spiritually meaningless" (1989, 18).

I turn to Taylor because I wonder whether my insistence that the conduct of life is more than expression is bounded by Taylor's conception of moral space and its inevitable frameworks. I hope not. If he is right, I not only have to spend the day in explanation but my whole life. "One could put it this way," Taylor writes: "because we cannot but orient ourselves to the good, and thus determine our place relative to it and hence determine the direction of our lives, we must inescapably understand our lives in narrative form, as a quest" (1989, 51–52).

In presenting his case, Taylor has a threat in mind: naturalism. He fears that we might regard our moral space as the result of something "adventitious," and that is his word, though I am happy to take it as my own, even my ownmost. He doesn't offer a gallery of villains who propose such a view, but one could imagine evolutionary psychologists, historical materialists, and genealogists alike presenting frameworks, moral or otherwise, in terms of the adventitious, that is, as derivative. Perhaps Taylor doesn't engage particular views because he regards the point as formal, something like: my rivals may confront me with discoveries of the adventitious but such findings are nevertheless discoveries, in other words, actions that derive their bearings from some sense of the good at which they aim. Yes, one can have different frameworks and thus rival, even evolving goods, but the very idea of a framework and the moral space it provides remains aloof from the high seas of material and cultural *metabolé*.

A very long road awaits one who would prove that frameworks are in fact grand adventures in the adventitious, so let me limit my resistance to an observation that I find telling. Moral space seems to be the kind of thing that infants and children grow into, and out of which the very aged and infirm can fall. And no doubt the same is true of the species, that is, even if Nietzsche is wrong about how we came to make promises, there is no longer any good reason to think that our teleological bearings are something other than adventitious in an evolutionary sense. In other words, moral space is a *result*, hence subject to liminal zones and transitions. And those are zones in which we can find ourselves as if on a stair, unsure of where we've been, unsure of where we're going, to recall the second sentence of Emerson's "Experience." I thus do not think that moral space marks anything like a transcendental condition. Instead it names a long-standing location where we have found ourselves. But it is not immune to the kind of dislocation that occurs when we find the where of our finding.

One could imagine Taylor objecting: but the very language of finding begs the question. What good orients that reflexivity, that practice of self-knowledge? What gives that activity meaning? In reply I would say: it depends on where I find myself. If I find myself at a point of genesis with regard to moral space, as I do when I read Emerson despite (or even because of) his theological insistences, I am inclined to say: nothing gives meaning to the emergence of something like a bearing toward the good or the way in which my fingers tug at it, into it, fingering the seam. And in saying this, I find myself quoting the essay "Circles," which says, with startling clarity: "The way of life is wonderful: it is by abandonment" (Emerson, CW2, 190). "Abandonment" is the decisive term. Where do we find ourselves? Abandoned to some where of finding, perhaps oriented toward the good, one that might bring a whole life together, imbue it with meaning. But there is no "good" toward which the finding of moral space is itself oriented and thus should we find ourselves committed to settling moral ranges, that affirmation will require a term like "abandonment," in the sense of surrender, though also leave-taking and departure—possibilities foregone, locales abandoned.

In pushing past the limits that Charles Taylor would draw around the conduct of life, I am not abandoning in toto the form of life he outlines in *Sources of the Self*. I do not mind spending an hour or two in explanation, as I hope this essay makes clear. But I am trying to engage that form and self-knowledge more generally without phrases such as "transcendental conditions." Such terms efface their own finding, their own telling, hide the ways along which such terms were chanced upon, essayed, converted, transformed. Keeping to Emerson, I would say they hide their own whimsy, adding that "whim-wham," which gave us "whim," denotes an ornamental object without a purpose beyond the flourish it bestows. And wonderfully, the phrase has no known origin.

—III. Unlike Taylor in *Sources of the Self*, Charles Scott has perched himself at the rim of where we find ourselves. In a series of books since 1990, his work has moved in and out of moral space and so it seems to conduct itself at the precise juncture that awaits whoever abandons "transcendental conditions" with regard to where we find ourselves. Refusing any deep distinction between the moral and ethical, Scott conceives of ethics as a "body of values by which a culture understands and interprets itself with regard to what is good and bad" (1990, 4) in each and every instance. That is, ethics (like a "framework" in Taylor's sense) governs the conduct of life in a way that brings it unity and ultimate purpose, either by orienting each action toward the good or giving it the pristine form of the right.

Scott does not define ethics in order to propose his own body of values, however. Rather, he wishes to interrogate how bodies of values conduct life. Books like *The Question of Ethics* seek to (1) uncover the adventitious in the manifold genesis of such bodies, and (2) expose the violence wrought by such bodies upon the characters and lives they norm. The point of the first exercise, conducted along the lines of Nietzschean and Foucaultian genealogy, is to underscore the accidental origins of any body of values (e.g., the fury of priests or the drift of confessional practices into doctors' offices and school boards). And Scott takes such analyses to open sites of possibility where something like necessity once claimed us. They enable us to look away, as Nietzsche might say. The second exercise, as I understand it, affects a nondialectical immanent critique. The critique is immanent because it exposes how a body of values conducts a life very close to what it purports to ward off.

Kant's genuinely *good* will is a site where such a critique might take hold. On my reading, repurposed from the pages of *Dialectic of Enlightenment*, Kant's version of morality masks a sadomasochistic asceticism that wills, as universal law, the renunciation of inclination for the purpose of renunciation—or so it seems given Kant's rigid metaphysics of the will. First, the *Critique of Pure Reason* limits causality to the phenomenal and hence to the materially observable, and in that realm, the will is not given as free (or even given, but that is a matter for another essay). It thus seems as if

Kant's moral theory not only asks us to renounce the only known source of motivation, but also in the name of a purity that is in principle unachievable. But what about Kant's distinction between choosing (*Willkür*) and willing (*Wille*) in his *Metaphysics of Morals* (1999, 6:211–6.214)? According to Kant, choosing makes use of various concepts (e.g., wants and imperatives), whereas willing concerns the grounds of those concepts and whether they are rational. If we only will what is universalizable, and if we only choose what we rationally will, autonomy results. But Kant never succeeds in establishing the reality of a will that has no "determining ground." Moreover, by isolating the rational will from the capacity to choose, Kant must explain how choosing decides between the full array of motivations at its disposal, which reintroduces the very problem the distinction hoped to solve. It thus seems that by renouncing inclination in the name of what can only be another inclination, an asceticism of the highest order is on offer.

I have worked into Kant along lines operative in Scott's work, exposing something other than the good will in Kant's account of the good will. And in a way, this is a kind of immanent critique. Kant's thought of the good will fails to be good on his own terms. Something else is at work. Yet unlike Hegel, Scott does not pursue critiques of this sort in order to redeem the inner truth of our ways of inhabiting the world, which in this case, would leave us with a better will if not a wholly good one. Nor does he "cancel" bodies of values whenever they conduct futures at odds with themselves. In fact, in Scott's work, these currents do not proceed in any linear, developmental manner. Instead, they move toward possibilities for other ways of inhabiting the world, and without the need to dismiss rivals with terms like false consciousness or irrationality.

Though I have highlighted the interruptive force of Scott's movement in and out of moral space, indeterminate negation does not exhaust the impact of his writing. As it proceeds, Scott's work finds itself claimed by various affective attitudes, what I have cast as a way (or part of a way) of conducting life. And his are characteristically affirmative. Let me try to be concrete. Imagine that you find yourself always searching for the good, living the quest vouchsafed by moral space. Suddenly, you find your way to its rim and turn, startled. The road taken might not have been taken. If you are at all like me, you will feel astonished by the accidental cast of it all, that moral space was and endures when it could just as well not have been, at least not in this singular manner. The earth might never have congealed and hardened to the point that we have somewhere to make a stand, and we might never have tilted upright on two legs such that we could stand, and so we might never have acquired the metaphor, "take a stand." Or evolution might have unfolded us into brains whose deep motivational centers worked more or less unchecked in the presence of foes or food. Or no one might have fallen (as, one falls in love) for the idea that mortal life is worth living if and only if it secures a heavenly bridegroom.

I turn to astonishment because it seems to arise in the very movement in and out of moral space that characterizes Scott's texts. "Astonishment," he writes, "is, as it were, an awareness of an escape from meanings and completed totalities" (2002, 15). In other words, astonishment is not some good toward which Scott's thought moves but a way in which we appear as we find ourselves in our adventitious origins. Scott's affirmation of astonishment is thus not bound by moral space, though, as the preceding discussion attests, I could imagine being astonished by moral space, by the vast, inspiring, and sometimes terrible orders it raises.

But perhaps this is too abstract. Let me thus turn your attention to Scott's recollection of an encounter with Wal-Mart. Scott finds Wal-Mart in a moral space whose telos is an ever-increasing profit margin. So oriented, Wal-Mart is more or less indifferent to both the overall economic well-being of the communities it purports to serve and the welfare of those lives that enable ridiculously cheap goods to appear on its shelves. Early one morning, gazing into the heavens, astonished by their sheer indifference to our fate as well as by the beauty to be found there despite that indifference (or even because of it), Scott found himself thinking of Wal-Mart. And it dawned on him that Wal-Mart's indifference was nothing in comparison to the utter indifference of the heavens whose sublime mechanics flow through the formation of our planet and the lives still evolving on it, including a life, straight out of Arkansas, that lived to "stomp the comp," that is, Sam Walton. So struck, Scott's thought began to move and Wal-Mart began to rise. Scott writes: "I can say retrospectively that there was something beautiful about Wal-Mart in that moment, although I hardly noticed it in the shock of its arrival. It shone without glare in its translation. In that appearance there was nothing of care or value. Certainly no competitiveness. It was just there in an element of indifference that it could not own or trade; it was taken from itself and remained in a beautiful event of con-fusion that didn't last very long" (2007, 158). In Scott's recollection, one finds a kind of rapt and pleasured attention to the sheer presence of things in their indifference, to what the rocker Robert Pollard has called "the cruel and sometimes perfect impartiality of the sun." And as his essay ends, Scott proposes that a beauty of this sort draws us out of moral space insofar as moral space eclipses the shining of that indifferent light. "In this indifference," he claims, "we can find something of beauty in Wal-Mart's appearance, something surprising that can lift people's spirits from the circumspection of our ethos.... Indifference to lives seems to be part of this strangeness that is part of the draw in beautiful appearances" (ibid., 160).

I have pursued this extended example because it shows how movement in and out of moral space can generate nonmoral ways of conducting life, such as with astonishment and a dazed feel for the beauty of cosmic indifference. The example also shows how self-finding conducts life in a manner that does more than reiterate antecedent states of affairs we might be tempted to term transcendental conditions; it can be generative and transfigurative on its own.

Being astonished, attending to beauty, Scott weaves these occurrences into something of an ethos, though he more or less admits in *The Lives of Things* that he has yet to come to terms with this term: "Whatever we decide to call it, in speaking of it, I wish to speak of an affirmation of things as we find them appearing, an affirmation of what we find of the world by our most determined and experimental knowledge, and of the ways we find things occurring in the world. These affirmations occur in a release of people and things to their epiphanies with emptiness—in an absence of expectation for meanings or glories that transcend worldly occurrence" (2002, 183). Returning to this passage again, I am struck by its recurring use of "find" and I take its repetition to indicate that what lurks in this term "ethos," at least as Scott employs it, is something close to what I have been elaborating in my conversions and transformations of Emerson. Confronted by Emerson's query, Scott would reply, I imagine, that we find ourselves (that is, how we inhabit the world), in an affirmative release (perhaps an abandonment) to the conduct of life as we find it in our way.

I note the intersection of these Emersonian terms and Scott's affirmative ethos for several reasons. First, I find the conductivity of the term "ethos" constraining in this context. It doesn't do justice, to my ear at least, to the myriad activities through which we find ourselves conducting life, activities that allow an ethos to be an ethos. Not that we are given to ourselves in an event fully accountable within the terms of agency, Hegel's brilliance notwithstanding. But I would insist that how we conspire with our fate, with the indifferent cast of our lives, becomes part of the fate wherein we later find ourselves conducting life. I have thus proposed a different run of terms and phrases for what one could call an ethos.[1] Second, I think the intersection of these Emersonian terms with Scott's work shows how the latter involves a recoiling praxis of self-knowledge, that Scott's work wins its affirmations by attending, unreservedly, to where it finds itself. But Scott's achievement occurs in such a way, and this is my third point, that the practice of self-knowledge is freed from the limits of moral space and so it acquires a richer, more intense conductivity than Emerson's thought can vouchsafe (at least in its theodical moments). Finally, I think my Emersonian language, particularly "conduct" and "abandonment," allows me to locate a thought that I would amend.

Return, if you would, to the constellation Wal-Mart and the translation Scott witnessed.

What gives me pause is that without care or value, without competitiveness, I don't think we can speak any longer of "Wal-Mart," either in its general character, what a Hegelian social theorist might term its historical essence, or in the singularity of each store (to the degree that something like singularity obtains there). Wal-Mart has an organizing logic that distinguishes a characteristic way of inhabiting the world, of conducting life. (Otherwise it couldn't replicate itself with such wild success and we wouldn't be able to speak of its "business model.") Moreover, it is a logic organized around the competitive pursuit and accumulation of capital. But if we erase that logic, we lose what gives Wal-Mart its character. And so, I don't think "Wal-Mart" survives the "translation" that Scott's sidereal gaze affects. Instead, that astonishment abandons "Wal-Mart" and converts it into some other phenomenon that shimmers with a kind of beauty that awaits those who step *jenseits* moral space.

I underscore the disappearance or conversion of Wal-Mart in Scott's translating vision in order to suggest something more general. Astonishment, for all its open regard, is derivative. Said otherwise, there is no simple "release of people and things to their epiphanies with emptiness," only a release to where we find ourselves conducting life in some particular, factically situated fashion. But I don't say this to advance perspectivalism, let alone idealism. (I'm unwilling to employ the tenets of either to capture the ways in which we conduct life.) Rather, my point is that any responsive regard for the world, moral or otherwise, is always conducting life and thus is always something more than a simple release.[2]

I suppose I also underscore the derivative nature of astonishment to facilitate a return to Emerson. Near the close of "Experience," he recalls the lords of life and confesses: "I dare not assume to give their order, but I name them as I find them in my way. I know better than to claim any completeness for my picture. I am a fragment, and this is a fragment of me" (CW3, 47). Because each self-finding is bound to its where, it is partial, a fragment of a larger event to which it belongs and knows it belongs given the marks and traces that its own transformations retain; moral space is partial, astonishment is partial, an eye for the beauty of the heavens is a partial eye. And so I would stress, with what I hope is nuance, that we find ourselves in our partialities, continuous as they are with the world, and I would share with you the joy and astonishment I find in that occurrence, that is, "I am a fragment" need not ring with melancholy, for that is all I have ever found myself to be.

——IV. But is it enough? Charles Taylor's objection to moving *jenseits* moral space is not only descriptive but normative—such a bearing risks, perhaps inevitably finds spiritual meaninglessness. The charge is dramatic and reflects serious concerns. Spiritual meaninglessness names, I presume, the discovery—the finding—that life is not worth living. But what kind of discovery is this? It may be that, all told, life's burdens and losses so outweigh its consolations that one would rather have never been born. This is a calculative discovery. Or, it may be that spiritual meaning only occurs within moral space, and thus, by definition, a life outside moral space is meaningless. This is a categorical discovery, and probably the one that Taylor has in mind, since he is likely to argue that the measure relied on in the calculative option sets one within the confines of moral space. It runs like this. If one finds X meaningful, one will find oneself in moral space oriented toward a good toward which one is more or less well on the way. A phenomenon is meaningful, therefore, because its realization inches one along. And even if one fails, at least one tried.

Before addressing it, let me try to clarify the question before us. "Astonishment" is one thing, "affirmation" another. The former unsettles, the latter settles, and at least in two senses. It finds value of some sort in the affirmed, thus settling the question of its worth, and it declares that one will settle there, bind oneself to the affirmed, say for an afternoon, as with a movie, for the period of a contract, as with a job, perhaps even for a foreseeable life, as when we say "I do." But what does affirmation entail for those who do not affirm on the basis of a good within moral space?

I want to reply by way of a poem, or rather, part of a poem I've already invoked. "The Flames" recounts a bus trip in which the speaker awakens to find a farmhouse ablaze, a "fire burning furiously in the dark" (Johnson 1982, 55–56). Recalling what was seen, the speaker then remembers "something I could only have imagined," a sound—"reins breaking / the bones in the farmer's hands / as the horses reared and flew back into the flames / he wanted to take away from." And that memory of what was never perceived (and most likely never happened) forces an inward turn, which closes the poem.

My thoughts are like that,
turning and going back where nothing wants them,
where the door opens and a road
of light falls through it
from behind you and pain
starts to whisper with your voice;
where you stand inside your own absence,
your eyes still smoky from dreaming,
the ruthless iron press
of love and failure making
a speechless church out of your dark
and invisible face.

By unsettling moral space, in finding its adventitious roots, and in keeping them adventitious, in other words, sporadic, arriving from we know not whence, one has the sense of thoughts that travel where no one wants to go, particularly if, as Taylor has it, personhood congeals in the stances one assumes in moral space. But even more trenchantly, the adventitious is subjectless, and irrespective of whether the arrival thereby named is natural, historical, or both. (Evolution is historical through and through.) It stands neither as the act of an agent nor the mode of a substance, and thus, strictly speaking, it also is not "accidental," a privative term meaning insubstantial in a strict sense. To think a human phenomenon through the adventitious is thus to think one's own absence, to step behind the back of one's self-regulating systems, conscious or otherwise, and to tarry there without finding any of the great author-functions of philosophy, such as divinity, the cogito, *Geist*, the working class, self-interest, the unconscious, the transcendental ego, the inductive generalizer of infinite inquiry, or the pragmatic reckoner.

"The Flames" is a poem of the adventitious. Following out the memory of a perception that never happened, it finds words on a whim. But as it reaches the limits of its saying it persists, joining the conflagration, fanning it with "eyes still smoky from dreaming," finding his or her *I* now a *you* who is not another *I*, but speechless, unable to reply. Yet neither is it an *it*, just some function of a representational system. It has a certain bearing, a way of carrying itself and the world, a way of orienting itself within the world, even a way of bringing forth certain futures. Somewhere between a *what* and a *who*, traced at the grammatical edge of a phenomenological reduction, the speaker witnesses a countenance of mute praise behind the visible face, a "speechless church." One might think a church only a house of worship. But in demarcating a sacred space, in claiming it, in calling for a bearing distinct from how we get about malls and offices, a church proclaims hallelujah in wood, stone, or steel (or charged tissue). Manifesting praise, it exhorts others to do likewise.

By finding a figure of praise inside his or her own absence, the speaker articulates a kind of affirmation that might allow us to begin to think affirmation in a nonmoral sense. In "The Flames," praise arises in our absence but nevertheless courses through the "ruthless iron press / of love and failure," a wonderful phrase that grants qualitatively rich occurrences (being in love, failing) the character giving power that Platonists reserve for *eidos*. As with Emerson and Taylor, the presumption is that conduct conveys who we are. But in Johnson's lines (to the degree they are his), something pulses beyond the reach of any self-styling, tracking, and/or recuperating ipseity. The poem presents praise *in*, which is not to say *of* the absence of authorship for that with which and as which we pass, say how we fall in love, the way it claims us, even if we resist, or the way in which our failures come about through bad luck, the stumbles of others, even our own weaknesses. These are defining occurrences and Johnson's poem is thinking of a praise that arises with them in their occurrence without graphing them as advances or regressions in moral space. Praise, like the image in the eye of Rilke's panther pacing about its cage, one that "runs through the limb's strained silence, and in the heart subsides." A surge of feeling, a "dance of strength around a middle" that rises up and passes away (1955/1966, band 2, 505). Yet whereas the will of Rilke's caged panther is driven back into itself, and Rilke writes of *ein grosser Wille*, the speaker in Johnson's poem is bearing witness to what exists in its evanescence, whose roots lie in *vanescere*, "to vanish," and *vanus*, "empty."

This is praise in an extramoral sense. It is not buoyed by any measure, ethical or otherwise. Because it does not occur by way of some transcendent guarantee, one that insures that the praised is praiseworthy, this is praise without measure. Second, in this sense praise does not arise in the form of a judgment, that is, it is not the product of a subject who deems something praiseworthy, say life or chaos or the sublimity of an expanding universe (or the electrical currents that enable our conduct). That is not its grammar we might say, albeit poorly, metaphorizing sentences to address what does not occur as sentences.

Before saying more about why it lies beyond ethics, let me concretize the praise poetized in "The Flames." This is not the stoic freedom that Hegel properly chastises, a relentless negation cast as if it were something positive, say acceptance (Hegel 1977, 119–122). Nor is this the *amor fati* that Adorno rightly insists is born in the prison, a cosmological identification with the aggressor, the love of that which one has seen and accepted for what it is—destiny (Adorno 1974, 98). In either case, what is accepted or even loved has been won through the labor of the concept: the not-me that the stoic ignores, the destiny that a lover of fate embraces. Said otherwise, in either case judgment foregrounds affirmation, erecting itself atop a reality with which it makes its peace. In pushing past that foreground, stepping into its own absence, Johnson's poem finds a praise whose affirmation does not arise through the recoils of reflexivity.

Another Johnson poem, "The Heavens," complements this thought.

> From mind to mind
> I am acquainted with the struggles
> of these stars. The very same
> chemistry wages itself minutely
> in my person.
> It is all one intolerable war.
> I don't care if we're fugitives,
> we are ceaselessly exalted, rising
> like the drowned out of our shirts (1995, 162)

This poem comes to mind whenever I encounter a thought of measureless affirmation. It acknowledges and embraces what I have been terming the adventitious in its who, its "mind to mind," which I take in an intra- and intersubjective sense. In the iron-press of love and failure, *our* being rises as us from we know not whence, to rewrite Emerson's phrase. Whereas "The Flames" reaches into our absence, "The Heavens" embraces our fugitive status in the "intolerable war" of energy transfer, which knows only frictions. Fugitive? We seek different terms than chemistry affords, "I" and "you," "love" and "failure," terms of our own finding and making, terms appropriate for beings that can be created and destroyed, for beings that have a "minute" sense of "my person." But like "The Flames," if from the lips of a visible face, it also gives praise to what enables us to be us, claiming that, even if we are fugitives from the impersonal mechanics of heartbeats and tides, eyesight and sun spots, we are exalted: we rise, intensify, and take place in and with praise (to recall three meanings of "exalt").

But why is a measureless praise that exceeds the confines of the judgment, both in terms of form and content, outside moral space? Most immediately, it remains immanent to its occurrence, selves and the world relentlessly unfolding, and thus its affirmation avoids the lifelong reaches that moral space aims to survey. More generally, though, it seems to operate with an extramoral sense. Irrespective of whether one distinguishes ethics from morality, both require (1) a measure (or value or principle), even if given as affect, which distinguishes moral from immoral, ethical from unethical, (2) a capacity to apprehend that measure, (3) a capacity to judge the world according to that measure, and (4) a capacity to commit to a life in accordance with that measure. But the praise that Johnson's poems present does not conform to that *Gestalt*, or pattern, even form, but remains immersed in the prereflective currents of the conduct of life. Instead, it arises in and keeps to an abandonment to the pulsing currents it conducts.

But is it enough? Is something like spiritual meaning possible for those who abandon themselves to affirmations without measure, affirmations that do not commence with judgments but with the current of a nonreflexive occurrence? Meaning, in its spiritual (or existential) form, confers worth on actions and events, particularly when suffering and loss is involved. In other words, "meaning," when found, allows one to affirmatively reply when asked: "was it worth it?" (A negative reply might be: "well, that was a waste of time," which for a mortal being, is living death.)

The praise I found in "The Heavens" is emphatic on this very score. "I don't care if we are fugitives, we are ceaselessly exalted." And the "speechless church" in "The Flames" bears its own, clear reply. Set into a fully discursive register, the claim is that the "ruthless iron press / of love and failure" confers meaning in its occurrence, or it doesn't. Meaning, like our being, descends into us (or rises with us) from we know not where, or it doesn't. It arrives ahead of criteria and thus we find it in our way, or we do not.

Admittedly, if meaning arrives with the adventitious, no life will ever appear to itself as a whole, and thus, with regard to a life, the question, was it worth it, proves abstract, except in a calculative sense. This is not Heidegger's point in *Being and Time*, which rests on the fact that our death, which defines us in part, will never be disclosed to us given that its appearance announces our disappearance. Nor is this the karmic point that Aristotle considers, namely, that the very activity or being-at-work of our lives (our *energeia*), continues after our deaths, such that what we stood for only comes to light in our wake. It differs because these problems arise when our time runs out. But to be adventitious is to be riddled, at heart, by subjectless occurrences, including the emergence of the species and its, our, breathtaking nervous energies; including the emergence of moral space and one's language; including the fact that one's parents met, stressed character, and afforded one opportunities wherein, without the threat of violence, one could to *thine own self be true*; including the sheer luck that one's talents and auto-affections coincided; including the raced and gendered privilege that no one batted an eye when one presumed to speak; including a remarkable fortune—so many teachers taught courses as if their subjects mattered to students who mattered; including the fact that one never died driving drunk or went to jail for a freezer full of LSD; including the historical fact that such a thing as the *profession* of philosophy brought more than a living wage and allowed one to structure a life around reading and talking (about reading and talking about life) until, at fifty, one turns around and wonders whether the whole shebang has been the slow unfolding of a vocation or a series of collisions and responses, fugitively managed, each testifying, in its occurrence, to its worth (or not).

But if the unity of *a* life splinters with the adventitious, then meanings and purposes, actions and events, come into their own occurrence and are allowed to remain there. And that entices me to return to the limits of moral space. What would otherwise be just a chapter in a novel might become a story in itself, possibly a lyric poem, singular and radiant in its occurrence, or even an inception still seeking the genre of its expression. Not that one couldn't or shouldn't embrace the novel form and labor to set each episode into an unfolding drama unmoored from the locales and peoples of the epic. *Walden* does just that, but only after Thoreau abandoned the thought that he might record each turn and tick in his effort to "live deliberately, to front only the essential facts of life" (1971, 90). In fact, and I would underscore this finding, catching the adventitious in the emergence and maintenance of moral space is not to dismiss moral space but to find it anew, ripe for further explorations and essays. Yes, like Wal-Mart amid the constellations it will be transfigured, but so too will we.

NOTES

1. In *Emerson and Self-Culture*, I was happier to commit to the language of ethos, but that was within the praxis of self-culture. Now I am now considering events that elude the reach of any self-fashioning or recuperating labors (Lysaker 2008, 126–127).

2. In *Emerson and Self-Culture*, I develop this thought into the claim that human conduct inevitably reforms the world in which it finds itself. One thus does not elect to become a reformer; reform is part of the way of abandonment (Lysaker 2008).

NOT WITH SYLLABLES BUT MEN

Art is the Urge.
—*Ralph Waldo Emerson*

Poetry is the *gai science*. The trait of the poet is that he builds, adds, and affirms.
—*Ralph Waldo Emerson*

There are at least two Emersons, or rather, a manifold Emerson and no less than two sets of Emersonians. One cluster, currently vigorous, valorizes Emerson's recoiling perspectivalism, his recurring insistence that phenomena such as moods and temperament (or tropes, for that matter) foreshorten whatever clarity one might find in "kingdoms of cause and effect," in the "middle region," "amid surfaces," or even along the "subterranean and invisible tunnels and channels of life," to invoke the varied, ecopsychic geography of "Experience." Another bunch is drawn to the ecstatic sallies that depart these regions in an effort to map our condition, to "expand our orbit" as "Circles" would have it, to find the shores of our departures and ports for our bearing, happy to let the latter become the former in time. But this group has been less vocal of late, which leads me to fear that we might be overly domesticating Emerson, trimming whatever shoots rise above the nominalist, often pragmatic contours of our critical present. I offer this essay as something of a counter swing, therefore, the kind of "yes but" reversal one might find in an essay such as "Nominalist and Realist."

"Man lives by pulses," Emerson writes in "Experience" (CW3, 39). I wish to explore one set. They arrive courtesy of the muses and stand among the wildest phenomena in Emerson's corpus, namely, art and poetry. A kind of unbridled enthusiasm for the work of art spans Emerson's corpus. Several lectures struggle to fathom art's power. Some concern particular artists and poets such as Milton, Michelangelo, Hafiz, and Shakespeare, while others pursue more general themes such as the nature of art and poetic figuration as well as their import for self-knowledge and self-culture. And these themes appear across his career, from early lectures on "Biography" (1835) and "English Literature" (1835–1836) to later ones such as "Poetry and English Poetry" (1854), the series "Life and Literature" (1861), and the very late pair "Imagination" and "Poetry" (1872).

Questions concerning art and poetry also appear in most of the essay collections, such as "Art" (*Essays: First Series*), "The Poet" (*Essays: Second Series*), "Beauty" (*Conduct of Life*), "Art" (*Society and Solitude*), and "Poetry and the Imagination" (*Letters and Social Aims*). Equally significant is the organization of the first two collections. *Essays: First Series* closes with "Art" and *Essays: Second Series* commences with "The Poet." On the one hand, essays that begin these collections orient a whole that, by its very nature, eschews an axiomatic or even inferential structure in favor of leitmotifs and whatever pools and eddies their confluence generates. On the other hand, essays that are given the final word or words accentuate leading lines of thought, thereby returning the reader to previous essays with an eye for their more salient concerns, even if the closing essay foregoes a summation, as with "Art." It is thus noteworthy that two of Emerson's most significant collections give pride of place to two essays focused on the power of art and poetry.[1]

In Emerson's writings on art and poetry, poetry is the favored child (though in a qualified sense, as we will see). Besides being a poet in his own right, Emerson also edited *Parnassus* in 1875, a collection of poems that he copied out over the years from the likes of Herrick, Wordsworth, and Shakespeare, as well as the occasional woman poet, for example, Julia Ward Howe, Lady Anne Lindsay, and a Mrs. Barbauld.[2] Also, *Representative Men* gives us essays on Shakespeare ("or, the Poet") and Goethe ("or, the Writer"), but none on sculptors or painters, though he praises sculpture in the late lecture, "Art," which he delivered several times between 1861 and 1869. And yet, in order to offer this praise, he quotes, in full, a nine-stanza poem by the English poet, John Sterling, and closes the lecture with that poem, thus giving the final word to poetry (LL2, 224–225). But most importantly, none of Emerson's remarks on painting or sculpture rise to the rhapsody of "The

Poet," which holds that a poet is the "principal event in chronology" and the "true and only doctor," that poetry is "true science," and that poets are "liberating gods." For Emerson, poetry, though not exclusively, best exemplifies the transformative power of art.

Because Emerson finds poetic language so remarkable, I want to come to terms with his assertions on its behalf, to determine why, on his view, poetry is healing and liberatory, and to determine how it manages such remarkable feats. To that end, I will focus on the "The Poet" from *Essays: Second Series*. Presuming that "Poetry and Imagination" (1875) was in part assembled by his daughter, Ellen, and his literary executor, James Elliot Cabot, "The Poet" marks Emerson's most sustained treatment. Moreover, Emerson's feel for poetic figuration does not dramatically change over the course of his career.[3] But "The Poet" has its limits. Notably, it offers few concrete analyses of how poetic language achieves (or approximates) its end. Other texts must come into play, therefore, including various poems (or parts of poems), though not necessarily Emerson's own.

"Poetry," Emerson writes in a lecture of 1841, "finds its origin in that *need of expression* which is a primary impulse of nature" (EL3, 348–349). "The Poet" from 1844, elaborates: "For all men live by truth, and stand in need of expression. In love, in art, in avarice, in politics, in labor, in games, we study to utter our painful secret. The man is only half himself, the other half is his expression" (CW3, 4). I begin with these remarks because a perceived need lies at the heart of Emerson's high esteem for poets. Humans, he believes, must manifest their character, express it in a wealth of performances, a wealth equal to the richness of that character. Or they suffer. "That man is serene who does not feel himself pinched and wronged by his condition but whose condition in general and in particular allows the utterance of his mind; and that man who cannot utter himself goes moaning all the day" (EL3, 349). Where Adam Smith sees an innate need to truck, barter, and exchange, Emerson sees a broader trajectory: a need to find and say one's part within the world one inhabits.

Notably, this broader trajectory is at once intellectual and practical. It begins in actions: gardening, clothing, what we buy and where. But it culminates in a recognition of the truth of those actions, that is, the expression we seek must successfully reflect us back to ourselves, and for that, we need words. In his concept of "expression," therefore, Emerson weds a sense of human restlessness, what Nietzsche later presents as proactive desires, with the desire to understand that Aristotle finds integral to being human. And it is within that braid of lack and burgeoning surplus that the need for poetry germinates.

Unfortunately, most fail to find adequate expression. "We but half express ourselves," says "Self-Reliance," "and are ashamed of that divine idea which each of us represents" (CW2, 28). The problem is not merely one of cowardice, however. As the essay "The Poet" explains: "the great majority of men seem to be minors, who have not come into possession of their own, or mutes, who cannot *report the conversation they have had with nature*" (CW3, 4). This remark is interesting in at least two ways (or three, since it offers a poetic redirection of Kant's claim that preenlightenment culture and character has not yet reached maturity or *Mündigkeit*). First, it suggests that many of us, even courageous ones, lack the ability to express all that we are. Second, we now have a better sense of what "expression" (and what a human life) entails: a manifestation of our character as it arises within an ongoing conversation with nature. What is to be expressed is not some internal state of affairs but the truth of our character as it appears to us, as it is disclosed in what the essay "Experience" terms "the world I converse with in the city and in the farms" (CW3, 48). To be precise, Emerson denies neither interiority, that is, manifold self-relations such as feeling inspired or self-trust, nor its influence. Rather, his claim is that interiority bears the impress of manifold worldly relations such that the truth of our condition is the whole in which the genuine character of our relations appears.[4]

Let me underscore that the issue before us is one of genuine relation. The whole that is the true is not an undifferentiated unity, some perpetually congealing globe of divine essence. Instead, it involves multiple interactions and the differences (and the differentiation) those interactions presume. Moreover, for Emerson, as for Hegel, our thicket of relations relentlessly becomes, as does all of nature: "That rushing stream will not stop to be observed. We can never surprise nature in a corner; never find the end of a thread; never tell where to set the first stone. . . . If anything could stand still, it would be crushed and dissipated by the torrent it resisted, and if it were a mind, would be crazed; as insane persons are those who hold fast to one thought, and do not flow with the course of nature" (CW1, 124). Bringing this thought from "The Method of Nature" into the task of self-expression, we could say, therefore, that our expressions must keep pace with our perpetual expression, for each marks an expression whose truth must be found: "All is progress, and ascension, and metamorphosis. Chyle becomes blood, bone, tooth, nail, hair, skin, according to exigency, and, so, over the animal, its soul runs out to the expression and incarnation of all its inmost self—as is the bird to the bird's nest. We have not seen the bird till we have seen its egg and its nest. The nest is part of the bird, so is of man the house, the temple, the garden, the laboratory, the school, the state house, the theater, the Academy of Music" (LL2, 221). This thought from the 1861 lecture "Art" suggests that each new manifestation potentially unveils a new side of our character. If we are to give voice to our existence, therefore, manifest and recognize it for what it is, we must learn to track ourselves wherever we go, even into that very tracking. And so, we who are cowards, or minors, or mutes (or all of the above), come to rely on poets. "For, the experience of each new age requires a new confession, and the world seems always waiting for its poet" (CW3, 7).

But how does poetry pursue this task? "The Poet" replies: "the poet ... re-attaches things to nature and the Whole" (CW3, 11). What we lack and what the poet offers is a sense for the whole drama to which we belong: "Every man should be so much an artist, that he could report in conversation what had befallen him. Yet, in our experience, the rays and appulses have sufficient force to arrive at the senses, but not enough to reach the quick, and compel the reproduction of themselves in speech. The poet is the person in whom these powers are in balance, the man without impediment, who sees and handles that which others dream of, *traverses the whole scale of experience*, and is representative of man, in virtue of being the largest power to receive and to impart" (CW3, 5). We know parts and many of us can analyze them. We name the qualities of things, some primary, most less so. We trace consequents back to their antecedents in discrete ecologies of cause an effect. But most of us cannot bring together work and play, body and mind, human and animal, life and death, the terrestrial with the celestial, all of the ways we inhabit the world. That requires what "Circles" names a "bolder generalization" that takes up diverse accounts and finds in their pools and eddies broader phenomena, constants even, at least for the time being.[5]

Consider Heraclitus, whom Emerson names and implicitly quotes in the first paragraph of "The Poet": "But the highest minds of the world have never ceased to explore the double meaning, or, shall I say, the quadruple or the centruple, or much more manifold meaning, of every sensuous fact: Orpheus, Empedocles, Heraclitus, Plato, Plutarch, Dante, Swedenborg, and the masters of sculpture, picture, and poetry. For we are not pans and barrows, nor even porters of the fire and torch-bearers, but children of the fire, made of it, and only the same divinity transmuted, and at two or three removes, when we know least about it" (CW3, 3). Emerson follows Heraclitus and uses "fire" as an analogical universal figure, one whose manifold meaning names a basic aspect of all things and sets us along a continuum with everything that comes to be and passes away, and insistently so—we are not pans or barrows or porters but "children of the fire, made of it."[6]

One way that poets reattach things to the whole thus involves analogical symbols that purport to name recurring aspects of all things. This means that for Emerson, "poetry" names the figurative power of language, not simply verse. Whenever analogy, symbol, allegory, metaphor, metonymy, or synecdoche operate, the gesture is poetic on Emerson's terms. (This is why Plato proves a poet: cave, chariot, divided line, the *demiurgos* slapping form onto matter.)

Note, however, the origin of such figuration: the selfsame conversation with nature that each tries to grasp. "Things admit of being used as symbols, because nature is a symbol, in the whole, and in every part" (CW3, 8). And "we are symbols, and inhabit symbols; workman, work, and tools, words and things, birth and death, all are emblems; but we sympathize with the symbols, and, being infatuated with the economical uses of things, we do not know that they are thoughts. The poet, by an ulterior intellectual perception, gives them the power which makes their old use forgotten, and puts eyes, and a tongue, into every dumb and inanimate object" (CW3, 12). These passages are remarkable in their reflexivity. If poetry reattaches things to the whole, its own figurative power also must belong to that whole. Otherwise, its figurations are actually detachments and enclosures. Emerson rejects such discontinuities, however, insisting that the "poet names things because he sees it, or comes one step nearer to it than any other. This expression, or naming, is not art, but a second nature, grown out of the first, as a leaf out of a tree" (CW3, 13). It is necessary, therefore, that successful figurations track their own figurative sallies, and in a manner that belongs as much to the whole as that which they poetically figure.

A second path lies with particulars through which broad nature appears. According to Emerson, "there is no fact in nature which does not carry the whole sense of nature; and the distinctions which we make in events, and in affairs, of low and high, honest and base, disappear when nature is used as a symbol" (CW3, 10–11). Begin with a tree and soon you will find the history of soil, the history of planters and woodsman, the history of rain and thus of tides, hence the moon, and of global industry, and one will find the sun ninety-three million miles away *and* inclining along the heliotropic arc of a house plant. All that seemed distant and long gone proves near when some particular is seen as the meeting place of everything else.

One can witness such figuration in Robert Pinsky's "Shirt" (1990, 53–55). It begins concretely.

> The back, the yoke, the yardage. Lapped seams,
> The nearly invisible stitches along the collar (lines 1–2)

The effect of this concreteness is to open up the assemblage that each shirt is, which allows the stanza to effortlessly continue:

> along the collar
> Turned in a sweatshop by Koreans or Malaysians. (lines 2–3)

And so we are off and running, finding in the shirt on our backs a history of global labor, though our weavers may live closer to home.

> George Herbert, your descendant is a Black
> Lady in South Carolina, her name is Irma
> And she inspected my shirt. (lines 38–40)

The poem thus sets something seemingly self-contained, a shirt, into a larger economy of forces and events. And it sets itself therein as well, continuing:

> Its color and fit
> And feel and its clean smell have satisfied
> Both her and me. We have culled its cost and quality
> Down to the buttons of simulated bone. (lines 40–43)

This penultimate stanza is striking in its irony and implicit reflexivity. On first blush, the speaker appears as a consumer who shares the inspector's estimation of the shirt's quality. But on another level, the speaker, who has recalled sweatshops and the Triangle Factory fire of 1911 in which 146 garment workers lost their lives, opens a dialogue with the inspector about the cost and quality of the shirt, "Down to the buttons of *simulated* bone." In other words, down to the buttons, this is an unconvincing performance, and neither thinks that what has passed through their hands is satisfactory. More importantly, in addressing Irma Herbert in the third person, the speaker sets the poem into a larger conversation with other points and persons in the network of global labor, thus reattaching itself to the world to which it has returned our shirts—one in which, on the poem's own admission, the final word has not yet been uttered. But not just this poem, that is, "poetry" in a more general sense is drawn back to its entanglements. By naming Irma as George Herbert's descendant (1593–1633), the poem reattaches even the most metaphysical of poems to the world that bears their karmic impress. One may insist:

> Open the bones, and you shall nothing find
> In the best face but filth, when, Lord, in thee
> The beauty lies in the discovery. (Fowler 1991, 304)

But even poems of praise remain bound to mortal bodies, to patterns of breath, for example, though also to more than human bodies, at least in most cases, say trees for paper, glass and plastic for monitors, hence sand, petroleum, and much, much more. Said otherwise, the discovery of beauty, even divine beauty, has its own bones, and "Shirt" is insistent that we track what is thereby simulated.

It is precisely because the poet unveils an enveloping world, one that so often eludes us, that he or she proves a liberating god:[7] "We are like persons who come out of a cave or cellar into the open air. This is the effect on us of tropes, fables, oracles, and all poetic forms. Poets are thus liberating gods. Men have really got a new sense, and found within their world, another world, or nest of worlds; for, the metamorphoses once seen, we divine that it does not stop" (CW3, 17). A good deal is at work in this passage. Let's begin with the notion of liberation, which runs in two directions. "In my daily work I incline to repeat my old steps, and do not believe in remedial force, in the power of change and reform," Emerson says in "Circles." "But some Petrarch or Ariosto . . . breaks up my whole chain of habits, and I open my eye on my own possibilities. He claps wings to the sides of all the solid old lumber of the world, and I am capable once more of choosing a straight path in theory and practice" (CW2, 185). Again, the issue is intellectual and practical. A genuine poetic disclosure turns us around; it interrupts old habits as it opens new vistas.

As "Shirt" evinces, concretion is everything in these transformations. Images focus and convert us. But atop them, or rather, through them, the poet's achievement expands. Once we witness a particular wax cosmological—a shirt, a tree, some pale light—it should dawn on us that any particular could play that role, even our own lives. In "The System," John Ashbery says this to haunting effect (2008, 280).

> The system was breaking down. The one who had wandered
> alone past so many happenings and events began to feel, backing
> up along the primal vein that led to his center, the beginning
> of a hiccup that would, if left to gather, explode the center to
> the extremities of life (lines 1–5)

If we work toward our center, riding the thought that each relates to each, we undo the distinction between near and far, high and low. And without such demarcations, including inside and out (or with and without), systems give way. All at once, the center is everywhere. This is quintessential Emerson. Again, "there is no fact of nature which does not carry the whole sense of nature" (CW3, 10). But that is not all. In our continuity with nature, and in nature's relentless unfolding: "There is no outside, no inclosing wall, no circumference to us" (CW2, 181). But even the quintessential can be difficult to say without risking a circumference, and difficult to hear since everything seems to say it, even one's hearing. This may be why Ashbery figures such realizations as an occasional feeling in the opening lines of *Flow Chart* (Ashbery 1991, 3).

> Still in the published city but not yet
> overtaken by a new form of despair, I ask
> the diagram: is it the foretaste of pain
> it might easily be? Or an emptiness
> so sudden it leaves the girders
> whanging in the absence of wind,
> the sky milk-blue and astringent? We know life is so busy,
> but a larger activity shrouds it, and this is something
> we can never feel, except occasionally, in small signs
> put up to warn us and as soon expunged, in part
> or wholly. (lines 1–11)[8]

With Emerson in mind, particularly the line "character evermore publishes itself," I want to take "the published city" in terms of a thoroughly symbolic nature, one that includes sentences and sunsets, characters and characters, one worthy of the phrase "larger activity," though it remains (and will remain) to be said what kind of "action" this is (CW2, 90).[9] Second, I would add that only within the "published city" does the whole appear, that is, each appearing requires some other that indicates the appearing, if obliquely. "Direct strokes she never gave us the power to make," Emerson observes in "Experience," continuing, "all our blows glance, all our hits are accidents" (CW3, 29–30). And art works are no different. "Our arts are happy hits," we find in *Society and Solitude* (CW7, 23). But how could it be otherwise? How could a part indicate a self-differentiating, ecstatic whole to another part, except by way of suggestion, one whose reach, affectively effective, exceeds what either part could concretely synthesize?[10] The whole, this larger "activity" that binds speakers, addressees, and all that concerns them (and no doubt much that doesn't), rushes into us as a feeling, a presence without circumference, a presence felt just at that point where our symbols break open and suggest more than they could possibly mean, a point where we find ourselves "like a traveler, surprised by a mountain echo, whose trivial word returns to him in romantic thunders," to return again to *Society and Solitude* (CW7, 23).

In a more general way, feeling is integral to the full range of poetic liberations that Emerson imagines.[11] Introducing *Parnassus*, he says: "Whatever language the bard uses, the secret of tone is at the heart of the poem. Every great master is such by this power ... The true inspiration always brings it. Perhaps it cannot be analyzed; but we all yield to it" (P, x). Here we enter the murky field of voice, that characteristic tone with which a poem or occasionally a corpus addresses its subject matter and readership. Perhaps these lines from Whitman's "I Sing the Body Electric" will prove concrete (1982, 250–258).

> O my Body! I dare not desert the likes of you in other men and women, nor the like of the parts of you;
> I believe the likes of you are to stand or fall with the likes of the Soul, (and that they are the soul;)
> I believe the likes of you shall stand or fall with my poems—and that they are poems;
> (lines 131–133)

This poem overflows with enthusiasm, such as in the great length of each line. Interestingly, Emerson himself says: "the length of lines in songs and poems is determined by the inhalation and exhalation of the lungs," which I take to image a certain capacity for expression and thus for life (CW8, 24). But not just by way of line length, at least not in the case of these lines from Whitman, which brim with affirmation in the exclamation and declaration that open each line recalled: "O my Body!" "I believe." "I believe." And the repetition deepens the thematic point: the body is a fit subject for praise, even veneration, since the repeated "I believe" recalls a *Credo*.

For Emerson, the poem's mood creates a space wherein one can assume the possibilities it figures. In "Persian Poetry," he writes: "Every song in Hafiz affords new proof of the unimportance of your subject to success, provided only the treatment is cordial" (CW8, 133). In this context, "cordial" has powerful overtones, though one might miss them if one only thinks of a sweet aperitif or chocolate. But a return to the 1828 edition of Webster's dictionary gives us two other applicable meanings: (1) hearty and sincere as well as (2) invigorating and reviving.[12] What Emerson finds in Hafiz is a tone or mood that both radiates sincerity and invigorates whoever receives it. And in invigorating the reader, such a tone reattaches us to the whole at the level of affect and action, that is, it recalls us from dulled habit, possibly despair, and allows us to find and pursue possibility in the world at our door.[13]

If we focus on the invigorating tones of certain poets, I think we can see why Emerson terms the poet the "true and only doctor." She or he gives us back a kind of youth, renewed vigor. In "Culture," Emerson suggests, "Incapacity of melioration is the only mortal distemper" (CW6, 74). Whitman's lines, in their verve and exultation, cure such distemper. With rhythm and sound and sense they instill a visceral confidence in a life that will not treat the body as the soul's poor relation. And even Pinsky's poem is never overcome by disclosures that remind us of the bleak entanglements we wear. In fact, at the level of tone, and in the poise of its lines and images, there is a confidence that these stories can be told, and that conversations with the likes of Irma Herbert can be pursued, and that poems, if they do not forget the body, will help us pursue them.

In several ways, then, poets reattach us to the whole, thus empowering, Emerson believes, our own self-expression. Poetic figures help us see the world to which we belong (and the worlds within those worlds as well as what is, properly speaking, not a world but a "larger activity"), and in such a way that we inhabit that world with greater richness. In fact, on this view, the opening of such futures is the yet to be written verse of every truly great poem. As Emerson suggests: "He is the true Orpheus who writes his ode, not with syllables, but men" (CW7, 37).[14] The suggestion is not as strange as it sounds. Every poetic figuration is an action—it "adorns nature with a new thing" and "Words are also actions"—and every action a symbolic expression of the character of the actor and the ecology in which that action arose (CW3, 6). Emerson can thus, in a somewhat strict sense, regard the world as a poem in need of further elaboration, and he can regard each elaboration as the inception of futures whose future poems we will be, as "principal events in chronology," to recall one of his more robust phrases. Turning to Emerson's figurations, then, the world is less a stage than a poem in the process of perpetual revision or turning, as in the turns of a trope, from *tropos*, meaning manner and style, or even way of becoming, given the root verb *trepein*, to turn. "Nature itself is a vast trope," Emerson writes in "Poetry and Imagination," continuing, "and all particular natures are tropes" (CW8, 7). I am happy to confess, then, that I find something startlingly plausible in Whitman's wild suggestion that the likes of bodies should stand and fall with his poems and that they are poems.

I have been working my way into some of Emerson's strongest claims on behalf of poetry, for example, that the poet is a liberating god, the true doctor, and the inception of a chronology. I have also tried to show how and why Emerson thinks of nature and our role therein as an ongoing poem of visions and revisions that a moment might replace. But I have yet to pursue the thought that poetry is in some way a "true science." Admittedly, the claim is somewhat odd, as is the later assertion that the "Poet is a better logician than the analyzer" (LL1, 304). I think we can track these thoughts, however. Moreover, doing so should lead us into a variety of critical contexts that will help us evaluate the position I've been elaborating.

Emerson's decision to present poetry as a kind of knowledge stems in part from a struggle with Plato that appears at various points within "The Poet," most often through rhetorical revisions. According to Emerson, the poet, contra arguments found in the *Republic*, possesses a higher kind of seeing that brings him or her closer to what is to be known, and it is on that basis that the poet leads us out of the fabled cave. Moreover, that higher seeing does not result from the *elenchus* but from the kind of rhapsody that makes poets such a potential threat in the *Republic* and the rhapsode such an ass in *Ion*. Moreover, in a revision of a core image from the *Phaedrus*, Emerson orients the soul away from a mind-governed chariot toward an instinct propelled steed. "The traveler who has lost his way, throws his reins on his horse's neck and trusts to the instinct of the animal to find his road, so must we do with the divine animal who carries us through this world" (CW3, 16). At various points, then, Emerson, often by mere inversion, insists that Plato is wrong to distrust inspiration and its persuasions, and wrong to claim that poetry only offers replicas of replicas.

And yet, a recurring thought underwrites these revisions. According to Emerson, the poet, qua sayer, surpasses the knower because the poet "uses forms according to life, and not according to the form," which leads Emerson to conclude, "This is true Science" (CW3, 13).[15] The key to this thought is Emerson's claim that the bird can only be known through the egg and the nest. The suggestion is that the character of any being lies in its expressions (including its relations), and that no single expression—no particular form, for example, wing, beak, flying creature, egg layer, etc.—provides the whole story of any being that becomes. It inevitably omits dimensions and mistakes a partial for a complete development. And the problem only intensifies if we move to the whole, which is Emerson's principal concern in "The Poet." The whole not only manifests in every part, it also appears in and as dynamic differentiation such that the whole is at once tern and warbler, minnow and pitcher plant, gravity and RNA codon. And no form can capture this dynamic multiplicity, nor its movement, nor its differentiated continuity within and across that movement, nor its appearing to poets and dullards alike. As Emerson says, "because ecstasy is the law and cause of nature, therefore you cannot interpret it in too high and deep a sense," that is, again, there is no circumference, and forms, by definition, exact just that (CW1, 132). But the Emersonian poet does not rest with forms. Instead, she or he presents forms that, in their evolving interanimation, suggest the life therein, and so his or her "speech flows with the flowing of nature" (CW2, 12).

"This preference of the genius to the parts," writes Emerson, "is the secret of that deification of art, which is found in all superior minds" (CW3, 137). No one expects to find the meaning of a poem in one word or in all its words taken as an aggregate. So too, Emerson thinks, no one should seek a form for the whole or assemble it one necessary and sufficient condition at a time. Or, in his words, "Natural objects, if individually described, and out of connection, are not yet known, since they are really parts of a symmetrical universe, like words of a sentence" (CW8, 4). So too with us, that is, we are parts of a whole and our lives are drawn there-from (and there-on). And so poetry, which can indicate that whole through figure and feeling, can claim a kind of knowing that trumps a knowledge assembled out of universals, no matter how broadly (or compositely) drawn.[16]

Emerson's feel for poetry's power is thus epistemologically ambitious, which makes him an interesting interlocutor for someone like Richard Rorty who also prefers the poet to Platonic metaphysics, particularly with regard to languages of self-expression, or, in Rorty's words, self-creation. But Rorty eschews any epistemic register at this point, setting practices of self-creation in direct contrast to practices of self-knowledge (1989, 27–28). As we have seen, Emerson binds the two; deeper self-knowledge enables broader and richer self-creation. Now, on one level, Rorty could agree. Given a vocabulary, for example, a Neoplatonic, expressivist metaphysics, certain forays might count as self-knowledge and one might revise a life on that basis; for example, one might no longer eat animal flesh upon discovering that nature does not admit of fundamentally distinct natural kinds but is rather continuous. But vocabularies are invented, not discovered, and thus local gains in self-knowledge lose their epistemic sheen when their dependence on nonreferential, hence non-truth-functional vocabularies becomes apparent.

If we follow Emerson here, an interesting argument awaits. First, Emerson could agree that there are no finished or final vocabularies. As he says in "Circles," in a line already partially cited: "Every ultimate fact is only the first of a new series. Every general law only a particular fact of some more general law presently to disclose itself. There is no outside, no inclosing-wall, no circumference to us" (CW2, 181). Moreover, Emerson acknowledges the perspectival nature of every orientation. In "The Poet," he locates creativity in moods to which the poet resigns him or herself. And then in "Nominalist and Realist," he exclaims: "If only we could have security against moods!" and be certain that today's inspiration would not be replaced by tomorrow's despair or, worse still, the "same immeasurable credulity will be demanded for new audacities" (CW3, 144–145). But does it follow from our subjection to apparently inevitable and incalculable successions that we should abandon any epistemic sense with regard to phenomena such as vocabularies?

Emerson believes that at least one epistemic dimension persists in events of poetic figuration; apposition, what we might think of in terms of phenomenological fit.[17] According to Emerson, poetry involves an "abandonment to the nature of things," which requires "suffering the ethereal tides to roll and circulate through him: then he is caught up into the life of the Universe" (CW3, 15–16). As the language of "abandonment" and "suffering" indicate, phenomenological fit is not determined according to egological acts that compare concepts and sense data. Rather, mood and feel run the show, as when we say that something doesn't sit right with us. But let me be more concrete.

Rorty presents psychoanalysis as an instance of strong poetry fit for projects of self-creation (1989, 30–36). He valorizes the talking cure because it grants everyone their own personal, epic drama, as opposed to Nietzsche, who viewed most lives like the way Peter Warlock purportedly reviewed a Vaughan Williams symphony: "a little too much like a cow looking over a gate." But is a democratic air sufficient to recommend psychoanalysis as a language for self-creation? Rorty prefers this line of evaluation because it relies on terms such as "useful" and "interesting" as opposed to "true" or "false." But does not a vocabulary have to make sense in a general way? Doesn't it have to sit right with us? Repression, displacement, and sublimation—these terms make a good deal of sense in our conversation with nature, whereas the thought of libidinal energy running like steam through pipes fares less well for many. But the issue is not whether Freud works *for you*. Rather, my point concerns how it *works or does not work*, and to that question, apposition or phenomenological fit seems relevant.

I suppose Emerson would have another worry about Rorty's impatience with the language of self-knowledge within practices of self-expression. What are we to make of tropes like "vocabulary"? I ask because it seems to function like a circumference beyond which we cannot reach, even though it invites all kinds of questions. For example, how are vocabularies acquired in the process of human development? One might reply, "they are acquired as we learn a language," but what learning processes are operative in that transition? The question is forceful. It indicates that in order for the form "vocabulary" to do the work it does, it arises in the course of a life already unfolding, that is, in order to account for its own emergence, the rhetoric of a "vocabulary" must reach beyond its limits. Similarly, one can ask: are vocabularies discrete? Clearly not, so how do they interact? How do Newtonian mechanics and psychoanalysis interact? Where do they meet? Again, the questions have force because they rush to the limit that "vocabulary" marks and push into questions of genesis, emergence, transformation, and decay.

At points of genesis and transformation, Rorty begins to appear rather Kantian. I say this because the term "vocabulary" seems to frustrate lines of inquiry that the term itself awakens. Ask about the genesis of a vocabulary and one will meet with the claim that such questions only can arise and be pursued within a vocabulary. In other words, for Rorty, "vocabulary" *functions* as an a priori condition for the possibility of experience, inquiry, or poetry, and I think Emerson would resist the drift of "vocabulary" to the point of a quasi-Kantian limit. "There is not outside, no inclosing-wall, no circumference to us," he insists, and rightfully so. Not only do vocabularies have origins and porous limits, thus indicating a site where they emerge and interact, but the very term has its own porous lineage as well, such as, in Dewey's "pattern of inquiry," Quine's "web of inquiry," and Kuhn's "paradigms," as well in the various situations to which each term is a response. It thus strikes me that "vocabulary" itself gives the lie to the limit it would police. Or, to put the matter in Emersonian terms, whenever "vocabulary" marks a limit that cannot be surpassed, its advocates use life according to a form when they should be using forms according to life as they find it in their way.

Given Rorty's pragmatism, I realize the irony of my charge. But Rorty's focus on the "useful" and "interesting" takes its leave from certain commitments that do not seem open to revision, and the rhetoric of "vocabulary" is one. One other, which Emerson would also resist, involves the pragmatic strategist who picks and chooses among vocabularies according to his or her purposes, such as, psychoanalysis for private lives, liberalism for public ones. According to Emerson, it is unthinkable that we could choose our basic orientations in the cosmos, and poetry makes this plain. "In our way of talking," Emerson writes, "we say, 'That is yours, this is mine;' but the poet knows well that it is not his; that it is as strange and beautiful to him as to you" (CW3, 22–23). On Emerson's terms, our bearings take their leave from events that claim us prior to anything like choice. "He is the poet, and shall draw us with love and terror, who sees, through the flowing vest, the firm nature, and can declare it" (CW3, 21). But we need not be swayed by Emerson's account—call it a phenomenology of conversion—in order to see a more general point. To the degree that the pragmatic reckoner is a rhetorical figure that functions as a practical substratum in Rorty's thought, it circumscribes our condition in a manner that, like "vocabulary," unconvincingly suppresses its own genesis and the waves of relations that circulate along, through, and beyond the hem of any circumference.

I have been defending Emerson's enthusiasms for poetry against possible objections from the likes of platonists and Richard Rorty. My hope is that such contrasts allow the power of Emerson's position to appear in starker relief. I think the same might result from another contrast, though this one involves one of Emerson's strongest readers, Stanley Cavell. In particular, I want to use Emerson's career-long affirmation of poetry to resist Cavell's efforts to set Emerson along a continuum shared by Wittgenstein's pronouncement in section 116 of *Philosophical Investigations*, namely that: "What we do is lead/bring [*führen*] words back from their metaphysical to their everyday use."[18]

Cavell connects Emerson's thought to section 116 of *Philosophical Investigations* in several places.[19] I find the richest connection in the "Introduction" to *Conditions Handsome and Unhandsome*: "Wittgenstein's return of words to their everyday use may be said to return words to the *actual life of language* in a life momentarily freed of illusion; Emerson's return of words may be said to return them to the *life of language,* to language and life transfigured, as an eventual everyday" (1990, 21—emphases added). What strikes me as odd is the perceived analogy between (1) a return to the "actual life of language," what Wittgenstein names their *Heim*, their home, which he casts in terms of the everyday, the *alltäglich,* and (2) a return to the "life of language," what in Emerson's terms can only be the whole, and thus a good deal more than language, as we have seen, though one should also note that for Emerson, the poet: "has no definitions, but he is commanded by nature, by the living power which he feels to be there present" (CW3, 10). But setting this aside, the path taken by Emerson's poet toward the eventual everyday cannot be found in the uses that Wittgenstein presents as the home of philosophical terms such as knowledge, being, object, I, sentence, name, etc. Emerson repeatedly presents the poet as abandoning conventional usages. "His mastery of his native tongue was more than to use as well as any before," Emerson says of Milton; "he cast it into new forms. He uttered in it things unheard before" (EL1, 153). And all to the good since everyday usage often fails to keep pace with souls that become—"the experience of each new age requires a new confession, and the world seems always waiting for its poet" (CW3, 7).

One might recall me to Emerson's fondness for the low and the common, to use the language of "The American Scholar," or to his observation in "The Poet" that the "meaner the type by which a law is expressed, the more pungent it is, and the more lasting in the memories of men" (CW3, 11). Fair enough, but these mean types are not left in the hands of everyday usage, hence Emerson's insistence that the person of "poetic temperament" "delights in this victory of genius over custom" (EL1, 346). And one sees this in "Shirt." The poem transforms our sense of "shirt," turning the word and the clothes we wear into allegories of global labor, alienated labor, and the history of exploitation that haunts the garment industry. But it does not do so by returning the word to any everyday meaning.

Emerson's "The Poet" is a rich and remarkable essay and his occasionally wild affirmation of poetic figuration is provocative and instructive to those willing to track its celebrations and aversions. Of late, the theme and the essay have been eclipsed by essays like "Experience," which square more easily, at least initially, with a generation willing to live with the masters of suspicion and their fiercest heirs. Buell does devote an entire chapter of *Emerson* to "poetics," but his discussion strongly favors the self-interrupting style that characterizes "Experience," as does Richard Deming's *Listening on All Sides*, which claims that Emerson's poetics "enact a constitutive skepticism" (Buell 2003, 107–157; Deming 2007, 4). I hope I have provided a broader expanse for the more affirmative dimensions of Emerson's thought.

I would close with something other than a move in Emersonian scholarship, however. Poetry is the issue, and that need of expression that poetry answers by reattaching us within the whole. Yes, Emerson's poetics reach well past the task of reading poems but they include that task. Let me close in the company of a particular poem, therefore.

"Star Turn," by Charles Wright, and the volume to which it in part belongs, *Appalachia*, surveys more than a world and compels me to a reckoning. Not that I could offer a complete reading of either. How could I? Nor is my goal a scholarly explanation. That will not enable me to "stand before the secret of the world, there where Being passes into Appearance, and Unity into Variety." (CW3, 9). Nor will it allow me to find myself in a poem in an Emersonian manner. Following Wright's "meter making argument," will, however. I will thus assemble, juxtapose, and briefly interpret lines and images in order to provide a condensed sense of finding ourselves beneath the sky one night in *Appalachia*.

> *Star Turn*
> Nothing is quite as secretive as the way the stars
> Take off their bandages and stare out
> At the night,
> That dark rehearsal hall,
> And whisper their little songs,
> The alpha and beta ones, the ones from the great fire.
> Nothing is quite as gun shy,
> the invalid, broken pieces
> Drifting and rootless, rising and falling, forever
> Deeper into the darkness,
> Nightly they give us their dumb show, nightly they flash us
> Their message and melody,
> frost-sealed, our lidless companions.
> (Wright, 1998, 7)

It is easy to get lost in Charles Wright's *Appalachia*. It's much less easy to find your way out even though the collection almost always provides a sense of when—February in the year of the rat, a rainy Saturday, the Fourth of July, a day in late Spring given over to dandelions and violets.[20] As to where, the locales are familiar—a yard with a "high privet hedge on two sides," Montana, before a west window, somewhere this side of the Blue Ridge, in a deck chair. And yet, the map always points elsewhere, and in all directions: over the ridge, into mole holes, into the past, back toward language, and ever in the vicinity of the "secret landscape behind the landscape we look at here." But it only points—the map has no pages for the underside or for that side of the Blue Ridge that will tell me which side this side is. So while I always know I am *here* in *Appalachia*, I no longer know where here is.

Each poem delivers concrete, just so observations, their tone matter of fact, with the matter singing lead. Therefore, no grand conceptual or existential labor is required to imagine oneself speaker or addressee, which is to say, the voice throughout is representative in manner if not fact. Not that one is somehow expected let alone coerced to agree. "Just look and see and feel it out"; that is what I hear in the friction of fingertip and paper, or however poems convey their invitations.

Emerson's founding query, "where do we find ourselves?" resounds across *Appalachia*. With each reading I reply: amid images—so much flora, so little fauna; in *The Appalachian Book of the Dead* with its praise (for present and past) and its preparation for the final departure; in memory of memories; in books, among authors and their characters, with artists, thus in dialogues involving the likes of Chekov, Meng Chiao, Giorgio Morandi, Larry Leavis, Borges, the *T'ao Ch'ing*; and in a narrative accreted poem by poem (or is it image by image?), each mapping, as best it can, a "secret landscape behind the landscape we look at here."

> Just under the surface of the earth
> The traffic continues to glide by
> all night with its lights off. (lines 25–27)[21]

Where do we find ourselves? One might expect to find "us" in the interval figured by the "by." But subterranean traffic does not consider us, nor are we there to witness let alone direct the geophysical undulations that occasionally crest as our lives.

When looking down only goes so far it pays to look up. *Appalachia* knows many skies—some blue in mid-August, some "Blue as a new translation of Longinus on the sublime." But peel back that blue or wait on its unraveling and the twinkle, twinkle of what remains will flash into (and out of) view, fugitives from "the great fire," once burnt twice gun shy. These are less than boon companions. Lidless hence unblinking, one might also think them loyal, unflinching. In a sense they are; they persist. But they are mute *and* stupid (that *dumb*), and so their mix of rumble and pink noise is probably only the slow, dying echo of what they fail to be privy to but nevertheless convey—the recurring explosions from which they were flung to drift. Still they seem closer to "the great fire," the Heraclitean generator, that which can never be created nor destroyed, that which percolates as flora, fauna, you, me. Or rather I feel closer to that fire when I look into those eyes and recall my from-where and whither, my what if's and if only's—the rehearsal where I try to be thankful for my mortal heats in what is always the twilight of their cooling.

But that's me in *Appalachia*, which is why I keep looking up when the sky turns. Those are the times of my life, of a life that can be mine for the time being, mine in turn, turn, turn. I share this confession because *Appalachia* also offers an occasional afternoon when all is a hush and each companion—cloud, hedge, left and right, barn swallows, and the back porch—is:

> blown with silence, until the grass grieves.
> Until there is nothing else. (lines 17–18)[22]

This is a whole, though one without a here, without a now—or just a now, a *nunc stans* in which nothing else stands, not even someone to say, if only *sotto voce*, "at last."

There's a saying that greets those who enter *Appalachia*. "Our lives can't be lived in flames." Quite true; we walk along cooled traces. And yet, at each turn I find myself a child of the great fire, its cough, its little song, sidereal in a manner not struck dumb by the great kaboom. But that is to say, and perhaps only to say, that unlike the keeper of all I've heard in *Appalachia*, I haven't looked, all my life, for "this slow light, this smallish light" that hushes all the rest. And I don't think I can. That's posthumous work, and I have other tasks for the time being.

NOTES

1. Note also that the last collection, *Letters and Social Aims*, opens with "Poetry and the Imagination," though I hesitate to make too much of that volume given how much of its shape is due to hands other than Emerson's. For a detailed account of the book's editorial history, see Ronald Bosco's massive historical introduction to volume 8 in *The Collected Works of Ralph Waldo Emerson* (Cambridge: Harvard University Press, 2010).

2. A review of *Parnassus* indicates Emerson's conception of gender. The text is arranged thematically. Under "Human Life," one finds the subtopics "Home, Woman, Love, Friendship, Manners, Holy Days, Holidays." Under "Contemplative—Moral—Religious," one finds the subtopics "Man, Virtue, Honor, Time, Fate, Sleep, Dreams, Life, Death, Immortality, Hymns and Odes." This suggests that Emerson understands men and women to have distinct temperaments or ways of inhabiting the cosmos, and that each is fitted for different subject matters. But that is an issue for another time.

3. Both "The Poet" (1844) and "Poetry and English Poetry" (1854), for example, present poetry as the true science, and precisely because it finds unity beneath change, wholeness across nature's diverse forms and trajectories. (Notably, "Poetry and Imagination" concurs.) In order to further defend the claim that Emerson maintains a consistent (which is not to say identical) conception of poetry throughout his career, I will illustrate agreements between texts of different periods, although I will not call particular attention to this agreement.

4. The sources of Emerson's metaphysical holism are no doubt manifold, drawing from Neoplatonic thought and Vedanta as well as German idealism. I note this to underscore Buell's important insistence that Emerson's thought springs from and wishes to return to world culture and neither from nor toward a purely domestic let alone exceptionalist discussion (Buell 2003).

5. Note that with regard to such expansions, "Circles" also defers to literary works. "Literature is a point outside our hodiernal circle, through which a new one may be described. The use of literature is to afford us a platform whence we may command a view of our present life, a purchase by which we may move it" (CW2, 185). And to the poet in particular. "Therefore, we value the poet. All the argument, and all the wisdom, is not in the encyclopedia, or the treatise on metaphysics, or the Body of Divinity, but in the sonnet or the play" (ibid.).

6. In "Poetry and English Poetry," Emerson aligns figuration of this sort with metonymy, which he defines as "seeing the same sense in divers things" (LL1, 303). Because this is a rather loose definition that focuses more on analogical sense than actual poetic operations, I am not employing the analysis here.

7. I think the use of "god" is designed to both: (1) deify the poet, rendering him or her a "divine" who provides ongoing revelation, and (2) continue the process, begun in "The Divinity School Address," of rendering Jesus ontologically unexceptional.

8. In an early lecture on Michelangelo, Emerson claims that the whole cannot be understood, only felt. Ralph Waldo Emerson, *The Early Lectures of Ralph Waldo Emerson. Volume I: 1833–1836* (Cambridge: Harvard University Press, 1959), 101.

9. Whether "activity" fruitfully accounts for the dynamics of synchronic and diachronic webs of relation is a matter I have addressed in *You Must Change Your Life*, principally through the poetry of Charles Simic, though also in terms of Ammons's *Garbage* and Stevens's "Reality Is an August Activity of the Imagination" (Lysaker 2002).

10. In *Emerson's Fall*, Barbara Packer also finds the inevitability of suggestion in Emerson's poet (1982, 193). For her, this primarily is due to nature's ongoing ecstasies. I would add that part-whole problems thicken the issue and further note that suggestiveness has affective dimensions.

11. This is true on the side of the text and the reader, as Richard Deming notes: "At the very least, I would venture to say that affect, emotional valence, is one measure of response and investment" (2007, 128). That said, I think the distinction between thought and feeling will not hold up when we think-feel our way into the larger activity that Ashbery poetizes in "The System" and *Flow Chart*.

12. In "Poetry and Imagination," Emerson laments, "And the fault of our popular poetry is that it is not sincere" (CW8, 15).

13. Emerson reports: "It is much to know that poetry has been written this very day, under this very roof, by your side. What! that wonderful spirit has not expired! these stony moments are still sparkling and animated! I had fancied that the oracles were all silent, and nature had spent her fires, and behold! all night, from every pore, these fine auroras have been streaming" (CW3, 7).

14. This line from "Poetry and Imagination" has a partner in "Art" from *Essays: First Series*. "There is higher work for Art than the arts.... Nothing less than the creation of man and nature is its end. A man should find in it an outlet for his whole energy.... Art should exhilarate ... and its highest effect is to make new artists" (CW2, 215–216).

15. "The Poet" actually addresses a triumvirate: the sayer, the knower, and the doer. In the first Shakespeare lecture of 1835, the trio includes the Imaginative, the Reflective, and the Practical (EL1, 303). In the 1841 lecture, "The Poet," the poet is the "universal knower and singer" (EL3, 357). Finally, sayer, knower, and doer also appear in an 1845 journal entry (JMN9, 338).

16. Emerson's critique of Platonism is akin to his critique of sensuous science. "Science was false by being unpoetical. It assumed to explain a reptile or mollusk, and isolated it,—which is hunting for life in graveyards. Reptile or mollusk or man or angel only exist in system, in relation" (CW8, 5).

17. In 1824, Emerson observes: "Metaphysicians are mortified to find how entirely the whole materials of understanding are derived from sense.... I fear the progress of Metaphysical Philosophy may be found to consist in else than the progressive introduction of apposite metaphors" (JMN2, 224).

18. See Ludwig Wittgenstein, *Philosophical Investigations* (Oxford: Blackwell Publishers, 2001). To be clear, my resistance is not to the whole of Cavell's reading; far from it, as my *Emerson and Self-Culture* makes clear. Cavell's feel for Emerson's nonconformist, revisionary writings, such as Poirier's feel for Emerson's punning, is exemplary.

19. I know of five: Postscript A to "Being Odd, Getting Even," from *In Quest of the Ordinary* (Cavell 1988, 130–136); "Finding as Founding: Taking Steps in Emerson's 'Experience,'" from *This New Yet Unapproachable America: Lectures after Emerson after Wittgenstein* (Cavell 1989, 77–118); the "Introduction" to *Conditions Handsome and Unhandsome* (Cavell 1990, 1–32); "Aversive Thinking" from the same volume (33–63); and "Emerson's Constitutional Amending," in: *Philosophical Passages: Wittgenstein, Emerson, Austin, Derrida* (Cavell 1995, 192–214).

20. With few exceptions, I won't list the poems (and lines) from which I've drawn the images and phrases. What follows is thus a venture in a kind of reading that presumes that poems address us with something like the visions Emerson accords them, and it receives them as such.

21. These lines close "remembering Spello, Sitting Outside in Prampolini's Garden" (Wright 1998, 58).

22. These lines conclude the poem "Opus Posthumous III" as well as the volume.

ESSAYING AMERICA

American life storms about us daily, and is slow to find a tongue.
—Ralph Waldo Emerson

—I. Early in his *Meditations*, Descartes suggests that one, at least once, should set one's epistemic bushel in order, as if beliefs were apples to be sorted. But that's not quite right, even though he uses the image in his replies to the seventh set of objections. Descartes' principal concern is not each and every belief but the ways in which he justifies them. It is thus not a stretch to find a kind of ethics of belief in the *Meditations*, at least with regard to *scientia*. (Regarding the epistemic challenges of everyday life, Descartes is quite clear in his synopsis that "no sane person ever seriously doubted these things," in other words, "that there really is a world, and that humans have bodies and so on" [1984, 11].) At its heart, then, and all doctrine aside, Cartesian philosophy responds to a call that asks us to formulate a rational basis for our epistemic commitments.[1]

I feel a similar obligation, though my concern does not lie with how to conduct myself in the way of belief, or better yet, with how to formulate commitments to assertoric speech acts. In its briefest form, and arising as a question, it runs: "Am I an American philosopher"? But that wording is infelicitous insofar as it seems to concern a factual matter, whereas my issue is not whether I satisfy the semantic conditions for the terms "philosopher" and "American." Rather, I wonder whether I might or might not or, better still, should or should not take myself to be an "American" in my approach to philosophy. Should a certain kind of "Americanness" or "America" (for lack of better words) inflect how I pursue philosophy? Should I commit to being an "American" philosopher?

My question is *presentist*. How should I conduct myself, here and now, in the field of meanings and beings that interanimate one another in the term "America"? With Cartesian inflections, and a bit of the later Wittgenstein, I might say: the term "American" has become questionable. I am dubious of its merits and now I am unsure of how to proceed. (No doubt this Cartesian Wittgenstein also can be found in texts signed "Cavell.") But since my lineage lies more with Aristotle and his post-Kantian heirs, I prefer to present my quandary this way: is there something living in "America" on which I can hang my philosophical hat? Is there a project to be found on that vast geography that I can recognize as my own, or make my own? Note that my concern is not whether there is some period or school of thought—call it "American"—that I might term true or false, plausible or dubious. I am not bobbing for apples. The question, instead, concerns a project, one whose manner of engaging the world I too might conduct.[2]

In its focus on present concerns, my question arises in a complex modernity, a slice of which I find in Foucault's occasional praise for Kant's brief essay, "What Is Enlightenment?" According to Foucault, the piece takes the present to be a matter of philosophical concern—"It is a reflection by Kant on the contemporary status of his own enterprise" (1997, 309). More elaborately, Foucault writes: "When in 1784 Kant asked 'What is Enlightenment?' he meant, 'What is going on just now? What is happening to us? What is this world, this period, this precise moment in which we are living?'" (2000, 335). Foucault is drawn to this piece because in it, Kant defines his project by way of a stance toward the present, one he aligns with *Aufklärung*.

I do not want to defend Foucault's reading at all points. In this public brief, Kant puts the stamp of his "mature" philosophical project, call it critique, on the terms of his present, the *Aufklärung*, while barely engaging the concreteness of that present, his bargaining with Frederick aside. His "what's going on" is thus almost categorically different than Marvin Gaye's. But let's stay with Foucault, who is also struck by the particularly modern character of the stance Kant assumes. Kant's present is not derivative. He neither sets it within an epochal history—for example, by locating himself relative to some founding period, say post "Sage Kings"—nor regards his moment as an omen of things to come—as some do even now, insisting that current events indicate a foretold end drawn nigh.[3] Instead, Kant takes his reflections to concern what we might term that which is occurring "just now," from the Latin *modus*, which in part prefigures the term "modernity." Second, he finds "just now" to name a possibility, a time in which something else might happen, an *Ausgang*, an exit that could inaugurate a transformation. Third, and more specifically, this moment of possible enlightenment, what I am terming "just now," arises for Kant in an ongoing process, at once personal and collective, wherein persons assume the burden of modifying, to use Foucault's words, the "preexisting relation linking will, authority, and the use of reason" (1997, 305). Kant's present is thus one in which, on the basis of a public self-critique, human beings might replace extant authorities with, of all things, themselves, or at least, a kind of praxis that remains in some sense ours, though we might equally *be* through its form giving powers. And this is the crux of Foucault's enthusiasm for Kant's modest piece. It offers the beginning of what Foucault himself affirms, namely "a philosophical ethos that could be described as a permanent critique of our historical era" (ibid., 312).

I invoke Foucault for several reasons. In addressing "America," I also wish to refuse the "blackmail of the enlightenment," which requires us to be for or against the whole nest of concepts and activities associated with figures such as Kant, Voltaire, Adam Smith, etc. In fact, I wish to eschew efforts to engage the past by way of epochs or even purportedly univocal authors, committing instead to a slower, more nuanced trudge through texts and their polyphonic trajectories. Third, and at the outset, I wish to set aside any intellectual nationalism that presumes a phenomenon like "America" could only be essayed by native sons and daughters. As I shall argue, "America" is too global a phenomenon to warrant such an approach. Finally, Foucault offers me a way of philosophically engaging my present, of asking (in a way where the "us" names "we philosophers"): "What is going on just now? What is happening to us? What is this world, this period, this precise moment in which we are living?" And when I ask those questions, I am compelled to answer, "in large part, America," which returns me to my initial question.

In taking "America" to pose a question, my orientation is not limited to a Foucaultian modernity that has committed itself to an ongoing (rather than permanent) critique of the present. I find myself quoting other voices as well. One comes from a text penned forty years after Kant's contribution to the *Berlinische Montatschrift*. It asks: "Where do we find ourselves?" And it answers: "In a series of which we do not know the extremes, and believe that it has none. We wake and find ourselves on a stair" (CW3, 27). These lines, which open Emerson's "Experience" also arise in a "just now" that may prove to be a moment of transition, even transformation. "Where do we find ourselves" thus also inaugurates a kind modernity, though one somewhat different than Kant's.

Kant's modernity arises in the now of critique, a trope of supreme self-possession, of autonomy. Not only does critique promise to expel dogmatism but also to return us to an unconditioned ground, one thought in terms of reason's own activity. Foucault addresses us from points, or better yet, events, that have proven the undoing of this conception of humanity. And yet, a kind of self-possession persists in his transformative recovery of Kant, even as it rejects a dichotomy between autonomy and heteronomy. Foucault addresses his present with the vigor of an articulated ethos. Yes, "this historico-critical attitude must also be an experimental one," but its refusals are stark (not transcendental, not revolutionary) and its core commitment, even mood—what he at one point calls "our impatience for liberty"—is persistently audible (1997, 316, 319). Emerson's essay begins quite differently. He is bewildered and dislocated, surviving, but disoriented—"We have enough to live and bring the year about, but not an ounce to impart and invest" (CW3, 27). His essay's present thus proves questionable precisely because Emerson lacks the kind of bearing an ethos might provide. In "Experience," he has, to use Cavell's apt language, lost his footing and thus he seeks some traction in a world full of succession (hence death) that is framed by moods and temperament, which, along with succession, give rise to illusions, isolation, disagreement, and, at times, despair. "Ghostlike we glide through nature, and should not know our place again" (ibid.).

I invoke Emerson's essay because a brief tour of "America" leaves me disoriented. Permit me a somewhat free association. Franklin, Sequoyah, sequoias, John Dewey, the Brooklyn Bridge, Mother Jones, MLK, Guantanamo Bay, "Dead Indian Road," the Grand Canyon, Nebraska, Nike, Coca-Cola, the Trail of Tears, Joe DiMaggio, McDonald's, Hiroshima, slavery, the Spanish-American War, Elizabeth Bishop, the telephone, Utah, the phonograph, genocide, "amber waves of grain," Jane Adams, buffalo, Jane Addams, New Mexico, analytic philosophy, the Pinkerton's, "Fuck the Police," a rocket's red glare, pragmatism, Cassius Clay, transcendentalism, oak and birch, Wind River, NYC, death of God theology, Nashville, the Eastern Diamondback Rattlesnake, Appalachia, Coltrane, Hank Williams, Big Cypress, Chuck Berry, the Cascades, Dylan, Will Oldham, Youngstown, "Song of Myself," Hollywood, Vegas, Emily Dickinson, Charles Simic, Chocolate City, Mount Rushmore, the Chattahoochee, the Lincoln Memorial, April 4th, July 4th, Shiloh, Tammy Fay Baker, the KKK, Harvard, Spellman, Viet Nam, and so on.

How does one find one's footing on this vast terrain? There are so many trajectories, such violence, so many ways of inhabiting language, land, and life? The issue is not simply what events and persons might, just now, offer philosophy a future. Rather, the issue is, which of these fates exemplifies an "American" character that one might make one's own?

Where do we find ourselves? I find myself exploring "America" in a kind of bewilderment amid its vastness, diversity, and violence even as I address that maelstrom bent on antiauthoritarian critique, what Emerson might recognize as self-trust in its aversion to conformity. And first and foremost, it is the violence that claims my attention. In fact, in surveying my long list of "fellow Americans," the following injunction came to mind: "Language must be raked, the secrets of slaughter-houses and infamous holes that cannot front the day, must be ransacked, to tell what negro slavery has been" (CW10, 303). Emerson's offers this with slavery on his mind, and his insistence calls to mind Walter Benjamin's later demand that we read history against the grain. Why? "There is no document of culture which is not at the same time a document of barbarism" (2003, 392). Rake the languages of cultural achievement and you'll uncover occupied territories, institutional violence, and victims. What road couldn't bear the name, "Dead Indian Road," a name borne by a road outside Ashland, Oregon, into the 1990s? Can one invoke "the great experiment" without simultaneously recalling "the great conquest"? Not that each venture in American history is genocidal. But genocide touches each American venture simply in virtue of the land on which it embarks.[4]

I began with a question of commitment. Is there something in the term "American" to which I can commit as a philosopher, some project that I might make my own, thus making me an "American philosopher"? In taking up the question, one I've bound to Emerson's provocation, "Where do we find ourselves," I found myself within the kind of critical bearing that Foucault elaborates even as I found myself bewildered by, even adrift in the diverse and contradictory vastness that "America" contains. And now a third mood has seized me; even as I glide ghost-like beneath spacious skies I find other ghosts, haints that haunt America's touchstones, marking them as sites of great, unresolved violence. I underscore this mood because it charges me, "do not add yet another handful of dirt to those graves you walk beside as if they were thoroughfares and nothing more." In other words, an insistent countermemory is part and parcel of the antiauthoritarianism in which this question of America has arisen for me. "Every age," Benjamin writes, "must strive anew to wrest tradition away from the conformism that is working to overpower it" (2003, 391).

—II. Set aside, for a moment, this complex "America" and turn to "philosophy." Richard Rorty gave us many notable remarks, several in the spur of a moment. One, which I heard and now paraphrase, is that philosophy is more or less what people in philosophy departments do. The remark, characteristically deflationary, was designed to dodge metaphilosophical wrestling matches. In short, for Rorty, questions concerning the nature of philosophy, like questions concerning the nature of truth, were uninteresting and better left to the social sciences. Because Rorty did not consider "truth" an explanatory notion, he thought its meaning lay in the conditions under which communities say "yes" and "no" to assertoric speech acts. Similarly, Rorty's quip about philosophical trends seems to say: if you want to know what a philosopher is, "track and tag," that is, study them in the wild and generalize. No doubt there will be exceptions, but presuming a representative sample, this should produce a reliable portrait or set of portraits.

I'm not inclined to proceed in this fashion. Even presuming the adequacy of a third person answer to the question, "what is philosophy," one quickly finds that contrarian self-definition has usually been integral to philosophy, particularly during its most fertile periods, for example, Plato against the Sophists; James and Dewey against an anglicized Hegel; Carol Gilligan, Nell Nodding, and Eva Kittay against atomistic conceptions of the subject. The best one can expect from a social scientist, therefore (and I would set intellectual historians in that group), is a bewildering report detailing a series of successions and contestations.

But I'd rather not presume the adequacy of third-person answers to the question, "what is philosophy." In presenting philosophy by way of schools or even basic theses, one misses the phenomenon. Philosophical perspectives are not natural or even unnatural kinds that can be sufficiently accounted for in an intellectual taxonomy. Because they entail validity claims that seek recognition and acceptance in a *sensus communis*, one grasps philosophical positions only when one takes up their claims as an addressee. In other words, philosophy requires that observers become participants if they wish to say, "I understand this position." Otherwise, the observer behaves like a parent who hears a child's objection to a rule and ignores it, qua objection, explaining it instead, for example, as evidence of some developmental "stage."

If I am right, if philosophy is always interrogating its proper fields of inquiry and its bearings therein, and, more importantly, if the nature of philosophy only becomes apparent when one does philosophy, any answer to the question, "what is philosophy?" must be worked out within the living contestations that make up philosophy's ongoing history, that is, one must venture an account and, should questions arise, defend it in the company of others. I might put this point another way. Philosophy is not an event like a thunderstorm; it is a "praxis," a self-mediating activity that articulates its own ends and selects its own means in the course of its unfolding; one might say, it deliberates and commits on the basis of deliberation. As such, the nature of philosophy must be determined through its own exercise. Should it arrive at commitments wholly outside its own moments of reception, questioning, interrogation, response, anticipated objections, and commitment, it will cease to be philosophy.

Let me put the matter in the most general way. At stake is how philosophy, as an activity, engages its own facticity. My claim is that as a praxis, philosophy takes facticity to name a site from which it emerges, but it articulates that site in order to return to it in the thick of self-interrogation and, if need be, self-transformation. Everything else is a kind of positivism. Yes, philosophy is factically determined, which is to say, it is situated, which is to say, it is enabled and constrained by conditions to which it does not stand as author: terms and phrases, argumentative forms, rhetorical genres, institutional settings, power relations that establish possible speakers and addresses, etc. But such determinations are matters to be interrogated, accepted or rejected, or possibly reconstructed. Thus, while philosophy might commit to a state of affairs (a belief, an evaluation, a prescription), it shouldn't identify with any, which is why the nature of philosophy, in principle, is always to be determined, in both a practical and temporal sense.[5]

In presenting "philosophy" to the praxis of philosophy as a matter to be determined, one should not forget that such an activity is bound to language, that language marks a principal site where philosophy works out its character and the commitments it is willing to venture. And in thinking of those ventures, I also would call your attention to a cluster of activities that I have come to think through the verb "essay," meaning "to put to the test," "to perform in an experimental manner," and "to venture." I am drawn to this verb because it highlights the manner in which philosophy aims to inhabit the language it inherits from history, ordinary language, culture, what I have been terming "facticity." I am also drawn to the verb because it also recalls the genre of the essay, a personal, probing, nonsystematic form, which inhabits its language here and now in the hopes of proving equal to the occasion in which it finds itself, an occasion I have termed "America."

Earlier I claimed that philosophy offers validity claims that seek recognition and acceptance in a *sensus communis,* and I just claimed that philosophy is, in part, a matter of inhabiting language, of essaying possibilities found there. The praxis of philosophy is thus not simply or even principally a subjective affair. Rather, it begins and always returns to intersubjectivity, to communication or the Logos, that is, speech. As Dewey writes in *Experi-*

ence and Nature: "If we had not talked with others and they with us, we should never talk to and with ourselves" (1981, 135). To speak then of essaying the issue of "American philosophy" is to speak of a way of addressing another, here *you*. What follows (and what has just occurred) is thus a move in a conversation, a move that offers a possible future to all who would engage this rhetorical venture, including the reasons I offer on its behalf. Will it open such a future? I leave that to you, as I must; a concrete future is something no speaker can bring about for another, let alone guarantee.

—III. Returning to the American grain, permit me an anecdote. When I was a graduate student in the early nineties, living in Nashville, attending Vanderbilt, the meaning of the Confederate flag became a center of annual debate among students. For some it meant and means "state's rights." For others, it expresses an economically vibrant Southeast. And there are those for whom it remains a symbol that reasserts the legitimacy of slavery and expresses contempt for African Americans and their long-suffering fate. And no doubt for some it symbolizes a devil may care rebelliousness. Looking back to the early nineties, I know those annual debates taught me something valuable. An unbelievable number of people think meaning stems much more than less from intention. But that is absurd. First, meaning is intersubjective, and thus an account of each sign must think it from the side of speaker and addressee, much as Tom Petty came to think his own deployment of the confederate flag.[6] Second, individuals form their intentions in part through extant meanings, that is, their thoughts already occupy a position of generalized alterity to any concrete speaker or addressee, including oneself. Individuals do not decide, ex cathedra, the meaning of long-standing signs, therefore. Nor can they simply delimit the meaning of those symbols by stipulation. Such decisions and delimitations, even those most creative ones, prove this through their negativity—they are revisions, redeterminations of what has a polysemic objectivity that overdetermines the meaning of their presentation in the social realm to which all language belongs. (If you doubt me, stipulate that raising just your middle finger means: "Tea, please?" Or, when someone asks you what can be done with a philosophy major, reply as if "done" meant something like *energeia* in Aristotle and propose that it allows you to better pursue *eudaimonia*.)

I recall the Confederate flag because it makes plain that I cannot credibly stipulate the meaning of "American" and then assume it as a possible future for how I wish to philosophize. Instead, I must come to terms with the polysemic objectivity of the phenomenon and explore the life conducted therein if I am to determine whether I should be party to it qua philosopher.

Where do we find ourselves? "America." But where do we find "America"? At one level, "America" names the United States of America, a geographically bounded phenomenon constituted in 1787, but underway, in fits and starts, already by May 14, 1607, in Jamestown, Virginia. Because I am currently a citizen of the United States, evidenced by my passport, the taxes I pay, the laws I regard as "laws," and so forth, I am factually "American" in that sense. The question, though, is what does that geopolitical phenomenon entail and how should I engage it as a philosopher.[7]

I find that qua nation-state, the United States is first and foremost a geopolitical empire, which has systematically translated its military and economic might into a formal and informal politics of "conquest, annexation and administration" (Hobsbawm 1989, 57). This is not to say that each bit of legislative activity is designed to secure the empire. My claim is only that the character of American social life, here and abroad, is heavily determined by the global presence, stature, and strategies of American economic and military might. To put the matter in social-theoretical terms, "empire" is a plausible name for the ebb and flow of American social life.

Let me briefly justify why I regard "America" as an empire. As of March 2015, total military personnel stood at 3,163,098, with an active duty force of 1,354,532 as of June 30, 2015. US armed forces can be found all over the world. The United States maintains several military outposts outside its own fifty states, for example, and please note the strategic breadth of these examples: Guam, Japan, South Korea, Kosovo, Germany, Greenland, and Cuba. As of March 2015, almost eighty thousand troops were stationed across Europe, the bulk located in Germany, almost ninety thousand troops were in East Asia and the Pacific, and just under six thousand in all of Africa.[8] Of note, these are active duty military personnel not serving in combat zones. If one adds those remaining in Iraq and Afghanistan, which are not included in the report, the presence of US armed forces outside of domestic territories is startling. It is difficult to dispute, therefore, that a kind of *pax* Americana is a global phenomenon. Of course, "pax" is a matter of where, when, and for whom. In the 1990s alone, US troops were deployed over fifty times for "other than normally peacetime purposes" and over thirty times between 2000 and 2004.[9] Since World War II, the United States also has repeatedly underwritten coups of democratically elected governments, including Iran in 1953, the Dominican Republic in 1963, and Chile in 1973, to name relatively uncontroversial examples. As a world presence, then, "America" truly is a global superpower, and it inhabits the globe as such.

Not setting the guns aside, let me also observe that there are well over two thousand multinational US corporations, each of which "holds at least a 10% direct ownership stake in at least one foreign business enterprise."[10] Proctor and Gamble, for example, "the world's largest consumer products maker," has operations in over ninety countries and sales in over 150.[11] On the legislative side, a series of trade acts and treaties open and regulate or deregulate markets wherein these multinationals operate, and the US military, whether directly (e.g., the invasion of Iraq) or through aid (see the following discussion of "Plan Colombia"), often serves to protect and/or further those interests. Finally, economic aid often flows from the United States into countries where burgeoning markets might be found, and it often arrives with requirements that these markets open to US commercial interests.[12] In short, the legislative, military, and economic projects of the United States and its citizens cover the globe and flow into one another in systematic, strategic ways. And that, I think, warrants the term "empire."[13]

If we ask what orients this empire, it seems that economic interests lie at the forefront. In fact, a look at multiple global ventures suggests that the United States is, in large measure, a complex nest of commercial ventures that pursue global economic opportunities in a world that, in part, is secured by the US military, US foreign aid, and various trade acts and treaties enacted by US legislatures and signed into law by US presidents. And to the degree that this is true, the principal social form of these United States is the commodity, the principal mode of its global social relations, exchange. Concretely, this means that in and for this empire, the world of persons and things, as well as the networks that sustain them, is principally (though not exclusively) interpreted and engaged in terms of their ability to facilitate the production and exchange of commodities.

Empires are not self-executing, however. Instead, they are reproduced through a host of events and actions carried out by the like of persons, institutions, and symbolic orders.[14] To term the United States an "empire" is thus to implicate its citizens in the project of empire. Said more precisely, to be a US citizen and/or to be party to the exchange relations of its multinationals (whether as an employee, shareholder, or consumer) is to be a contributing member of this empire. "Empire America" is thus a global phenomenon that is woven through our clothes, fuels our cars, and drives the political-economic imagination of the United States.

Where do we find ourselves? In large measure, "Empire America" is my answer. But let me draw this portrait a bit more concretely by way of Colombia. The Clinton administration initiated Plan Colombia, a program that has involved over $5 billion, most of which has been military related.[15] (The aid also includes military personnel, including eight hundred troops and three hundred civil contractors in 2005.) While the plan had several goals, including diminishing drug trafficking and improving Colombia's human rights record, economic concerns were also at the forefront. In a 2001 Congressional Research Service report to Congress (RL30330), Nina Serafino reports that: "Colombia is the United States' seventh largest oil supplier, and its fourth largest trading partner in Latin America. US Firms have provided some 40 percent of Colombia's foreign direct investment, of which petroleum investments are an important part." It is worth underscoring that the presence of significant economic interests and large-scale military aid are not unrelated, or so I conclude from the fact that the Congressional Research Service report notes in a section titled "Maintain U.S. Trade and Investment" that security concerns are very high among foreign investors. In fact, this is the only concern the report notes in this section. Plan Colombia and its various extensions are thus clear evidence of an empire systematically woven out of legislation, multinational investment, and military might.

Of course, "empire" is not just any word. It connotes illegitimate violence and imperialism. Those connotations apply. Even while the US government claimed to be combating human rights abuses by way of Plan Colombia, its own multinational firms, whose interests the plan also promotes, were embroiled in those various abuses. In 2007, Drummond Ltd. was sued for allegedly hiring paramilitaries to assassinate three union leaders, but it was acquitted in 2007. Also in 2007, Chiquita was fined for financing paramilitaries with $1.7 million. In 2001, Coca-Cola was sued for allegedly hiring paramilitaries to kill, threaten, torture, and kidnap Colombian trade unionists. While the suit never came to trial in the United States and thus Coke's guilt was never established, it is important to note that between 1989 and 2005, eight union leaders associated with Columbian bottling plants subcontracted by Coca-Cola, and exclusively by Coca-Cola, were assassinated. Moreover, paramilitary organizations have often taken direct roles in Coke's Colombian labor disputes. Lesley Gill reports: "In 2004, for example, as Coca-Cola workers in seven cities participated in a hunger strike to protest the closure of several bottling operations, paramilitaries in Bucaramanga sent a message to a local SINALTRAINAL president Efrain Guerrereo by killing his brother and sister-in-law and their son" (2007, 246). It is clear, therefore, that even if it did not sponsor the violence (which remains to be determined), Coke profited from paramilitary assaults on trade unions and personnel while working to consolidate and standardize bottling in Colombia.[16] I thus find it appropriate that the sponsors of a global boycott of Coca-Cola should rely on an image that Emerson invoked when memorializing the slave trade in the British West Indies. "The media may not have publicized it—but the internet has—and a lot of people will now realize that

that metallic taste in coca cola is in fact the bitter taste in the blood of murdered trade unionists."[17]

No doubt, paramilitary organizations complicate the picture. Whose interest do they represent and defend, and to what degree are US multinationals and the US government responsible for their actions? No successful account of empire can overlook the ways in which foreign states and their citizens, through legal and extralegal means, carry out the global economic project of America. In fact, foreign legislation, like subcontracted work, needs to be "raked" and read "against the grain" if one is to grasp the empire-laced dimensions of these phenomena. But we needn't solve that general problem just now. Instead, we need only observe that in the case of Colombia, "both Colombian and international human rights organizations have repeatedly documented and reported on continued military-paramilitary collaboration."[18] This suggests, therefore, that US military aid has funded paramilitary violence in Colombia. True, one might leverage aid as a means for reform. But Amnesty International reports that the Bush administration restricted provisions that required the "Secretary of State to certify Colombia's progress on human rights criteria before aid can be distributed," and dramatically so. Initially, 100 percent of the aid was governed by this proviso, but that level was reduced to a mere 25 percent. I thus find it difficult not to conclude Plan Colombia values secure markets for US multinationals over basic human rights, even lives.

——IV. Where do we find ourselves? Here is the more general observation, which I have only begun to substantiate. As a geopolitical entity, "America" names a globally operative, dominant force, which often operates through violence or its threat, whether in the form of a global, standing arming, actual invasions, or military/paramilitary operations sponsored by and/or beneficial to US dollars. As far as the ends orienting these activities, the commodity form seems to drive the moral imagination of the US government and the multinational parent companies that are incorporated under US law. While these phenomena do not exhaust political activities of the United States, they do form the nation's chief, global characteristic, particularly if one looks at the United States from a global perspective.

Let's return to flags. In a way, I am asking whether one, qua philosopher, should pledge allegiance to a flag that waves for a globally militarized empire. I put the matter this way because, should I align the name of philosophy with the name "American," I seem to do just that. The argument runs like this. If I were to present myself as a "Confederate Philosopher," I think my philosophizing would be entangled in the objective polysemy of that term.

Similarly, if I present myself as an "American Philosopher," the full meaning of the term also comes into play and that troubles me, for I do not wish to be a philosopher of empire.

But how exactly does one become a "philosopher of empire" through identification as an American philosopher? First, if the term "American" aligns principally with the project of American global capitalism as conducted in countries like Colombia, then the phrase "American philosophy" seems to align philosophy with global capitalism. Second, and more generally, in aligning "philosophy" and "America," one presents the latter as a home for philosophy, and this seems odd if not outright farcical. As a militarized empire that willingly subverts the rule of law and pursues violence for commercial ends, the United States seems hostile to the kind of logos that philosophy requires: the formation of belief, value, and policy through dialogue and open inquiry. In fact, this "America" seems openly hostile to the kind of self-definition that philosophy entails, at least where that practice undermines profits. In other words, to my ears, the phrase "American philosophy" verges on contradiction, saying something like "antiphilosophy philosophy." And this feeling only deepens when I look at our domestic politics, which are a mockery of open dialogue and debate. Even our educational institutions are turning their backs on philosophy and the humanities in general in the name of a value-added education that will—I think you know the phrase—make our students competitive in a global economy.

Finding myself, here and now, caught up in the event that is "America," I am tempted to renounce it in the name of philosophy and, more importantly, the praxis conducted in the name of philosophy. But things are not so easy. As I have argued elsewhere, following Adorno, there is no way out of this entanglement (Lysaker 2007). Global capital, including Coca-Cola, underwrites my salary and the research account that enables me to travel to meetings and share work with colleagues and friends. Any renunciation is thus only a protest with regard to the fates that course through my praxis, irrespective of my intentions. Like it or not, I am a symbol of empire. My conduct conducts it, and that holds true whether I shop at Wal-Mart or teach Marx. Nevertheless, I will not silently present myself as a philosopher in the land of antiphilosophy, but protest that entanglement, as I have here, in the hope of spurring others and myself into futures more hospitable to the life that philosophy in principle affirms.

You might wish to remind me: "America" is not *reducible* to global empire. In fact, there seem to be American traditions of justice that I can bring to bear against our nation's crimes. In the name of philosophy, therefore, one might prove "American" by taking one's leave from figures such as

Thoreau, Jane Addams, or Martin Luther King. More generally, one might find a cultural tradition or set of traditions that can be named "American" and that run counter to the lines of empire I am protesting.

I have no interest in suggesting that somehow these thinkers are harbingers of empire. But I would like to pause and ask what renders an intellectual phenomenon, particularly a philosophical praxis, "American." I pause because what attracts me to philosophers such as Emerson or Dewey, for example, the former's essayistic form or the latter's functional account of the human organism, is unrepresentative when we consider what most of their (or my) fellow citizens believe. One might find other thinkers who shared their views and term the larger conversation "American," for example, transcendentalism or pragmatism, but a large number of their peers, including highly learned ones, did not share their views, and I presume that was not because they were somehow not American or un-American. In fact, if we were to look at the sum total of US born and/or raised philosophers, trends like transcendentalism and pragmatism seem the exception rather than the rule. It thus seems a mistake to consider these phenomena representatively "American," even within philosophical circles.

My worry runs deeper than truth in advertising, however. In presenting the grand figures of transcendentalism and pragmatism as "American," we threaten to render obscure if not illegible the American character that surrounded each and to which each movement is a decided protest. My fear is that we obscure deep, historically pervasive trajectories when we champion figures such as Emerson and Dewey as representatives of some general American character at work in philosophy or the culture at large.[19] I would thus prefer that we engage them as exceptions to a more pervasive national character, which they were, as Emerson knew all too well. "Things are in the saddle," he mused, "And ride mankind" (CW9, 148). And others had similar thoughts. Looking toward the future, Jane Addams wrote: "It will certainly be embarrassing to have our age written down triumphant in the matter of inventions, in that our factories were filled with intricate machines, the result of advancing mathematical and mechanical knowledge in relation to manufacturing processes, but defeated in that it lost its head over the achievement and forgot the men" (1964, 206–207). And well before his deep engagement with Marxism, W. E. B. Du Bois wrote: "Atlanta is not the first or the last maiden whom greed of gold has led to defile the temple of Love; and not maids alone, but men in the race of life, sink from the high and generous ideals of youth to the gambler's code of the Bourse; and in all our Nation's striving is not the Gospel of Work befouled by the Gospel of Pay?" (2007, 38–60). Out of honesty with ourselves and those with whom we "share" the planet, I request that we present our conversations with luminaries such as Addams, Dewey, Du Bois, and Emerson in a manner that keeps our national character unobscured.²⁰

"American" also obscures whenever I enter the heart of a supposedly core American thinker. Consider this list of principal influences: Vedanta, Plato, Plotinus, Montaigne, Scottish Common-Sense philosophy, and Kant (via Coleridge and de Staël). This remarkable list underwrites Emerson's corpus. And one can find the not so subtle hand of these inheritances in several of his principal themes (nature, intuition, and genius), as well as his exquisite mode of presentation, the essay. "American" just doesn't do justice to the full range of Emerson's intellectual inheritance, therefore. "But it situates his texts in a historical context to which his work is a response and that fact is obscured if we do not address him as an 'American' thinker." Up to a point, point taken, but again, I worry about an overly general designation. The real issues lie with the specific events to which Emerson is responding, such as Harvard's slavish dependence on European texts or the panic of 1837. And given that so many "Americans" responded to these matters in non-Emersonian ways, I don't think "America" or "American" serves us very well if we wish to name the situatedness of Emerson's thought.²¹

I suppose another reason prompts me not to identify my philosophical practice with "America." I not only want the full character of the nation front and center, but, given the palpable evils of empire, I want it contested. By drawing figures such as Emerson and Addams outside of a discussion of some purported national character and its autochthonous roots, we are better able to essay their texts over and against the United States' more obvious national character. Not that one should only read these figures at points where they resist empire. One should certainly expose moments where they further empire, perhaps unwittingly. But if they do help us undermine the tropes that galvanize empire, such as commodity fetishism and liberal atomism, then those entangled in the projects of empire should resist those projects, and doing so in the name of purported native sons and daughters may rouse a few sleepwalkers and weaken a few master narratives. Even better, it may teach us a few new steps.²²

You might be wondering: "Are you suggesting that we drop altogether the term 'American' in our explanatory ventures?" Not if Emerson is right when he says: "The near explains the far. The drop is a small ocean. A man is related to all nature. This perception of the worth of the vulgar is fruitful in discoveries" (CW1, 68). The thought suggests that we could engage the term "American," and whatever texts it once gathered, as a site in which multiple forces converge and become legible in rather particular ways, that is, as a locale where what is local and not local meet and transform one another. In other words, although "American" doesn't explain much, it could initiate a certain set of inquiries that focus on points (e.g., Concord, Chicago, Atlanta) where forces (e.g., a legislative act, a book, an institution) converge. Read in this way, "American" (and "America"), or so I propose, will name sites of ongoing multicultural events and collisions that often do not add up to anything like a national character, and which call for thorough interrogation and, when the violence is apparent, a kind of witnessing.[23]

I should stress that my position is more realist than nominalist, at least in a historical sense, and thus I do not object, in principle, to organizing semiotic events in general terms. (As Dewey has it, in full Hegelian mode: "But the whole history of science, art and morals proves that the mind that appears *in* individuals is not as such individual mind" [1981, 170].) Cornel West's recent review of the black prophetic tradition lines up a series of thinkers and activists in a forceful, at times inspiring way, including the likes of Ella Baker, whom I did not know, as well as Du Bois, whose multidisciplinary and polygenre writing offers more of a future the more I read it (West and Buschendorf 2014). But in each case, Baker and Du Bois, "America" and "American" must be taken as a polyphonic, dialectical image in which myriad differences and struggles, within and without, are allowed to breathe.

—V. There is always music in my head. Some offer examples (Bach and Coltrane) others touchstone lines—"The best you can be is the beast that they don't want to see," from J. Robins of *Burning Airlines*. One line in particular has recurred throughout the writing of this essay. "But if you go carrying pictures of chairman Mao / You ain't going to make it with anyone anyhow." While I don't know (and very much doubt) that it's gonna be alright, I do worry that declaring philosophical independence from "America" is too strong a gesture, one that, in the name of an eventual reconstruction, undermines the kind of solidarity such a reconstruction requires. Perhaps I would be better off protesting "America" in the name of some "America to come," one along the lines envisaged by Guillermo Gómez-Peña (1996):

> standing on the map of my political desires
> I toast to a borderless future
> (*I raise my glass of wine toward the moon*)
> with . . .
> our Alaskan hair
> our Canadian head
> our U.S. torso

> our Mexican genitalia
> our Central American cojones
> our Caribbean sperm
> our South American legs
> our Patagonian feet
> our Antarctic nails
> jumping borders at ease
> jumping borders with pleasures
> amen, hey man.

There is a great deal to say about these lines which close the essay "Freefalling toward a Borderless Future," for example, the persistence of borders—jumped with ease, jumped with pleasure—within this body politics. But the general thought would be, perhaps "America" might become a more inclusive ideal, one covering the whole of the Americas, not just the United States. While the scale of this vision daunts me, and while the image of a "body politic" connotes a kind of coordinate unity that rings various alarms, the question at hand is whether this or any ideal should bear the name "America." What do we gain if we wed our romance to a new yet undiscovered America, no matter where it dawns?[24] These are nearly impossible calculations, but the concern is not ill-founded or posed and so I find myself obligated to offer something of a reply, if only a brief one. "America," whether a city on the hill or a continent (or two) connotes a nation-state and I don't see how such a figure either can make sense of or justly maintain global economic networks. But more importantly, the "America to come" must so resolutely not be a militarized empire that the future so named, if it is to be a future, really lies on the far side of what "America" has become. And for the moment, I would not obscure the task at hand. Finally, I would rely on another term to call us to our better selves, if only because it insists, from the ground up, that no one be unduly favored. But that would require another discussion, one concerning "justice," a term that bucks and sways under the weight of words for peoples, nations, even cultures.

Where do we find ourselves? I raised the question within a modernity averse to conformity, bewildered in a landscape of immense diversity and violence, and committed to raking any language that not only obscures the victims of historical injustice, but further buries them in history.[25] My reply has centered on the word "America." But I do not think that only US citizens should or would answer in this way. "America" is a global phenomenon, an empire of might and money that principally engages the world with an eye on the commodities it might yield and the profits they might generate, and along the way, persons are more or less mere means to this rather indeterminate end.

And that is my principal reason for not enlisting in the project of "American Philosophy." Philosophy withers within a militarized empire ensnared by exchange relations that revolve around the commodity form. Moreover, I do not want to obscure the barbaric fact of empire by presenting "America" in the terms assembled in texts signed Emerson, Addams, Du Bois, Dewey, etc. Rather, I want to inherit those texts over and against empire, particularly since so many of these authors protested the commodity-driven myopia in which they found themselves and their philosophical projects. Philosophy has almost always been an exception in America, and it is barely even that today.

But all forms of praxis bear their situations along with them, quoting, beyond the reach of intention, the world that enables them. I have thus elected to retain the word "American" as a marker for a fate requiring more (and more nuanced) analysis. "American" thus names a certain kind of situatedness, but not one with which philosophy should identify. Moreover, it less explains that situatedness than marks a site that has, in many ways, yet to be discovered in all its multiplicity. My venture thus both eschews and retains the word "American" in the realm of philosophical conduct, which is to say, I hereby declare my independence from "America" in the name of a philosophy that would be, or rather, that would enable, as best it can, something more, though I acknowledge, with the same breath, that for the time being "America" remains a condition for the possibility of that declaration and the independence to which it aspires.

NOTES

1. I think we would have a richer conception of philosophical modernity if we recalled, as Hegel did, Descartes' practical bearings alongside his dualism and circumscribed quest for certainty: "Descartes made a fresh start.... The thinking or philosophizing, the thought and the formation of reason in modern times, begins with him. The principle in this new era is thinking, the thinking that proceeds from itself" (1990, 131).

2. I won't elaborate the various modes of philosophical conduct at stake in what I do, except to observe (1) principal activities (teach, write, edit, review, publish), (2) nested addressees and enablers (students, publishers, friends, other professional philosophers, unknown friends and secret addresses), as well as (3) enabling conditions underwriting the whole shebang (global capital, civic, state, and federal agencies, etc.).

3. A brief Google search locates numerous websites insisting that the present is best understood through signs of our impending demise, for example, raptureready.com, contenderministries.org/prophecy/endtimes.php, and prophecyupdate.com.

4. A visit to native-languages.org/states.htm gives one the sense of how vastly and diversely inhabited the lands were that have become the United States.

5. I take myself to be saying something stronger than John McDermott, who claims: "It is this double aspect of being rooted in one's culture, while yet providing a philosophical

articulation which is transcendent of that culture, that characterizes the influential philosophical movements of the past" (quoted by Haddock Seigfried 1988, 835; (from McDermott 1986, 97.) In my view, not just the influential philosophies of the past, but also the praxis of philosophy itself is a self-transcending enterprise and thus never identifiable with any set of cultural conditions.

6. Petty, who grew up in Florida, displayed the flag on tour in 1985, which he came to regret. "To this day, I have good feelings for the South in many ways. There's some wonderful people down there. There are people still affected by what their relatives taught them. It isn't necessarily racism. They just don't like Yankees. They don't like the North. But when they wave that flag, they aren't stopping to think how it looks to a black person. I blame myself for not doing that. I should have gone around the fence and taken a good look at it. But honestly, it all stemmed from my trying to illustrate a character. I then just let it get out of control as a marketing device for the record. It was dumb and it shouldn't have happened" (Green 2015).

7. One might suggest that "America" could be taken to name a broader region, one running from the northernmost tip of North American to southernmost tip of South America. That may be a worthy dream, but at present, that geography does not involve any unified cultural outlook or political form that might allow us to speak of "the Americas" as more than a geographical region. I thus prefer to treat "America" (and "American") as radial categories whose principal referent concerns the United States.

8. These figures, which obviously do not include covert operatives, are publicly available from the Department of Defense website.

9. For a thorough recounting of US military action, see Richard F. Grimmett's "Instances of Use of United States Armed Forces Abroad, 1798–2004," Congressional Research Service report RL30172, as posted by the Naval Historical Center. The thorough and somewhat startling report can be found at: http://www.au.af.mil/au/awc/awcgate/crs/rl30172.htm.

10. I draw this definition from Matthew J. Slaughter's "How U.S. Multinational Companies Strengthen the U.S. Economy," 4.

11. Reported by the *Atlanta Journal-Constitution*, July 9, 2010, A14.

12. Kevin Watkins of Oxfam writes:
> much has been made of America's generosity towards Africa under the Africa Growth and Opportunity Act (AGOA). This provides what, on the surface, looks like free market access for a range of textile, garment and footwear products. Scratch the surface and you get a different picture. Under AGOA's so-called rules-of-origin provisions, the yarn and fabric used to make apparel exports must be made either in the United States or an eligible African country. If they are made in Africa, there is a ceiling of 1.5 per cent on the share of the US market that the products in question can account for. Moreover, the AGOA's coverage is less than comprehensive. There are some 900 tariff lines not covered, for which average tariffs exceed 11 percent.
>
> According to the International Monetary Fund (IMF), the benefits accruing to Africa from the AGOA would be some $420m, or five times greater, if the United States removed the rules-of-origin restrictions. But these restrictions reflect the realities of mercantilist trade policy. The underlying principle is that you can export to America, provided that the export in question uses American products rather than those of competitors. (Quoted in Shah 2014)

13. Hardt and Negri take "empire" to name a "new global form of sovereignty" that not only exceeds the control and reach of nation states but also decenters and deterritorializes such projects. I see the point. Multinationals, for example, wield influence across such boundaries, thus introducing a kind of global power that does not flow simply from (or answer to) nation-states. That said, I think they are wrong to deny that the United States forms the center of an imperialist project (Hardt and Negri 2000, xiv). In a country like Iraq or Colombia, for exam-

ple, the United States has systematically translated its military and economic might into a formal and informal politics of colonial control. Yes, that power bears the traces of forces that are not simply or even primarily "American," but for now, a kind of center still holds in these regions, and that center is much more than less a creature of the United States.

14. I cannot resolve, here and now, the long-standing dispute gathered by the term "methodological individualism." But I can state my position. While individual actions are meaningful variables in the life of social constellations such as families as well as economic and legal orders, such constellations have discernable logics that inform individual action in ways that cannot be interpreted as yet another instance of individual action or the causal influence of spatiotemporal objects. For example, family structures inform the behavior of all family members without flowing from the agency of any given member or all members taken as a sum.

15. My data is taken from several sources: a Witness for Peace brochure, "Putamayo, 2004: An Evaluation of Four Years of Plan Colombia in Putumayo"; Ari Paul, "Colombia's Agony, Coca-Cola's Responsibility, and America's Solidarity"; Lesley Gill, "Right There With You: Coca-Cola, Labor Restructuring and Political Violence in Colombia"; killercoke.org; and an Amnesty International paper titled "US Military Aid to Colombia." I have elected Colombia-US relations as a paradigm example because even though the second war in Iraq was an almost classical instance of an empire flexing its imperial might, it does not capture the principal way in which the American empire operates, although it certainly reminds other nations that the United States is capable of unilateral, military action under false pretenses. The Wittness for Peace brochure can be found at http://www.witnessforpeace.org/downloads/putu2004.pdf.

16. I should hasten to add that Coca-Cola has been sued in other locales as well. The *Atlanta Journal-Constitution* reported in March 2010 that Coca-Cola is being sued by Guatemalan union leaders, who claim the company is "not acting to stop violence against union leaders at Incasa, its Guatemalan bottler." (Jeremiah McWilliams. "Union Leaders in Guatemala sue Coca-Cola." 03 March, 2010. A. 11) Moreover, the *Wall Street Journal* reported in July 2010 that a cabinet in the state of Kerala, India, has established a "tribunal to recover payment worth 2.16 billion rupees ($48 million) from Hindustan Coca-Cola Beverages for alleged damage caused to the environment by it Plachimada bottling plant in Palakkad." (Arlene Chang. "Coke's Kerala Problems Bubble Up" http://blogs.wsj.com/indiarealtime/2010/07/05/cokes-kerala-problems-bubble-up/.)

17. From *Kirkby Times* (2003). Emerson's remark, which concerns the oblique presence of slave labor in sugar, reads: "The sugar they raised was excellent: nobody tasted blood in it" (CW10, 314).

18. Reported by Amnesty International in "US Military Aid to Colombia."

19. I find such histories in John Smith (1992) and John McDermott (2007). The former finds a characteristic "American" mode of philosophy, whereas the latter connects a characteristic mode of philosophizing with broader trends in American culture. More precisely, Smith presents a spirit of receptivity, feel for change, and concern for relevance, whereas McDermott's speaks of a philosophical orientation that is "indigenous to a culture which was attempting, within the ever-present framework of Western European civilization, to work out what Emerson plaintively called 'an original relation to the universe'" (61).

20. Since making this request in a public presentation, Scott Pratt and Erin McKenna have accepted it, if on amended terms. Their *American Philosophy: From Wounded Knee to the Present*, presents a genuinely diverse, inclusive American philosophy, with an emphasis on its resistances (2015). I still do not see what renders this tradition "American," however. Most of those who satisfy the conditions for "American" fall well outside the tradition Pratt and McKenna recount, including most American philosophers. And while I agree that my own position arises out of experiences and replies situated within the "American" event, I think the

full character of those experiences and replies exceed the reach of any national category, whether it names a nation-state or a linguistic-ethnic identity.

21. Charlene Haddock Seigfried, in "Advancing American Philosophy" (1998), finds "American" at once too broad and narrow an explanatory concept. It is too broad because it obscures the fact that there are many American philosophies, and it is too narrow because it limits to a particular, national history, phenomena that exceed it, namely, the particular thoughts ventured. I more or less share this view. If I add it to the concerns advanced here, I think it better to philosophize in the name of other, more precise designations, whether tied to points of view, for example, pragmatism and radical empiricism, or normative commitments, for example, social justice or the great community.

22. I thus take this essay to accept John Stuhr's request, in a reply to Haddock Seigfried, that interruptions of "American Philosophy" should do more than diagnose muddles (Stuhr 1998). First and foremost, they should seek advances. By articulating some new ways in which the America of "American Philosophy" should be interpreted, and by trying to model how that figure might be critically engaged, I hope some advances have been made.

23. While I am drawn to Doug Anderson's suggestion that philosophy aim to "maintain an experiential home" for an evolving, pluralistic "we," and that it do so through engagements with a broad range of cultural phenomena, I am averse to casting that project in terms of a "philosophy Americana" (Anderson 2006). For the reasons offered in this essay, I would rather meet elsewhere and have him (and me, and whatever "us" finds these remarks compelling) engage phenomena like pragmatism, country music, jazz, rap, Southern lit, confessional poetry, and transcendentalism, over and against what "America," in the full objectivity of that term, has come to be.

24. The phrase is Emerson's and runs, "I am ready to die out of nature, and be born again into this new yet unapproachable America I have found in the West" (CW3, 41). I would not preserve it in this context, however. It occurs in a paragraph that proposes a hidden divinity that each should let trump, as a "life above life," our material nature, and under no condition would I divinize "America" nor hitch my cart to the fable of what in "us changes not, and which ranks all sensations and states of mind" (CW3, 42).

25. Readers of Baudrillard might find it ironic that I have tried to contest "America" with a kind of modernity. According to Baudrillard, "America" names a "radical modernity" that escapes history to the degree that it is the "*only remaining primitive society*" (1988, 81, 7). In other words, "just now" is all there is to American temporality. I think Baudrillard is wrong on two accounts. Like all empires, "America" has a monumental history through which it reads its conquests. Second, there is more to the trope of modernity than the ahistorical primitivism that Baudrillard finds as he travels quickly (often by plane) across the United States, or so I have tried to show by way of a threefold mood of antiauthoritarian defiance that is bewildered before the immensity of a present (that isn't simply present) and gripped by a feel for the ways in which symbolic orders must be raked if the fullness of the present is to be adequately engaged, "adequacy" measured by the kinds of exits and possible transformations, even advances, one's bearing, even one's essay, helps effect.

LIVING MULTIPLICITY: A MATTER OF COURSE

> It is *so difficult* to find the beginning. Or, better: it is *difficult to begin* at the beginning. And not try to go further back.
> —Ludwig Wittgenstein

—I. We easily answer questions about ourselves. How are you? What do you do? What do you want to be? Are you happy with whom you've become? They do not pose extraordinary puzzles, even though our replies might draw from several wells. "How are you?" I am fine though my tooth hurts. Getting older, I guess. My job is driving me crazy. In love, still. "What do you do?" I am a professor. Is that the doing you had in mind? I ask because I do so much, at times, unwittingly. "What do you want to be?" *Not* a jerk. And like Thoreau, someone who, when it comes time to die, knows that he has lived. And in praise, I would add. "Are you happy with whom you've become?" I've become so many things... Some more than others, a few very much so, one or two, not at all. And there is more to come.

Of course, it matters who is asking. And where. And when. If I were writing this twenty-five years ago, when I was twenty-five, I would have replied differently. "How are you?" I am fine but I'm tired of being a graduate student. And I'm confused. How can one suck at love? (I mean me.) "What do you do?" Right now? I tutor athletes. "What do you want to be?" A professor. "Are you happy with whom you've become?" Still too soon to tell, but this is much better than sixteen. That was a mess.

If I were applying for a job or on a date, no doubt I'd answer differently still. Not that I would lie in such cases. But I would answer differently as different thoughts came to mind as I found myself in different situations. But that wouldn't surprise me, at least not at twenty-nine, nor at twenty, and now I expect it, even delight in it. Do different enough things, hang out with different enough people, and you'll prove kaleidoscopic, a spectacle, not yet a dog peddling the same old tricks.

Most of the questions we turn on our selves are answerable, at least with a reasonable degree of specificity; more than good enough for rock 'n' roll. But there are times when we stumble in reply. In "Santa Barbara Road," Robert Hass playfully presses his daughter (1989, 52).

> Household verses. "Who are you?"
> the rubber duck in my hand asked Kristin
> once, while she was bathing, three years old.
> "Kristin," she said, laughing, her delicious
> name, delicious self. "That's just your name,"
> the duck said. "Who are you?" "Kristin,"
> she said. "Kristin's a name. Who are you?"
> the duck asked. She said, shrugging,
> "Mommy, Daddy, Leif." (lines 21–29)

The puzzle is: who (or what) lies beneath our name? The poem seems to give a point to Kristin. Everyone else in the family answers to a name, why can't I? But after her first "Kristin," it also says "laughing, her delicious / name, delicious self," which intrigues. Is her delicious self in her name or in her laughing? Or in her laughing her reply by way of her name? And/or in her shrugging resort to the terms she has for the most important people in her life, terms that work, or used to work, to indicate who they were?

Kristin is three, of course. But the poem denies that innocence precludes insight of a sort. And it goes on to suggest, with varying waves at the Buddha (whose own name is displaced), that multiplying terms does not produce more satisfying answers.

> So many prisms to construct a moment!
> Spiderwebs set at all angles on a hedge:
> what Luke thought was going on, what Mr. Acker
> saw, and Richard, who had recently divorced,
> idly rolling a ball with someone else's child,
> healing slowly. (lines 63–67)

We live with a wide-ranging and relatively deep sense of ourselves, but when pressed to provide univocal replies, we struggle, and with good reason. We are polyphonic beings. Even our own being offers so many prisms to construct a moment. But we nevertheless find ourselves in that polyphony, say laughing, shrugging, recently divorced and rolling a ball with someone else's child, or fifty trying to imagine what I might have said at twenty-five to a question like: how do you see yourself in twenty-five years?

——II. The thought that selves are polyphonic has roots in Nietzsche. But that is just to name a site, even if I can point to a particular passage, section 12 of *Beyond Good and Evil*, which declares war against the "atomistic need" and risks "new versions and refinements of the soul hypothesis" (Nietzsche 1966, 20). I say this because Nietzsche is not without his predecessors, even progenitors. As Thoreau has it, with characteristic restraint: "It is difficult to begin without borrowing" (1971, 40–41). Emerson, as usual, is more explicit and upbeat: "Original power in men is usually accompanied with assimilating power" (CW8, 100).

The point by now is familiar, even uncontested. Were it not regularly ignored, I would not repeat it. But, to begin with Nietzsche is to begin after the beginning. There is my path to, from, and back to Nietzsche. There is Nietzsche's path to "Nietzsche." And there is a long, long history of squabbles about what we mean when we refer to our *selves*. And that is just to trip on the roots.

I pause before "Nietzsche" because, like many (though not enough), I wish his debts to Emerson were a matter of course.[1] It thus bears repeating that in coming after Nietzsche one also, at least at certain points, comes after Emerson, say through the thought that self-consciousness is principally responsive and never autonomous, or in their insistence that living things seek conditions conducive to growth, a state both think in terms of power. That said, two cautions quickly come to mind. Taking an author's proper name as a site is not equivalent to rendering him or her a sieve. Nor should it lead us to believe that a cultural-textual mapping of that site somehow provides the whole of what is found there. Thinkers like Nietzsche never simply quote. As Emerson says in "Quotation and Originality": "There are great ways of borrowing. Genius borrows nobly" (CW8, 100). I would also stress (my reasons to follow) that *quotation* names an event that has personal dimensions—it involves activities that no one can do for the one who quotes, which is why I am so taken by the line: "Original *power* in men is usually accompanied with assimilating *power*."[2] I would thus amend my earlier claim that commencing with Nietzsche begins after the beginning. Even as Emerson's focus on power (over freedom) testifies to that fact (and sets them both in line with Spinoza, though also with Aristotle, for whom the voluntary entails something other than autonomy), "Nietzsche" remains a beginning, better still, an inception, a beginning again.

One more thought by way of orientation toward questions concerning the self. "Whoever expresses to us a just thought, makes ridiculous the pains of the critic who should tell him where such a word had been said before" (CW8, 101). This is another variation on Emerson's devotion to power. Set here, it reminds me that Nietzsche does not quote, whomever he quotes, explicitly or otherwise, simply to quote. Rather, he quotes to orient and outfit himself for a task, even if it refracts or reorients the project. (We might say, Nietzsche, like Emerson, thinks through quotation, neither self-possessed nor dispossessed in the process.) In taking a proper name as a site, one need not abandon that site as a place of power that one might inherit, try out, essay. And that thought, even as it quotes Emerson, is the spirit in which I wish to proceed. Something startling comes to pass in Nietzsche's war on the atomistic need and in his revisions of the soul hypothesis, particularly given how both projects abandon the theodical hopes and pains that so often recur in Emerson's texts.[3]

—III. I want to restart by way of *Beyond Good and Evil*, section 12. It has cleared the way for and initiated the task to which I abandoned myself some years ago—reckoning with the phenomenon of human being, "the self" in a manner that (1) proceeds *jenseits* (understood in the sense of "beyond," even "outside") the *subiectum*, that principal figure of metaphysics, which invokes an enduring presence or ground, even a substratum (material or spiritual), while (2) still attending to the ways in which we find ourselves in ongoing disclosures of our being. Moreover, in a metatheoretical way, a few passages from *Beyond Good and Evil* orient how I approach questions concerning the self—but we'll come to that shortly.

Here is Nietzsche's provocation: "One must, however, go still further and declare war unto the finish, a merciless war upon the "atomistic need," which still leads a dangerous afterlife in places no one suspects, and similarly upon the more celebrated "metaphysical need":—also, above all, one must finish off the other, more calamitous atomism, which Christianity has taught best and longest, *the soul atomism*. Let this phrase be taken to indicate the belief that the soul is something imperishable, eternal, indivisible, a monad, an atom: this belief should be removed from science" (1966, 20). I do not wish to underplay the proactive language of "removal," of *hinausschaffen*, which denotes bringing something outside of an area (see Luther's translation of Leviticus 16:27), and, more recently and idiomatically, setting out the trash. Nietzsche is bellicose because he is deep in struggle, resisting certain currents, striving to intensify others. But for now, I want to present Nietzsche's request in the form of a negative hypothesis. It is infelicitous to posit the existence of a self that, in any enduring, self-identical manner, either perceptually underlies or agentially directs (self-consciously, unconsciously, or mechanically) human life. The thought is strong though not unique. Anticipations lie in Hume's *Treatise*, and the suggestion that we are clusters without cores informs John Dewey's *Human Nature and Conduct*. But I will develop it in my own way as I too work to expose and undermine lines of thought where soul atomism persists.

But given how section 12 continues, let's not rest with the negative hypothesis: "Between ourselves, it is not at all necessary to simultaneously get rid of 'the soul' and so dispense with one of the most ancient and venerable hypotheses: as customarily befalls clumsy naturalists who barely touch on 'the soul' and then lose it. Yet the way stands open for new versions and refinements of the soul-hypothesis: and concepts like 'mortal soul' and 'soul as subjective multiplicity' and 'soul as social structure of the drives and affects' henceforth want citizen's rights in science" (Nietzsche 1966, 20–21). While diagnosing various prejudices of the philosophers, Nietzsche calls for and begins the work of the new psychologist who offers concepts that (1) acknowledge the life they conduct, which, as mortal, involves growth and decay, and (2) attest to a kind of polyphony in our being, one somehow organized without seamless unity—more constellation than monad. In order to continue this line of reconstruction, I will try to concretize the thought of a *subjective multiplicity*, which I take to require (1) granting ontological primacy to multiplicity and (2) articulating how a kind of subjectivity (which I shall interpret as self-experience) arises through and in response to that multiplicity.

Before pursuing these tasks, allow me to remain with Nietzsche. I am struck that, on behalf of concepts like "soul as subjective multiplicity," he lays claims to the citizen's rights in science and maintains the language of hypothesis. And I don't regard these invocations as ironic. *Beyond Good and Evil* is a text written with the tension of a bow strung to the breaking point. Nietzsche, feeling that tension as a "need of the spirit," harnesses it with almost every word and phrase in the hopes that he'll be sprung beyond a form of life he finds less than lively. I thus find his invocations of "psychology" and "science" sincere. They reverberate with remarkable overtones, however. At the close of section 12, he suggests that something like the negative hypothesis thrusts one into a barren land where, mistrusting previous orientations, one must remake one's way (borrowing, quoting, collaborating).[4] In other words, displacing soul atomism disorients us, and we need to work to refind our footing. Nietzsche thus continues, "eventually, however, he [the new psychologist—JTL] knows that he has thereby precisely also condemned himself to *invention* (*Erfinden*)—and, who knows, perhaps to *discovery* (*Finden*)" (1966, 21). I underscore this passage because it casts "psychology" and "science" as more than explanatory discourses making predictions on the basis of recurring correlations among antecedents and consequences. For Nietzsche, and for me, systematic psychological inquiry is also the imaginative attempt to find one's way in precarious and even inhospitable climes, that is, these practices try to secure conditions in which a life might flourish. (Readers of *Beyond Good and Evil* might recall how section 13 insists that living things seek to discharge strength, to feel the surge of their life, and that mere survival is often an effect of this but almost never the goal, except in moments of extreme distress, as we're told in section 349 of *The Gay Science*.)

My negative hypothesis runs: it is infelicitous to posit the existence of a self that, in any enduring, self-identical manner, either perceptually underlies or agentially directs (self-consciously, unconsciously, or mechanically) human being. I know that many will resist this claim. You might agree that we present ourselves to ourselves in varied ways, and thus, in reflective moments, appear as a complex and differentiated, but that complexity is simply the varied appearance of a unified phenomenon.[5] This is not my position, and primarily because I cannot find any evidence of this supposedly unified phenomenon. As Hume argues, we have no knowledge of ourselves as having any "perfect identity and simplicity," as being a kind of being that exists independently of its activities. He continues, "I never catch *myself* at any time without a perception, and never can observe any thing but the perception.... I may venture to affirm of the rest of mankind, that they are nothing but a bundle or collection of perceptions, which succeed each other with an inconceivable rapidity, and are in a perpetual flux and movement" (1964, 252).

In this context, let's broaden the terrain to self-experience. To speak of a self-experience is to speak in part of a reflexive phenomenon, of finding oneself appearing in a particular manner, such as self-as-shopping, self-as-hungry, self-as-agile, self-as-female, self-as-Latino, or self-as-success. My claim is: when we try to locate the substantive or singular self presented in self-experience, we always find ourselves in various determinate ways but we never find some enduring, identical self thereby determined. And if we try to locate an enduring observational ego in the finding, we only encounter concrete self-experiences and never a bare, observational ego. True, the reflexivity of self-experience grammatically invokes a being that finds itself so positioned, but phenomenological reflection suggests that such reference is misleading. In fact, Emerson is more perspicacious when he writes: "Man is a stream whose source is hidden. Our being is descending into us from we know not whence" (CW2, 159).

If Emerson's image of the stream recalls you to William James, you might also recall that James believes Hume goes too far in his denial of an enduring ego. In large measure, James agrees with Kant that each thought is in some sense "mine," though he replaces the transcendental unity of apperception with an event wherein experiences are appropriated to a prevailing state of mind, which he terms a "Thought." But when pressed to account for this state of mind and its appropriations, he admits that each new experience is not appropriated to an ego or even to some prevailing "Thought," but to and by a stream of consciousness (or "sciousness"), since he regards the stream and the swimmer as facets of the same mad rush. Not that that the stream lacks a characteristic current according to James. It moves, he thinks, through the body and its "central adjustments." In fact, James goes so far as to term those ongoing adjustments the *"real nucleus of personal identity"* (1983). This more or less leaves us with an eroticized Hume, however (call him Nietzsche), with a being whose *"central active self"* is in fact the interplay of corporeal attractions and repulsions that are felt and undergone without being authored. Nietzsche would insist, however, that we not rest with a term like "nucleus" and its atomistic connotations. Do corporeal propulsions and repulsions admit of their own multiplicity, flowing from multiple corporeal sites within the brain and across the body? Do they come to pass as self-enclosed phenomena, or is each at once a projection into and a response to the world, such that they are in-the-world as Heidegger has it, or transactional in Dewey's idiom? And do explicit self-interpretations, for example, "I am scared," simply interpret this supposedly "central" active self or is a more complex phenomenon involved such that self-interpretations spawn their own interplay of corporeal adjustments which in turn call for further self-interpretation?

Galen Strawson is more confident that self-experience involves an encounter with something like an inner entity. He claims that "self-experience" involves "one's experience of oneself when one is considering oneself principally as an inner mental entity or 'self' of some sort" (2004, 429). Obviously, this view runs counter to mine, and on several fronts. But the real bone of contention lies with the claim that one experiences oneself as an "internal entity" that is a "self of some sort."

But "contention" may say too much. One cannot cleanly resolve a debate if the evidence that proves decisive for one view is not available to all interlocutors. Not that Strawson and I have nothing to say to one another, as Hume suggests when he claims that he cannot reason with another who finds more than perceptions when entering "most intimately into what I call *myself*" (2000). Strawson and I can always ask one another to look again and to more finely and discriminately describe what appears when we encounter ourselves. We also can consider the felicity of our terms—why "entity," why "inner," why "mental"? And we can genealogically explore the roots of what might seem like common sense in order to loosen its hold on us. I note these options because, although such exchanges constitute arguments (reasons are given in support of conclusions that one asks another to adopt), they are not easily resolved through appeals to verifying or falsifying data, appeals that we associate with the replicating strategies of the empirical sciences. And thus I do not note my disagreement with Strawson in order to definitively demonstrate the error of his ways, though later, I will explain why terms like "inner" and "entity" are ill-suited to the task at hand. But for now, my concern lies with how tricky philosophical psychology becomes when intuitions (or inventions) clash, and my goal, for the moment, is to acknowledge that trickiness, and only after that, return us to scenes wherein we find ourselves.

——IV. Talk about selves is not only tricky. It often breeds impatience. One might not mind being wrong about the Battle of Princeton, but it irks when we goof what we are. I thus imagine protests as I go, often involuntarily. "Be that as it may," one might say, "isn't what appears in phenomenological reflection ultimately the appearance of material elements whose interactions are best understood as causal connections? And so, shouldn't you focus your ventures upon a material substratum, thus limiting your claims to the kind of options that are possible for a being of our nature given the kind of forces one finds in a universe like ours?" I confess that I don't find this line of thought very promising. Humans are certainly beset by manifold forces. In fact, we find ourselves always already beset, hence Heidegger's felicitous conception of *Geworfenheit*, "thrownness." (We always find ourselves situated in ways we did not choose but must engage.) But even as conditioning events beset humans, they find themselves so affected. In other words, most of the time human beings are not simply subjected to causes (instantaneous death may be an exception). Instead, they explicitly undergo that subjection, that is, interpret and respond to it, and in a recursive manner, meaning, a prior adjustment becomes part of the situation that must again be assessed.[6]

We could put the matter more phenomenologically. In Hegel's words, human beings are for-themselves. Or, in Sartre's language, human being is a presence to itself. Or, in Heidegger's language: *dasein* is characterized by *Erschlossenheit*, disclosedness. I take this to mean, keeping to Heidegger, that humans are *opened* to themselves in the course of their *development* (*erschliessen* carries senses of opening and development). Less technically stated, humans exist in the ongoing event of finding themselves disclosed to themselves, for example, sweating on a humid day, challenged by mental illness, or touched by a gift. Regardless of which phenomenology one favors, the underlying point is that human lives have an ineliminable first-person dimension. In fact, for Heidegger, even *Angst* maintains this reflexive dimension—in anxiety, the utter retreat of beings as a whole is something one undergoes. Now, this is not to say that every facet of human being-in-the-world is laced with reflexivity. For example, Antonio Damasio (1999) reports that several brain-stem nuclei, some of which regulate states like body temperature, carry out operations that do not seem to be undergone as such. But enough of our being is for-itself that a felicitous account must take into account the reflexivity lacing our existence.

Let me now return to the thought that philosophical psychology should focus its ventures on the material substratum of our being. Because humans are for-themselves they cannot be identified with either a purported ground of their being or some consequent or set of consequents of that ground. Either moment, insofar as it can be presented as such, for example, given as evidence, is a disclosure of our being to our being, thus indicating that the ground or consequent is a matter to be interpreted and further engaged by the one undergoing it. And if there is a being that undergoes and further engages a given ground or consequent, that being cannot be reduced to either. I thus do not think that the future of philosophical psychology exclusively or even predominantly lies with explanations of how our being arises out of the causal interactions that are often presented as our material grounds. When it comes to understanding selfhood and self-experience, that kind of materialism only offers another atomism.

Now, to be clear, I am not claiming that human beings writ large, or even the fact of our reflexivity, occurs unrelated to events that we would term "causal." Rather, I am claiming that one cannot fathom human beings if one tries to locate the self in either its causal grounds or their purported effects, if only because the self occurs in an ongoing movement between these terms, with self-experience arising in the course of that movement. My objection thus lies with a metaphysical figure, that of a ground and its consequents, and the distortions that this particular conception of the *subiectum* brings to philosophical psychology.

Here is one distortion that I have termed "Henderson's two patients." Jamie Henderson is a neurosurgeon who works with neuroprosthetics including deep brain stimulators (DBSs), surgical implants designed to alleviate phenomena such as the tremors associated with Parkinson's. In a seminar on neurosurgery and patient freedom/autonomy sponsored by the Liberty

Fund, Henderson clearly articulated a common conundrum. The patient with whom he discusses the procedures, risks, and possible benefits associated with DBS has an obscure relation to the patient on whom he operates with unbelievable precision. It is as if all of the self-relations that occur in the consultation, for example, the patient's fears, hopes, and/or conceptual grasp of the procedure, as well as his or her consent, evaporate when it becomes a question of where to locate the DBS—none of them are or need to be taken into account in order to have a medically successful operation (legal issues notwithstanding). Surgically speaking, they seem irrelevant. And if they are surgically irrelevant, one wonders if they are immaterial in all contexts.

I appreciate the dilemma because I too am averse to substantial and discursive dualism. One cannot operate on mind-stuff, and trying to keep the two activities categorically distinct (consulting and operating) is just plain odd since the consult concerns the operation and its likely outcomes, which indicates an operative belief that Henderson's two patients are not categorically distinct. "If we operate, you can expect the following gains, the following losses, and for X amount of time. But overall, I think you'll feel more like your old self."

In order to avoid the conundrum of Henderson's two patients, we need terms in common, terms that operate similarly in the consult and the operation. I think I have such terms, and I propose to work toward them through the idea of the symptom. The operation and all of its miraculous, even awe-inspiring precision, is designed to alleviate or meliorate symptoms, and the consult concerns, in part, what symptoms will be alleviated, to what degree, how, and with what risks and side effects. My hunch, then, is that, if we concretely apprehend the phenomenon of the symptom, we will locate the site where Henderson's two patients flow into each other.

Among other things, tremors interfere with motility and it is because of such problems that we inquire into their causes in order to interrupt them. Skin cells continually die and are replaced, and at varying rates on different parts of the body, and differently on different bodies. There are causes of this, but we don't regard these deaths as symptoms because they do not interrupt most lives, although certain practices may require unbelievably smooth, flakeless skin, and in those cases, we may begin to "treat" the issue. A certain degree of knee pain may come and go in the course of a day for a bus driver but require extensive therapy for an Olympic athlete. Headaches are symptoms because they make it difficult to concentrate and carry out tasks. The fact that my left foot is a half size smaller and a half a size wider than my right is not a symptom because most shoes allow for that range. These examples suggest, I think, that "symptoms" occur as problematic situations that interrupt the ongoing activities and purposive trajectories of a person, that is, their conduct of life. Outside of that context (which includes the worldly conditions in which we find ourselves), symptoms do not occur. Nor would symptoms occur if we lacked self-experience. If we were not self-relating beings, finding ourselves, our lives could not be interrupted. One day I would have psoriasis, but that change would have no significance or meaning and thus never become a "symptom." It would be like a sheet of metal growing hotter as it nears the sun. Flaking paint is not a symptom for a car even if it means the body will eventually rust. Intense heat is not a symptom for clay even if the clay melts. Only a being whose life is disclosed to itself in the context of purposive trajectories has symptoms.

I am proposing that Henderson's two patients meet in the course of a purposive, reflexive life, one wherein we find ourselves en route to various ends, say a meal, a walk, a liaison, an exam. Each "patient" is in fact a moment within the course of a life, and surgeons and physicians have this context in mind when they consult with patients and when they operate. "Let's see if we can't get your life back on track. When properly placed, these gadgets can really help." Even the brain that receives a DBS is analyzed and manipulated with this context in mind. The intervention is not an attempt to return a "brain" to some purportedly normal state but to meliorate symptoms that have made life difficult for the person suffering from tremors and to mitigate whatever side effects might introduce new problematics. At least in these clinical settings, it is not the case, therefore, that the brain (or the body) is something like a substratum for the life that is the focus of consultations. Rather, the course of a purposive, reflexive life is the ur-phenomenon that orients how the brain is assessed and redressed.

I have never been able to venture this thought without provoking the charge of dualism. Let me repeat, therefore, that I am not claiming that humans have an immaterial nature that allows them to be more than their organicity would otherwise allow. Nor am I identifying the self of self-experience with some undetectable being *for* whom events like influences and self-experiences come to pass. As I've argued, I cannot lay my hands on any such phenomenon. I am a materialist through and through. And I do not know what it means to be otherwise. But I do not think that materialism (or naturalism) should generate hypotheses on the basis of a ground-consequent figure, such that matter is the ground whereas mind, selfhood, and sense of self are cast as its consequents. Nor, for that matter, do I think the mind or the soul is the ground such that our beliefs, acts, and desires are its consequents. The figure is altogether too clumsy to still claim citizen's rights in science.

—V. Proceeding phenomenologically, I have resisted the inscription of atomistic centers within self-experience, at least in the position of the experiencer and the experienced. I also have proposed that self-experience and selfhood not be thought in terms of ground-consequent figures. But Nietzsche's provocation also calls for and initiates a reconstruction. The beginnings of one lie in our discussion of Henderson's two patients, but let's develop it further through an account of self-experience. The grammar of self-experience is ambiguous along lines analogous to "experience." On the one hand, there is the experiencing or interpreting self, shorthand for the diverse processes by which human organisms track what befalls them, whether prereflectively (e.g., peripheral attention, working memory, or coretorso and refined-motor somatotopic mapping) or reflectively (e.g., through autobiography). On the other hand, there is the self that is experienced, shorthand for the diverse ways in which human facticity appears, for example, in affective bearings and social roles, such that it can be known and acted on. Both moments are integral; when turned toward itself, self-experience apprehends the self as a movement between an experiencer and the experienced. One is never without the other and not just in a grammatical sense. We never find ourselves simply as an experiencer, and as we encounter ourselves in our facticity, we also encounter how we encounter it, such as *fondly recalling* my thirties, *impatiently anticipating* my wife's return, *carefully* shaving while *seeing* my reflection in the mirror. How though should we conceptualize this interplay? On my account, which has evolved since 2002, self-experience has at least four analytically distinct moments, which I term the 4Ps.[7] It is: (1) positioned, (2) purposive, (3) partial, and (4) possibilized. And knowing this provides us with points (or sites) of self-knowledge, meaning, a purposive, reflexive life becomes more salient when its course is mapped at all four points.

Because we transpire in given, factical *situations*, self-experiences are *positioned*. In each case, the interpreting self and the self being interpreted are always positioned in "ecosocial history," that is (1) in synchrosomatic webs of relation and (2) diachronic histories, at once social and personal. Imagine yourself a wage laborer in a retail setting. The job *positions* you in a matrix of relations. Interpret them as you will, even strive to change them, but the job nevertheless stages large parts of one's time and world. Some of these relations are interpersonal, for example, you work alongside coworkers, a manager or two, perhaps an owner, customers, and your workplace overlaps with the work of UPS delivery personal, custodial and sanitation workers, etc. Where you work also positions or places you in a concrete environment, say a shopping mall with its regulated temperature, artificial light, recycled air, food court, soundscape, various insects, the occasional rat, and so forth. And you inhabit that concrete environment in terms of various corporeal orientations, such as working the floor and the register, thereby standing as opposed to sitting. Third, your calendar revolves, more or less, around your job: 8–5 every Wednesday through Sunday with a few holidays here and there and a few more twelve-hour days, filling in for ownership and worker turn over; such is the plight of an assistant manager. Fourth, if one works in the United States, wage labor involves one in a vast series of municipal, state, and federal laws as well as ongoing debates about where to set the minimum wage.

The example of wage labor illustrates a self whose job determinately (and corporeally) positions it in a synchronic web of intersubjective (e.g., coworkers), institutional (e.g., the IRS), and environmental relations (e.g., the mall, its internal ensemble of creatures and, for the sake of argument, the wet land it borders and partially fills). The example also illustrates how those relations are suffused with diachronic determinations: the era of the mall pre- or postinternet, the seasonal nature of retail sales, the history of the minimum wage, and the life calendar that a retail job arranges. To be a wage laborer is thus to be positioned in a diverse, synchronic, and diachronic field.

Among those diachronic determinations, one finds more than institutional and evolutionary histories. One is also there as a teenager, as a middle-aged man surviving an economic downturn, or as a lifer, one for whom selling shoes has been a career approaching its end. Within the currents of ecosocial history, one also experiences oneself in the course of one's life, and not simply through memories that might come to mind, or relative to a personal narrative that informs one's existential expectations. Institutional roles register and reflect our place in the life cycle back to us through anniversaries, formal or informal rules involving seniority, nicknames ("old man," "kid"), as well as our responses to and preferences for customers. (Shifting to my job, it is much different teaching undergraduates as a fifty-year-old than it was as a young man approaching thirty. Students respond to me differently, which gives me a new sense of my presumed place in the larger social fabric.) The diachronic dimensions of self-experience are thus personal as well sociohistorical. Or rather, there is a personal dimension to how ecosocial history unfolds in self-experience, and that dimension concerns the life that is in some sense ours.

Not only the object of self-experience is positioned in this manner. What proves salient and significant in self-experience modulates as my positioning changes. Move from a job interview to a date to a beer with a very good friend. In one context, possibly two, one's posture may prove salient, that is, one may sense oneself slouching and adjust. With a very good friend, I am not acutely aware of whether they are digging what I say. And in the job interview as opposed to the date, I focus much more on what I am saying (and how I am saying it), whereas I worry quite a bit more about the questions I ask on dates. Even my memory seems to function differently when my positioning shifts. Family gatherings trigger certain memories, first dates others, and job interviews still others. Desire too. Children raised together tend, overwhelmingly, not to be sexually attracted to one another whereas biologically related people raised separately and ignorant of their biological relation are as likely to have the hots for one another as any other pair. And now that I'm older, I tend to experience my own frustrations differently. Like many, I had more patience when I had a good deal of time ahead of me, less patience now. In short, the experiencing self seems thoroughly positioned as well.

Consider some other examples, attending to how positionality impacts both facets of self-experience. You are walking along a rough path, having a conversation. As you walk and talk, you continually adjust your footing without giving the adjustments a second thought. While this process is inordinately complex, it evidences how, even at the level of basic motor skills, self-experience is a matter finding oneself positioned in a determinate situation. One doesn't simply sense one's foot but one's foot in relation to the ground in the course of walking and only on the fringes of an attention intently focused on the conversation at hand. (Without the conversation, and if exercising, one's balance and gait will likely register differently.) Recall a time when you felt afraid. What all was disclosed in the feeling? Just the state of some isolated self? What then were you afraid of? Instead, one feels oneself threatened in some determinate, purposive context: walking to one's car, entering a bathroom, or sitting next to a stranger at an airport. And even if the threat is vague or indeterminate, that indeterminacy arises within a larger context, say a dimly lit alley, a strange group of people, or an uncertain future, each of which orients us differently. Finally, imagine a case of heartburn. The pain is clearly "in" your body, but your body or better still "you" remain in a determinate context that you engage given your discomfort. You stand up, you take deep breaths, and you walk around the room and eventually get a drink of water. Or, if you are at a meeting, you might try to block it out, or quietly regulate your breathing while answering a question, or excuse yourself. In other words, finding oneself with heartburn, feeling afraid, or adjusting one's footing involves finding oneself positioned (or better still, repositioned) in a determinate scene of ecosocial history. Or, in other words, while degrees and kinds of reflexivity lace our positionality, that reflexivity is always responding to our positionality.

You may wonder why I speak of "degrees" of reflexivity. I agree with Antonio Damasio's claim that "consciousness is not a monolith, at least not in humans: it can be separated into simple and complex kinds" (1999, 16). According to Damasio, what we normally term "consciousness" is in fact a multifaceted but acentered gathering of perceptions, feelings, attentions, emotions, and responses. Damasio thus distinguishes activities such as low-level attention, the ability to pay fleeting attention to salient events like a flash of light or sounds outside one's room, from higher-level attention, for example, the ability to attend to a colleague entering your office as "the entry of your colleague into your office." He distinguishes these in part because there exist conditions like akinetic mutism where low-level attention is possible but higher-level attention is "severely diminished or even suspended altogether" (101).

Consider Damasio's case of L. Following a stroke, L would not respond to questions (though she would occasionally say her name) and she "did not react to the presence of her relatives and friends" (1999, 102). Moreover, after regaining her speech and higher-order capacities of attention, "she had no recall of any particular experience during her long period of silence; she had never felt fear; had never been anxious; had never wished to communicate" (103). Unlike patients with locked-in syndrome, therefore, L seems to have lived without higher-order attention for several months although one would describe her as awake and capable of low-level attention.

This ability to distinguish higher-order from low-level attention suggests that human reflexivity does not involve a unified field of consciousness continually observing the course of our lives. Note that my claim is not that many cognitive acts are unconscious. Rather, what we call consciousness is itself a multiplicity operating at various levels that do not revolve around a central point of self-consciousness. But, one might object: isn't it possible that akinetic mutism entails the diminishment of what is otherwise a unified phenomenon? Doubtful. One can focus on a conversation in a crowded bar while low-level attention persists (cross-modally, I should add), without interrupting or even entering higher-level attention, although it might if one smelled enough smoke for a long enough time to stop and ask, "Is something burning?" I thus think that even in the absence of profound impairments, consciousness involves overlapping but distinct fields of awareness, and thus it is a mistake to say that some enduring, knowing self hovers at heart of all of the ways in which we are disclosed to ourselves over the course of our lives.

But let us return to self-experience and its positioning. Earlier I argued that causes and effects are phenomena for selves to interpret and redress. I thus do not believe that our positioning in ecosocial history, including the course of our lives, is simply a process of subjection. Yes, to be positioned is to be thrown into and exposed to determinate situations, and thus ecosocial history is something that a self undergoes rather than simply posits or constructs. But the mall's controlled air can prove too cold or too warm and thus one can put on a sweater or take one off. The customers can be irritating or engaging, and one can reply in kind (or not). One can take aspirin for an aching back or build up one's core to better withstand the rigors of standing all day. The building's teeming world of insects can be marveled at and/or poisoned. And so forth, that is, to be positioned in ecosocial history is to be exposed to a world opened for further interpretation and response. But that puts the point too passively. Ecosocial history is not simply open to interpretation and response; our course within it is interpretative and responsive from the outset. The mall's climate is controlled for and by reasons, and various interests mediate relations to customers.

That we interpret and respond to the various ways in which we are positioned indicates that we are *purposive*, striving to find our way through the folds of ecosocial history. We don't just register data, we reckon with its significance for our projects. The customer is irritating, but we need the sale to earn our commission. The food court only sells fatty food so we bring a lunch in order to maintain our weight. Our wage is lower than we like but we know that the owner is going through tough times so we don't ask for a raise but instead seek a few days of paid vacation when business is slow.

The purposive nature of the self is evident in other ways as well. As Dewey would have it, we don't just see but look, that is, one keeps an eye on the entrance to see who enters (Dewey 1972). We don't just hear; we listen. As a salesperson, one attends to the customer's voice in order to gauge increasing or decreasing enthusiasm. Of course, while doing so, one hears a great deal more: a phone, the whir of climate control devices, the buzz of fluorescent lights, the cough of an allergized coworker, and a good deal of indistinct tones coming from the corridors. But the point is not to claim that all of perception is a function of a single purposive focus. (Usually, multiple purposes are orienting us in multiple ways at any given time.) Rather, it is just to say, the being that the world washes over is proactively addressing (and redressing) the world. Think also of those times when the hair on your neck stood up and fear crept over you. Those instances illustrate that, prereflectively, we monitor the safety of the world in which we are positioned. Yes, the self is positioned in the world, but its position is usually oriented toward more or less determinate goals: safety, a meal, pleasure, a paycheck, meaning, etc.

Always already positioned and purposive, self-experience, like symptoms, seems bound to the course of a life, that is, the *self* that experiences and the *self* that is experienced is a moment within this more originary phenomenon. Neither comes to pass without being positioned in a factical situation with purposes in play. And this is why I speak of the *course* of a life. We always find our *selves* along paths already charted by the events of ecosocial history. And we proactively travel those paths with varying courses of action, say looking for a place to eat, feeling about a drawer for our keys, just trying to relax in a side room, away from the fray. Yes, we can be surprised. We may not be looking for food but driving to a meeting, and then, the sight of an intriguing restaurant may lead us to pull over for a quick bite. But surprises occur when one trajectory is interrupted by the appearance of something that suggests another, not when a purpose appears within an otherwise purposeless horizon. Even practices that call for detached observation or nonattached contemplation are themselves positioned and purposive. I bracket certain expectations and predilections in order to be a better scientist. I try to still my mind, the whirl of memories, desires, and grievances, in order to grow attuned with a certain way of the world, say its broad, cosmic transitions, events whose gaits are far slower than the stretch and contraction of mountains.

Reflexivity, whether reflectively or prereflectively operative, accompanies many of the ways in which we are positioned in the course of ecosocial history, which is why I speak of a *life* and not of self-consciousness or *sciousness*. When inhabiting social roles, when responding to desires, when growing tired or hungry, even when feeling shame or elation, reflexivity is a matter of finding oneself in these conditions, and they claim us behind our back, as it were. We can commit to the courses of action thereby indicated, for example, eat when hungry, steady ourselves when stumbling, flirt when attracted, or spit when drinking old milk (or swallow if we're guests at a brunch). We can play along with (or resist) race and gender privilege, or defer or stand up to our institutional superiors. But reflexivity, from prereflectively operative, corporeal adjustments to explicit self-narration, is a responsive phenomenon.

Because self-experiences are not exclusively or even principally the fruit of reflexive acts (though such acts are part and parcel of self-experience), it strikes me that we do more harm than good when we regard them as propositional attitudes. "Proposition" suggests that self-experience involves judgments about oneself, but that seems off. Yes, I may take how I find myself positioned and articulate it as a judgment, for example, I may discover how often I am a raced, by myself and others, and I may come to render it as "John is a white man," and that may empower certain practices of self-knowledge and transformation. But the event of finding myself so positioned usually does not arise within the activity of discursive judgment. If anything, judgments are responses one might make to self-experiences. In finding myself raced, I may labor to articulate, as precisely as possible, how that functions and with what effects, but experiencing the arbitrary favor of a waitress who had just unfairly treated a black patron grabs me, affectively and viscerally, before the grammar of a judgment can settle. I would thus take the language of "propositional attitude" and set it on the curb alongside the other trappings of soul atomism.

The positioning of self-experience also indicates that our lives and self-experience are neither internal nor external phenomena, at least not in any exclusive sense. My experiences may not be available to you as "experiences," but that does not mean that they are *inside* me, and it seems odd to claim that they are. "Inside" is a term for containers, and while my liver is within my body, my experiences carry too much of the world that concerns them to be *in* me in an analogous way. Said otherwise, our synchrosomatic and diachronic positioning in ecosocial history (recall our wage labor example) underwrites both the experiencing and the experienced self, which in turn sets self-experience *in* the world, as Heidegger struggles to say. Self-experience thus dialectically undoes the semantic logic of "inside" and "outside," even if it does not thereby provide more felicitous phrasing.

The positioned, purposive nature of self-experience indicates, I think, that self-experience, in both its subjective and objective moments (to the degree that kind of shading is helpful), occurs within (and never without) the course of a life. There is more to say about self-experience, however. In the proprioceptive feedback that allows me to drink my coffee and in a surge of anxiety before an audience, each self-experience is *partial*, the disclosure of a facet of all that I am. Drinking coffee in my office, I am also a professor, male, white, alert, middle-aged, a friend, healthy, etc. And even as my anxiety strikes, the same series applies, as well as an odd feeling of confidence given I have had butterflies several times before and there are friends in the audience whom I cannot disappoint.

Given the partiality of self-experience, our being often appears to us as a spectacle of sonority, coloration, harmony, and dissonance. And we can try to draw it together through explicit narratives that organize the course of our lives as we find and pursue them in ecosocial history. But such reconstructions are partial (through their positioning) in their own ways. First, long-term memory is selective relative to our positioning. The autobiography of a film star, writer, or politician usually focuses on events that led to their becoming an actor or writer and ignores all of the selves they did not become. Similarly, a career narrative in a grant or job application amplifies events that prepared one for the next step. And one can expect other inflections when friends reminisce or one tries to explain, if only to oneself, how one has come more or less to despise a colleague. Again, reflexivity is responsive and situated, and that doesn't change when we expand it into a life narrative. Second, most of what befalls us permanently fades from view if it doesn't prove significant. Our purposiveness thus infuses our personal history and its recall at the most basic levels.

In "Experience," Emerson announces: "I am a fragment, and this is a fragment of me" (CW3, 47). The remark is a rich one, particularly in the context of transcontinental romanticism. With regard to the "new" psychology initiated by Nietzsche, I think the line captures an essential facet of self-experience. We never find the whole of our being. Instead, self-experience, positioned as it is, concerns a moment in the course of our lives, such as self-as-husband in his late thirties, self-as-friend on a bender in his twenties; self-as-professor mid-career; self-as-white-man in his teens, again in his thirties, then again at on fifty amid recurring waves of recalcitrant racism and white privilege. To say that self-experience is partial is thus to insist on two things. Self-experience is mediated by how it is positioned, and what is thereby disclosed is only a part of a larger phenomenon.

The fragments of self-experience are not simply fragments of ourselves, however. Our positioning shows that our course is always already part and parcel of the course of ecosocial history, for example, self-as-unmarried in a heteronormative, breeding social scene; self-as-friend on a bender, sporting a tweed in a working-class bar in a part of town rarely visited by professionals let alone academics; self-as-academic in a family devoted to the "real" world of commerce and its bottomless line; self-as-white in the heat of El Paso, or walking with a pack of dogs along the coast of Maine, or somewhere, alone, in the Hindu Kush mountains, bitterly cold. Self-experience discloses that we are fragments of a larger order that envelops us, inside and out. To say that we are in-the-world is thus to say that the *self* of self-experience orients and finds itself always already in a determinate, ecosocial setting, and it cannot do otherwise. And the more historically we think, the more this sensibility settles. My lungs and my skeleton, my language (syntax and semantics), the availability of "the promise" as an act, that my family was almost exclusively nuclear, the presence of a "federal" government, traces of what is possibly common law, each carries (or quotes, as Emerson has it) the conditions of their own emergence, conditions that cannot be fully accounted for by a litany of self-conscious acts. And yet, they constitute me in part, which is to say, my facticity is bound to theirs, and if it were all stripped away, there would not be a self for me to experience nor would my experiencing self have any orientation from which to assess and redress the world.

One might say, like Dewey (1983) does, that the self of self-experience is a functional concept, unthinkable outside of a larger context that gives determinate character to its bearing. In other words, take away the world and the self disappears, just as "x" ceases to be a variable (and becomes just a letter) when taken out of equations like $3x = 12$. The language of "function" threatens to mislead, however. By stressing our fragmentary character, I am not dissolving the self into a larger network that thereby becomes the genuine phenomenon, as if we were mere organs in a larger body. Rather, to switch the metaphor, selves are stars in ecosocial history's genuine constellations. Intersubjectivity, by definition, involves at least two subjects involved in a reciprocal engagement, each aware that the other is aware of addressing and being addressed by each other. The norms governing institutional roles require that those who fill them spontaneously decide whether any given situation calls for a particular norm; none are self-executing. And as we now know all too well, human production and consumption is reshaping the earth topographically and atmospherically.

By settling unhappily in the metaphor of function, self-experience exposes at least one more dimension—it is *possibilized*. What appears in self-experience is not simply the quality of thing, as if we were substances carrying various accidents such as brown eyes, straight hair, short legs, the ability to form sentences, including some that make promises. As we discussed earlier, each of the ways in which we experience ourselves is a matter for further interpretation and possible redress or a possibility.[8] As I sit in my chair, I am adjusting my hips, more or less continually, and not in any explicit fashion. My leg begins to cramp and I stand to stretch. I slip and I regain my balance, more or less without thinking through all that is required to right myself. Instead, my awareness is filled with a mild panic. My concentration wanes so I yawn, stretch my face, and reread the passage. Thinking about peripheral attention, I begin to hear the air conditioner, like an old dot matrix printer in the ceiling, and I try to focus on the touch of the keyboard. I realize I am growing content with certain kinds of avoidance, so I resolve to be more engaged. Across our varying degrees of awareness, situations to which self-experience is bound carry varying significance, from the immediately forgettable (the feel of this chair and today's humidity) to the monumental. But that is the horizon that opens in the course of a life. We are creatures whose lives are at stake in the world as we find it, and with regard to all of the ways that we can be at stake: survival, pleasure, meaning, power, piety, moral goodness, profitability, dignity, beauty, etc.

Return to the thought of a symptom and our earlier discussions. When a symptom arises, one is challenged to address it. It does not occur as a new coat of paint or the flaking of an old one. It puts one's being in question, and in many ways, often complicating home life, work, our sense of self-worth, etc. It is something with which one has to deal, usually with the help of others; it arrives as a possibility for the course of our lives.

Returning from a funeral, I once saw a student sitting on a cement wall, a "forty" in his hands. He had the most far-away look. Eyes focused on nothing in particular, he seemed barely there. Because I knew that he struggled with mental illness, I went over to see if he needed help. But given his state, I had to proceed slowly, and so I sat on the wall some four feet away. His body clenched but he remained seated. After fifteen or so minutes, I asked, gently: "Do you know who I am?" He nodded but said nothing. He was clearly in the grip of an acute episode, paranoid through and through. Ten or so minutes later we began a very simple conversation, which evolved into a walk and a more complex conversation. But I was unable to get him to seek medical attention. (Later we met and things had eventually settled for him.)

What struck me across the entire encounter was not the kind of vacancy I typically associate with unfocused eyes. Instead, an utter concentration was apparent. He was hanging on for dear life. (Referring to his decision to stop his medication—or so I inferred and later corroborated—he kept saying: "I just wanted to take one step. But I fell.") I recall the event because it shows that, even in what appears to be the disintegration of self-experience, the reflexive, purposive course of a life persists. In fact, this person's very disintegration remained something to be interpreted ("I tried, but I fell") and redressed, say with alcohol, just sitting (in a very public space, we should note), a minimal conversation, and later, fleeing when my efforts to walk him to the counseling center proved too threatening.

The example of a symptom can mislead, however. It is not the case that our possibilization is limited to single, discrete disclosures. Self-experience is often organized around multiple positionings and purposes, which pose their own possibilities. You attend a work party with your new partner and struggle to remain attentive to your new partner as you make the rounds and pay (and receive) your social dues, particularly to your new manager, who is hosting. A former love interest also attends with a new partner, which awakens surprising feelings of jealousy that are difficult to ignore, and so you find yourself posing questions designed to expose the shallowness of your former lover's partner elect. In this case, self-experience inhabits several situations without disclosing some self presumably lying beneath the subjective multiplicity. Moreover, the surfeit occasionally proves too much for you to reflectively assess, so you step on to a balcony to settle down. Yes, the example is exaggerated. But it also captures the kind of multiplicity that is often operative in lives that are positioned in various ways at work, at home, while shopping on a Saturday or while driving or taking a train. That is, in the course of our lives, self-experience is rich with multiplicity, even though we answer (usually) to the same name wherever we go.

As I argued earlier, the multiplicity of self-experience is not the manifold appearing of some enduring, unified entity or being that we are. No such phenomenon can be found. When I speak of the course of a life and grant it primacy, I am not thereby indicating some *one* who lives it and stands as its ground. I recall this point because, should a multiplicity of positionings, reflexive capabilities, and purposive trajectories partially characterize the course of our lives, then we are, as Nietzsche suggests a multiplicity of souls, an interanimating system of possibilities, some known, some not.⁹ From prereflectively operative systems of self-regulation to social roles to our explicit (usually) manifold self-regard, we exist through and as the interaction of multiple, orienting phenomena: peripheral *and* focal attention; working, short-term, *and* long-term memory; core-torso *and* refined-motor, somatotopic mapping; immediate consciousness with its pulsing here and now; social roles grounded in a corporeal and cognitive savoir; narratival, extended consciousness with varying self-concepts. These are the phenomena that, through and with ecosocial history, constitute the currents that flow as the course of a life.

—VI. "But what renders any given multiplicity the course of *my* life? Distribute me as you will, I am still the one coming and going." The question is not unreasonable. Do we need a general vocabulary for the ways in which this multiplicity unfolds across the course of a life? Contrary to earlier writings, I no longer find it helpful to term the dynamic interplay among our partial positionings, reflexive capabilities, and purposive trajectories "dialogical." The metaphor does help show how the complexity of our being interanimates. Consider the following. A group of male friends loiter outside a bar. Suddenly, they are aggressively accosted by another group of men. Startled and threatened, many feel a strong inclination to flee; self-experience discloses self-as-threatened and starts to narrow to the horizon thereby opened. But those threatened also feel the tug of loyalty to their friends and elect to stay in the wake of that self-experience. Not that they deliberate, though they might. Rather, witnessing their friends in dire straits trounces the desire to flee and so they remain. Attending to this kind of complexity with a given course of action could lead one to cast the interplay of self-as-threatened and self-as-friend as a dialogue of sorts among something like a self-position. But dialogue too readily connotes (1) an "I" positioning itself and (2) a model of interaction that is derived from human conversation, which is misleading. In other words, I now think the metaphor is insufficiently apposite to the matter at hand, particularly since (3) it obscures the fundamentally purposive and proactive nature of human life and self-experience. Finally, (4) the language of self-position suggests subpersons, which exaggerates the relative independence of the manifold ways in which we are positioned and position ourselves. Moreover, it threatens to untether our positionings from the undercurrents of somatic-psycho systems that operate across being a friend, afraid, a worker, tired, a citizen, etc. But then neither am I drawn to binding, at an ontological level, our multiplicity to something like "narrative," which also hearkens back to reflective ego acts, that is to a narrator, which (1) overly unifies the ways in which human organisms track and respond to what befalls them, while (2) obscuring the ways in which ecosocial history positions us and the ways in which we account for ourselves. In other words, "narrative" remains too haunted by soul atomism to maintain its citizen rights. For the time being, then, I am happy to speak of *the course of a life* that is characterized by multiplicity in its subjective and objective moments, each of which is interpretable through four analytically distinct terms.

Recall Hass's poem. "Who are you?" asked the rubber duck. By replying with her name, Kristin gestures towards the relational, purposive course her life had taken among parents, older brothers, baths, and picnics. Her name is a rough marker for that course. But in saying (or acknowledging) her name, isn't she suggesting something more, namely, that the course of her life is *hers*? Or, leaving her be, isn't each self-experience, despite this multiplicity, *mine*? And if so, doesn't that indicate that there is something more primordial buried in our manifold ways of being purposive and reflexive within a manifold field of positionings? Dan Zahavi's research suggests that a thorough phenomenological reduction uncovers a more basic mode of self-experience than I have offered, one he terms "ipseity," which names the sense we have that our experience is *mine* (Zahavi 2000; 2005). Ipseity is a phenomenological reconstruction of the following dimension of self-experience: we indirectly encounter ourselves continuously encountering the world—each memory, flight of imagination, and perception is *mine*, and thus I have a sense of myself as a "dative of manifestation," to recall Zahavi's elegant formulation. Moreover, "It is also possible to identify this pre-reflective sense of mineness with a minimal, or core, sense of self" (Zahavi 2005, 125).

I am unwilling to regard this "this pre-reflective sense of mineness" as "a minimal, or core, sense of self." First, the language of "mine" seems misplaced. "Mine" is a meaningful term when it further specifies something that might also be "yours" or "another's" but isn't. In the prereflective flow of experience, however, we are never faced with a plurality of experiences, some of which are another's, some of which are *mine*. Rather, the flow of experience is one's alone and confusion cannot arise, as the proponents of *ipseity* admit when they term the *mineness* of experience indubitable. This is not to claim that we might not term a belief, opinion, or even one's experience "mine," say when observing that we admire a movie that another disliked, or even as a shorthand for the reflective realization that another has her own experiences. But, at the prereflective level, mineness seems conceptually unhelpful. Second, the claim that mineness is a "quality" of the first-person givenness of experience seems descriptively false (Zahavi 2000, 69; 2005, 124). Yes, one experiences imagining and desiring and remembering, and those experiences remain somewhat continuous even when their objects change, or when mode of apprehension gives way to another. But that flowing awareness does not have a special quality of mineness, and neither does any particular experience. This is not to say that one is uncertain about whether this awareness is *mine*. One is not, but not because it has some quality of mineness. One's experience only appears to one. An object might appear in common, but one's experience of it does not. Likewise, another's anger or frustration might be apparent, but not in a manner that one distinguishes from one's own anger because the latter has the quality of mineness and the former does not. We may come to believe that everyone has their own point of view, but this belief does not indicate that one's experiences or the flow of experience has a quality of mineness. "Mineness" thus seems like a particularly awkward term from a phenomenological point of view.

The question of mineness aside, catching oneself in the continuity of one's experiences, say of wanting, recalling, and anticipating, does not disclose something like a minimal self, namely, the one to whom all this keeps appearing. The flow of apperceptive consciousness *may* be a necessary condition for self-experience but it is not a sufficient one. One's awareness of being the one to whom the world appears does not itself appear in a manner that is self-subsistent, that is, unbound to determinate worldly affairs. Such engagements are thus integral to the very sense of self that ipseity presumably involves: I am the dative of these imaginings, memories, feelings, etc. But, and this is the key, such engagements do not have their source in the flow of apperceptive awareness. One does not experience a self-same "I" generating and apprehending a memory, for example. Memories are often involuntary and prompted by various triggers. The imagination often surprises our awareness with its fancy. To the degree it is *mine* at all, it is mine as emergent from an opacity that is less mine than also me. If I take myself to be a dative of manifestation, therefore, I also sense that I am more than this awareness. I am also the being whose various acts, some reflective, some pre-reflective, allow the course of my life to appear to me. Ipseity does not offer a "minimal or core sense of self," therefore, but a partial one bound to a larger course. In other words, ipseity occurs in ongoing receptions and responses that are also integral to the self I am, and this indicates that, even in the dative, self-awareness is only a facet of a larger phenomenon of worldly engagement and disclosure.

We began with Nietzsche, though not without observing that by commencing with Nietzsche one also, to a point, comes after Emerson. "Experience" opens with the question: where do we find ourselves? Nietzsche's new psychology attracts, in part, because it helps us prepare a reply, and a reflexive one at that. We find ourselves in our findings, which are multiple in their purposes and positionings and bound at every turn to ecosocial history. Such is the course of our lives, which I have marked as the irreducible context out of which self-experience arises and to which it returns as we respond to the partiality and possibilization of our occurrence. Amid the flurry and fuss, hypotheses abound regarding who we are and who we are becoming in currents and countercurrents that never relent. Following Nietzsche, I have tried to displace the intuitability and undermine the plausibility of soul atomism, as well as the more general figure on which it rests, that of a ground and its consequents. But I also have tried to maintain a language of the soul, or rather, in my case, the self. I want a language that can find our finding. To that end, I have refused to reduce our subjective multiplicity and tried to defend its rights to citizenship in science, and then some.

NOTES

1. Among multiple studies, the following strike me as posing and pursuing some of the right questions: David Mikics's *The Romance of Individualism* (2003); Alan Levine's "Skeptical Triangle?" (2011, 223–264); and the special issue of *ESQ: A Journal of the American Renaissance*, edited by Michael Lopez (1997).

2. "Self-Reliance" puts this nicely. "The power which resides in him is new in nature, and none but he knows what that is which he can do, nor does he know until he has tried" (CW2, 28).

3. I agree with Alan Levine when he agrees with Walter Kaufman's observation that "one would never mistake a whole page of Emerson for a page of Nietzsche" (2011, 260), although a great deal hangs on what one finds on the page, such as doctrines, rhetorical logical operations, or voice. To my ear and eye, the death of God is what most separates these authors. Emerson's hope (and even his moments of despair), whether we locate them in a recurring tone or a concept like the double consciousness, revolves around his sense of final causes, which are almost always theological. His eschewal of linear inference also reflects a trust in the involuntary buoyed by his sense that each mind is a moment in ongoing revelation. Even his racialism and its embrace of the concept of arrested development is underwritten by his faith in a *Deus sive Natura*.

4. Most of the views presented here have emerged in an ongoing dialogue with my brother, Paul Lysaker, with whom I have written several articles and a book, *Schizophrenia and the Fate of the Self* (2008). And that dialogue has also been in dialogue with several other people such as Hubert Hermans and Giancarlo DiMaggio, even as each of us has enjoyed our own interlocutors, in my case, Mark Johnson. And then there is our reading. Beginning without borrowing is quite difficult it seems.

5. This seems to be the view that Ulrich Neisser presents in "Five Kinds of Self-Knowledge" (1988). While he considers five modes of self-knowledge, he leaves little doubt that each concerns a unified, enduring entity that is the self.

6. A complex issue underlies this claim, and several advances in neuroscience are required in order to clarify matters. Gerald Edelman speaks of reentry in order to describe how neural events are tracked in the brain (I don't say "by") and thus available to succeeding neural events, which I take to mean, previous corporeal adjustments become part of the situation with which later adjustments contend (2005, 32–47).

7. The evolution of this view can be seen across the following: "Being Interrupted" (Lysaker and Lysaker 2005); "Schizophrenia and the Experience of Intersubjectivity as Threat" (Lysaker, Johannesen, and Lysaker 2006); "I Am Not What I Seem to Be" (Lysaker 2006); *Schizophrenia and the Fate of the Self* (Lysaker and Lysaker 2008), and most recently, "Metacognition and the Prospect of Enhancing Self-management in Schizophrenia Spectrum Disorders" (Lysaker and Lysaker in press). Although the view has usually appeared in the context of its application to the challenges posed by schizophrenia, it is not simply a reconstruction of self-experience in schizophrenia, but a general account of self-experience that has proven fruitful in clinical efforts to explain or meliorate the challenges that schizophrenia brings in its wake.

8. I leave open whether the possibility of response adds up to something worthy of the name "freedom" or even "power." Given the decentered ways in which we respond, it is clear that we are not autonomous in any strict sense, and in another context, I would like to add the term to the pile growing around soul atomism. But I do think a kind of suitably revised version of de Beauvoir's freedom deserves the name, particularly if we think of ambiguity in terms of

ecosocial history's constellations, which include our own pale contributions. That she does becomes apparent, I think, when we read *Ethics of Ambiguity* (1976) and *The Second Sex* (2011) together, allowing each to inform the other.

9. I say "possibilities," not "potentialities." Given that we only are through our facticity, our being is not merely potential but actual. But as we've seen, facticity comes to pass in a manner open to address and redress, and thus, as Heidegger (1962) would have it, the possible names the occurrence of the actual for beings like us.

EMERSION, RACE, AND THE CONDUCT OF LIFE

> There is, indeed, this vice about men of thought, that,
> you cannot quite trust them, not as much as other men of the
> same natural probity without intellect, because they have a hankering
> to play Providence, and make a distinction in favor of themselves,
> from the rules which they apply to all the human race.
>
> —*Ralph Waldo Emerson*

—I. Work Undone: Emerson celebrates poets because they reattach things to the whole. In wild figurations they redraw nature's vast synchronic and diachronic dance. It is notable, therefore, that he includes the trope of "race" in the poem that fronts "The Poet," as if it names a key element in natural history.

> A moody child, and wildly wise
> Pursued the game with joyful eyes
> ...
> Through man, and woman, and sea, and star
> Saw the dance of nature forward far;
> Through worlds, and races, and terms, and times,
> Saw musical order, and pairing rhymes. (CW3, 1)

One has to wonder: what could "race" mean in such a context, particularly since Emerson employs the plural? And in what other contexts does Emerson employ the trope of race, and to what effect?

Several scholars have pursued this question. Philip Nicoloff's *Emerson on Race and History* more or less initiates the critical discussion in 1961, whereas Cornel West renewed it in 1989 with *The American Evasion of*

Philosophy. Since then, several others have furthered it from vantage points in literary studies, political theory, science studies, and intellectual history. For my part, following the approach I introduce and defend in *Emerson and Self-Culture* (2008), I will "take Emerson personally"; that is, I will take myself to be the addressee of his texts (or their "unknown friend," to use his own, magnificent image). This requires, I think, that I work out the degree to which, and on what terms, I am willing to accept or reject the thoughts that he essays and the manner in which he essays them; that is, I need to determine if, how, and why I will or will not allow his essays to reform what Thoreau has beautifully termed the "very atmosphere and medium through which we look" (1971, 90). It doesn't mean that I will ignore what many have said about race in Emerson. I will address this conversation whenever my thought enters it. But my central goal is to think with Emerson more than to think about him.

Taking Emerson personally, I want to begin with two particular reasons for pursuing this topic here and now. In *Emerson and Self-Culture*, I addressed the question of race in a brief but unsatisfactory manner. Not that I consider my account wrong. I still believe that Emerson takes "race" to indicate a kind of collective temperament widely distributed in populations associated with various nations and ethnicities, as he does, for example, when he lectures in 1843 and 1844 on "The Genius and National Character of the Anglo-Saxon Race," aligning Anglo-Saxons with a disposition toward "Conscience and Common Sense, or in the view of their objects, the love of Religion and the love of Commerce" (LL1, 9). But there is much more to say about how Emerson understands the roots of racial temperament and how the trope functions in his lifelong concern with self-culture. In that sense, (though not only in that sense), my project is unfinished. But more importantly, the trope of race continues to loom so large in local and global culture, and to turn so violently in the lives conducted therein, that, as a *topos* of history, it compels comment. In fact, a life that would be eloquent, that would attest, in word and deed, commitment and conduct, to all that it holds dear must declare how it comports itself toward a word that one cannot utter in English without drawing a hush of troubled anticipation. And since this eloquence is precisely what I seek and what Emerson's texts provoke and provisionally essay, I must say more.

—II. STAGES OF RACE: Without limiting ourselves to its approach and conceptions, let us begin with "Race" from *English Traits*. Investigating the global presence of Britain, Emerson asks: "What made these delicate natures? was it the air? was it the sea? was it the parentage?" (CW5, 26). And he answers: "It is race, is it not? that puts the hundred millions of India under the dominion of a remote island in the north of Europe" (CW5, 26). Here the question of race arises within the philosophy of history, the attempt to locate basic principles that govern the becoming of phenomena that not only endure but also evolve, for example, the family, civil society, and the state, to invoke a Hegelian triad. In "Race," Emerson is puzzled by the emergence of British colonial power, and he offers race as a force or principle responsible for its emergence.

Another rhetorical mode organizes Emerson's essay, however, and it is marked thematically and performatively. Emerson is quite clear that race is not the only force operative in history. At least two others are present, and they mitigate the influence of race, namely, "credence" and "civilization." The latter refers to the sedimented history of human learning, what we might term "culture" in an anthropological sense—that stock of practice-bound knowledge that allows emerging generations to use its predecessor's achievements, from wheels to constitutions, quasars to modal improvising. "It implies," he writes six years later, "the evolution of a highly organized man brought to supreme delicacy of sentiment, as in practical power, religion, liberty, sense of honor, and taste" (CW10, 394).

Civilization counters the play of race because it preserves and provides sedimented knowledges and action orientations, ways of assessing and addressing situations that never would have dawned on us if we were left to individual devices. But such forces are not self-executing, even if they have their own objectivity. They live and move through human lives, and if we were to disappear they would as well. Civilization is thus bound to and binds the conduct of life. "It is the learning the secret of cumulative power, of advancing on oneself," Emerson writes of civilization. "It implies a facility of association, power to compare, the ceasing from fixed ideas" (CW10, 394).

How though does one move from cumulative to personal power? How do general truths turn into individuated insights? At this juncture, credence transpires, that act, barely audible at times, even to ourselves, whereby we acknowledge the currents of civilization as valid, that is, worth acting upon. "Credence," as a trope of troping, marks the site of what I have come to term "the personal," those acts that no one else can do for us, such as understand, believe, commit, persevere, acknowledge, feel regret, or fall in love.[1] And that is a complex affair, one that involves an attentive reception, some degree of interpretation (and thus rearticulation), and possibly the giving of our selves to what these phenomena suggest, or not; our credence also may refuse to embrace what entices our allegiance.

Credence modulates race according to Emerson because it involves, recurringly, the ways in which we interpret and respond to what befalls us, to how I, for example, respond to being raced, say as a scholar writing on Emerson, a vacationer in Barbados, or a shopper at Kroger. Or, since so many of our projects involve others, as a coeditor of a volume, as a neighbor, or a teacher working with students on a thinker trapped in tropes that threaten to overshadow his commitments to emancipation. That I am raced in these arenas is a fact. How I take up and engage that fact is also a matter of credence.

As a site of reception and response, credence is a site of possible transformation. Unhappy with what my race and civilization provide, I might disavow or at least countermand both and try to revise some or much of what they bequeath. For example, I might write an essay titled "Race" and develop a way of gauging its place in the arc of my life. Practicing Emersonian self-culture, I might work toward my own creed, as it were, negotiating what currents of race and civilization I aim to conduct, protest, or battle vociferously, maintaining throughout a bearing averse to conformity and unafraid of earned inconsistencies. This is just what Emerson does in the essay "Race." The essay not only names "credence," it exemplifies it. At a performative level, then, "Race" leaves the philosophy of history and essays the sphere of self-culture; that is, it moves in the region of personal receptions of and responses to the ways in which our lives are conditioned.

But let me be more specific, and with regard to some other texts essential to those who would think about race in Emerson. In a now well-known but still powerful line from Emerson's 1844, "An Address on the Emancipation of the Negroes in the British West Indies," he insists, in effect, that we can misread history if we allow basic terms to function uncritically. I say "in effect" because his speech aims to disrupt the ease with which one might say the phrase "negro slavery." In fact, he insists: "Language must be raked, the secrets of slaughter-houses and infamous holes that cannot front the day, must be ransacked, to tell what negro-slavery has been" (CW10, 303). This ransacking, raking language, is a work of credence, a matter of not believing one has fully understood the words one has heard and read, of believing that one can draw closer to the truth if one works to hear new words in old ones, and of raking language to that end. This is less a matter of replacing one term with another, such as "negro slavery" with something like "genocide," than one of treating words and phrases as "infamous holes" from which one draws out buried crimes, perhaps locating "rape" within "plantation," "merciless beatings" within "slave," and an ideal and factual monstrosity within "master," one human being claiming, in word and deed, to own another, to have the right, at a whim, to starve or sell or fuck or kill or work and work and work another human being, and with a chuckle or a leer or even a look of distraction.

Emerson does not rake language simply in order to uncover the past, however. He also rakes it in order to open futures, which language might foreclose, thus turning credence back into cumulative power. Speaking one year later, to the day, commemorating again the emancipation of slaves from the British West Indies, Emerson wonders why he is not commemorating emancipation in his own land. Even more particularly, he wonders why the North continues to accept slavery, to remain party to it. He rejects that any seriously deny either the justness of the slave's cause or the sincerity of abolitionists, even if, like Emerson, one finds the most effective abolitionists "tedious monomaniacs" (EAW, 35).[2] And while self-interest leads some to ignore the horrors of slavery, he thinks that fails to account for the behavior of "northern People at large" (ibid.). Rather, a single word, incessantly repeated, keeps Northerners party to slavery through commissions and omissions. Not that each mouth and ear consciously takes this word it say, "slavery, let it be." But that is what the word really says, Emerson suggests.

> I think there is but one argument which has any real weight with the bulk of the Northern people, and which lies in one word—a word which I hear pronounced with a triumphant emphasis in bar-rooms, in shops, in streets, in kitchens, at musters, and at cattle shows. That word is *Niggers!*—a word which, cried by rowdy boys and rowdy men in the ear of this timid and skeptical generation, is reckoned stronger than heaven; it blows away with a jeer all the efforts of philanthropy, all the expostulations of pity, the cries of millions now for hundreds of years—all are answered by this insulting appellation. (EAW, 36)

Again we see the work of credence, Emerson not believing that this word, the N-word, which I shall not use again, passes innocently from lips to ears. And we see him believing that it enacts white supremacy and thereby conducts slavery, even in states that profess to have outlawed it. As he goes on to say: "It is the objection of an inferiority of race. They who say it and they who hear it, think it the voice of nature and fate pronouncing against the Abolitionist and the Philanthropist" (ibid.).

I am trying to render concrete my claim that self-culture, through credence, opens a site that can contest and possibly meliorate the fates that our conduct conducts. I do not wish to suggest, however, for Emerson or myself, that writing is the sole site where such reforms might be pursued. Writing (and speaking) is not the only activity that conducts the fates we wish were not. Wondering how England and its colonies made their peace with slavery in the West Indies, Emerson blames consumptive practices that happily received goods and ignored evils: "If any mention was made of homicide, madness, adultery, and intolerable tortures, we would let the church-bells ring louder, the church-organ swell its peal, and drown the hideous sound. The sugar they raised was excellent: nobody tasted blood in it. The coffee was fragrant; the tobacco was incense; the brandy made nations happy; the cotton clothed the world. What! all raised by these men, and no wages? Excellent! What a convenience! They seemed created by providence to bear the heat and the whipping, and make these fine articles" (CW10, 315). The teeth of this particular rake are multiform: they make explicit implicit affirmations; they set the effects of commodity fetishism within the operations of sense—what we taste, what we hear, what we smell; and they not only charge the sounds of praise with hypocrisy, but imply that by "drowning out the hideous sound," organs and bells prove more hideous still. But here the field, lined with textiles, liquor, tobacco, and sweeteners, concerns conduct, often unaccompanied by words, that is domestic, intimate, daily. In other words, through credence, not only language must be raked, but all of the activities that reproduce the ecosocial world in which we circulate.

Credence, performed through writing, opens a site where Emerson receives and contests whatever fates come his way. But this site, which is also a praxis, opens for Emerson's readers as well. Returning to "Race," the essay not only involves the experiments of its author, but also the credence of its readers. "Race," as much as his speeches about the West Indies, offers performances and determinations that seek but cannot compel the acknowledgment of its addressees. With every stance it adopts, it also asks, implicitly—you as well? As he addresses race, then, Emerson also addresses us, even calls us into the work of credence, which he can provoke, orient, even instruct by way of example, but which he cannot conduct. Credence is personal work. And he does not let us forget it.

Considered as a whole, the essay "Race" moves between the philosophies of history, where race is a force that drives global history, and self-culture, where race is forced into the crucible of credence, perhaps with transformative results. In the former, and this will become all too concrete, race is a force of fate. In the latter, race is a trope that each of us is called to essay, and thus a possibility in the sense of a site where our being is at stake, but in a way that calls for our reception and response. Not that the two modes of address carry equal weight. In an elemental way, Emerson's invocation of the philosophy of history is a move in his own self-culture, and as much on offer for our credence as any facet of his address. I thus give self-culture something like primacy in Emerson's approach to race. Yes, he was a student of and commented on the politics and science of his day, but he did so within a project that "The American Scholar" already described in 1837 as "the gradual domestication of Culture" and the "upbuilding of man" (CW1, 65).[3] If so, then "race" is a question because it is a meaningful variable in the "upbuilding" of man, marking a force with which domesticated Culture, that is, self-culture, must contend.[4]

At the risk of belaboring the point, I briefly want to show how a similar rhetorical stage operates in "Fate," where Emerson ventures some of his most striking and troubling thoughts about race. As "Fate" opens, Emerson announces that the "question of the times resolved itself into a practical question of the conduct of life. How shall I live?" (CW6, 1). While the "question of the times" is presented in terms of a "theory of the Age" or the "Spirit of the Times," in 1860, such theories involved if not revolved around the presumed force of race therein, and Emerson's essay is no exception. "Race" or "races" are explicitly invoked no fewer than twelve times and six more times in an implicit way, for example, by way of terms such as Circumstance, instinct, and creature (CW6, 4, 5, 7, 8, 10, 12, 13, 17, 19, 20, 22, 23, 26). I thus take the essay's opening observation to transpose the question of race from the stage of world history to the field of self-culture thought in terms of the "conduct of life." But "transpose" may be too tame. As the 1828 edition of Webster's presents it, "resolve" means "to separate the component parts of a compound substance; to reduce to first principles; as, to resolve a body into its component or constituent parts; to resolve a body into its elements." "Fate" thus engages the question of the times through key elements, including race and through it, temperament, but in a manner focused on the basic solution (or current) in which such elements move, that is, focused on practical questions concerning the conduct of life (for "resolve" also means "to melt or dissolve").

Stanley Cavell takes "Fate" in a different if aligned direction. He asks: "Could it be that the founder of American thinking, writing this essay in 1850, just months after the passage of the Fugitive Slave Law, whose support by Daniel Webster we know Emerson to have been unforgettably, unforgivingly horrified by, was in this essay, not thinking about the American institution of slavery? I think it cannot be" (2003, 194). Fair enough (or almost fair enough). But how was Emerson thinking about slavery, and to what degree? Cavell proceeds to read the entire essay as a performative enactment of freedom through philosophy that in principle rejects (and thus protests, categorically) slavery. And Emerson does so, Cavell suggests, because the prevailing polemics (as well as the compromise that hoped to close them, which Cavell reads as the leading effort to "solve" the times), fail to exemplify the discourse of free persons. This performative twist carries with it a tone of pain, Cavell thinks—who wouldn't want to say more about something so horrible—but Emerson, believing an uncompromised future still possible, bears his reticence with a hopeful if pained patience.

I cannot deny the inventiveness of Cavell's reading, and I love how "I think it cannot be" offers itself as Emersonian whimsy. Cavell no doubt thinks it more than whim, but he cannot spend, as the story goes, the day in explanation. But I am wholly unconvinced as well as troubled. Emerson had no problem stumping against slavery for much of the 1850s and throughout the war. Polemic and invective were thus pointed arrows in his quiver. "Well, now comes this conspiracy of Slavery," he writes in 1862, "—they call it an institution, I call it a destitution,—this stealing of men and setting them to work" (CW10, 403). Second, Cavell's reading elides how "Fate" rhetorically opens the whole collection, tuning its title and preparing us to think its many topics from the standpoint of the conduct of life (power, wealth, culture, and worship, for example). The book thus needs the essay "Fate" to negate the "question of the times" and the "theory of the age" at the most general level possible, not simply with regard to slavery. But more generally, as we have seen, race is a recurring subject for Emerson, and as a figure of fate, which he glosses as the "despotism of race" (CW6, 7). It is prima facie plausible, therefore, that Emerson would set race at the heart of an essay on "Fate" as a constant of history and save slavery for other occasions. As he tells himself in Notebook *IT*, assembled in the mid-1850s, "Some persons may be spared from politics, & from philanthropies, even. I have quite other slaves to free than those negroes, to wit, imprisoned spirits, imprisoned thoughts, far back in the brain of man,—far retired in the heaven of invention" (TN1, 160–161).

Such disagreements are not troublesome, however. But when Cavell's reading also leads us past some of Emerson's most troubling remarks about race, it undermines the effort to come to terms with the full complexity of Emerson's thought on the matter. And that is something we should not let stand, even if, I hasten to add, I share Cavell's sense that Emerson's example, in prose, enacts a freedom worthy of our allegiance.[5]

—III. "Race" as Temperament: We have stepped into questions concerning the conduct of life in order to clarify how Emerson takes up the issue of race. But what does race throw our way on his view? Accounting for the character of Anglo-Saxons, Emerson identifies three contributing races: Celts, Germans, and Northmen. What they contribute seems more interesting, however. "On the whole," he writes, "it is not so much a history of one or of certain tribes of Saxons, Jutes, or Frisians, coming from one place, and genetically identical, as it is an anthology of temperaments out of them all" (CW5, 28). Temperament and race are linked at the beginning and close of "Fate" as well (CW6, 5, 26). And "Experience" also ties the two. "On its own level, or in view of nature, temperament is final," Emerson writes, adding a few lines later, "Given such an embryo, such a history must follow" (CW3, 32). Of course, "embryo" need not be a figure of race, but Emerson so often casts humans in terms of blood, stock, and race, it would be a striking exception if he took the embryo to figure a beginning free of the inertia of race, particularly given this remark from "Fate," which occurs in the heart of a prolonged discussion of the "scale of the races, of temperaments" (CW6, 5). "When each comes forth from his mother's womb, the gate of gifts closes behind him.... So he has but one future, and that is already predetermined in his lobes, and described in that little fatty face, pig-eye, and squat form" (CW6, 6).[6]

According to Emerson, temperament names a kind of native outlook on the world, even a kind of genius, a standpoint of view and value that renders certain worldly features conspicuous, others murky, even opaque. In Emerson's terms, therefore, one's race provides dispositionally operative ways of conducting life. In the case of the Anglo-Saxon, this entails an inherited love of and talent for religious conscience and commerce. Among persons of African descent, Emerson finds a "more moral genius," one free of the spirit of revenge to the point of being joyful by predilection. As he writes in a late journal, "The negro, thanks to his temperament, appears to make the greatest amount of happiness out of the smallest capital" (JMN16 50).

As the figures of "parentage" and "embryo" make plain, Emerson takes race to have biological roots. Philip Nicoloff and Laura Dassow Walls have taught us that there are multiple reasons for this, many having to do with Emerson's meetings with then-contemporary naturalists and his broad reading of what passed for the science of his day (Nicoloff 1961; Walls 2003). Nineteenth-century science aside, such an approach to race is also in line with Emerson's metaphysics. Emerson treats race as a part of *natura naturata*, the profusion of forms that express the "quick cause" of *natura naturans*, nature's form-giving, protean power (CW3, 104). In fact, he sometimes uses the term "race" as a stand-in for "species," for example, when he speaks of "all the races of creatures" in "Nature," including the "lichen race" (CW3, 107, 105). "Race" thus has to have its roots in nature, for Emerson; he believes that humans, like roses, are products of nature, and thus kinds of humans, like kinds of roses, should also be treated as products of nature. As he records in journal E: "We are all boarders at one table,—White man, black man, ox and eagle, bee & worm" (JMN7, 382).

In Emerson's terms, then, "race" is part of how nature unfolds in and as human beings. But it does not do so statically or through the simple instancing of universals. As Walls makes abundantly clear, for Emerson, the fate of a race is bound to statistics and transmutation, also known as evolution (2003, 167). One sees the former in "Fate," when Emerson observes that in "every million there will be an astronomer, a mathematician, a comic poet, a mystic" (CW6, 10). Or, in language employed in a journal entry of 1853: "the race distributes amongst many individuals the sum of qualities that belong to the type" (JMN13, 194). Temperament is thus not simply a racial imprint, but an individually variable thing. To be raced is thus to be set along a continuum of intensities, some of which verge on being racially unrecognizable. Moreover, there will be exceptions, for example, British astronomers who were far less concerned with commercial affairs, such as Newton, Halley, and Sir Joseph Lockyer (1836–1920), who is credited with discovering "helium" in the solar spectrum.

Race is thus a variable affair according to Emerson. And that variability only intensifies if we set race within his philosophy of history, which presents each race, contrary to Knox, as a mixed phenomenon. "We are piqued with pure descent," he writes, "but nature loves inoculation. A child blends in his face the faces of both parents, and some feature from every ancestor who face hangs on the wall" (CW5, 27). And England is no different: "The English composite character betrays a mixed origin. Everything English is a fusion of distant and antagonistic elements" (ibid.). History brings more than mere mixing, however. In a manner somewhere between the positions we now associate with Darwin and Lemarque, Emerson holds that a race also reflects the history of its relations to geography and circumstance. "Certain temperaments suit the sky and soil of England," he writes, "say eight or ten or twenty varieties, as, out of a hundred pear-trees, eight or ten suit the soil of an orchard, and thrive" (CW5, 28).

Emerson's conception of race and its third-person operations is somewhat complex, therefore. While Emerson is more or less certain that various human "races" are forms of nature, their particular traits are variable across populations, admit of exceptions, and transmute or transform over time. Emerson thus cautions the readers of *English Traits* to use the tropes of race along pragmatic lines. "We must use the popular category," he writes, "as we do by the Linnæan classification, for convenience, and not as exact and final" (CW5, 29). I underscore Emerson's caution because it rhetorically embodies how his self-culture addresses and contests conditions that orient the conduct of life, raising credence, through self-reliant labors, over "quotation," a term Emerson often uses to name cultural and physiological influences, as well as their evolved intersection, which is precisely what a term such as "Anglo-Saxon" reflects. In fact, Emerson is occasionally ironic when treating the topic, as when he observes in the essay "Race": "Men hear gladly of the power of blood or race. Every body likes to know that his advantages cannot be attributed to air, soil, sea, or to local wealth, as mines or quarries, nor to laws and traditions, nor to fortune, but to superior brain, as it makes the praise more personal to him" (CW5, 25). I find irony here because Emerson shortly thereafter deploys terms such as soil and sea as contributing factors to a term such as "Anglo-Saxon," that is, for him, the contour of a race is inextricable from several of these influences. Moreover, what is personal about a physiological inheritance?

But not all Emerson's deployments of race show caution, let alone irony, as the following claim from "Fate" makes painfully plain. "As in every barrel of cowries, brought to New Bedford, there shall be one *orangia*, so too there will, in a dozen millions of Malays and Mahometans, be one or two astronomical skulls" (CW7, 10). The suggestion is remarkable for several reasons. First, what leads Emerson to treat "Mahometans" as a single race when he is willing to carve up Anglicans as well as Catholics into several races? Second, the analogy is frivolous in that it compares a haul of snails with sexual reproduction. But most troubling is the math. Earlier in the paragraph he spoke of one astronomer in a million. Apparently, this is only true of certain races; Malays and Mahometans are capable of only one or two astronomical skulls per twelve million. One wonders what calculator enables such calculations, and in the absence of one, it is hard not to attribute such claims to a version of white supremacy.

—IV. Guano, God, and Geology: We have explored some of the ways in which race operates in Emerson's thought: it is a variable and mixed form of nature that gives to each a variable temperament that informs, in part, how we receive and respond to the world, including ourselves. And we have noted Emerson's occasional caution with regard to the term's explanatory limits as well his rhetorical efforts to keep the trope, even in its most biological operations, within the essaying practices of self-culture. But there are times when Emerson offers bold claims about the relative capacities and limits of various races, claims that lack the epistemic humility that characterizes essays such as "Race" and escape the rhetorical confines of self-culture and its pursuit.

"We know in history what weight belongs to race," Emerson writes in "Fate." "The German and the Irish millions, like the negro, have a great deal of guano in their destiny. They are ferried over the Atlantic, and carted over America, to ditch and to drudge, to make corn cheap, and then to lie down prematurely to make a spot of green grass" (CW6, 9). This passage always catches me up short. Delivered from the platform of a philosophy of history, it declares that the life energies of certain races are little more than mulch for the strivings of other races. One labors for another who grows and expands in turn. And the difference that makes the difference in these cases is race, not individual choice, nor even poor moral luck on an individual scale. The operative force is race, and its appearance signals a statistically distributed fate, one that Emerson is occasionally confident enough to read and declare.[7]

There are other times, however, when Emerson's thought is unsettled, at least with the fate of those he terms "negroes." Consider these fragmented jottings from the journal "War," penned in 1863.

> Negroes good soldiers
> they love music, dress, order, parade,
> they have a couth temperament and *abandon*, & Gen H.'s opinion
>   of their desperate courage.
> Fitness of the hour. At this moment the Negro an object of kindness
>   to all nations.
> ...
> Periodicity of errors & periodicity of races & civilities.
> Negro nearer to geology than others.
> Exhausted perhaps in his first era
> ...
> Perhaps only his period is larger, & his return to light requires a better
>   medium than our immoral civilization allows (JMN15, 212–213)

This is Emerson working in the philosophy of history. He has a general sense of the character of those he terms "negroes," and he tries to square it with information flowing north from the fields of the Civil War. He is convinced that people of African descent emerged early in the course of human history, perhaps at its very dawn.[8] And he thinks, with anxiety, that this may indicate an arrested development, a development "exhausted" not long after its emergence.

It is important to underscore that Emerson does not take these speculations to bear upon the question of slavery. In reflecting on the "duty to our fellow man the Slave," Emerson insists in a lecture notebook compiled between 1836 and 1840, "We are to assert his right in all companies" (JMN12,

152).⁹ Moreover, "An amiable joyous race who for ages have not been permitted to unfold their natural powers we are to befriend" (ibid.). And he insists a year into the Civil War: "Emancipation is the demand of civilization. That is a principle; everything else is an intrigue" (CW10, 406). But Emerson has deep doubts that those he terms "negroes" have much to offer the world even if freed. After insisting upon their political equality, and after stating that Northern whites are obligated to befriend their cause, he continues: "I think it cannot be maintained by any candid person that the African race has ever occupied or do promise ever to occupy any very high place in the human family. Their present condition is the strongest proof that they cannot" (JMN12, 152). In 1863, however, he wonders whether new conditions, say civic friendship as opposed to the existential assaults of slavery, might not lead to different results. And as late as 1867, the question remained on his mind.¹⁰ But on the whole, Emerson seems convinced that those he terms "negroes" bring little by way of native temperament and talent to the table of civilization. Among them there is "honesty by temperament," but, he notes in 1866, the "way to wash the negro white is to educate him in the white man's Useful and fine Arts, & his ethics" (JMN16, 50). Emerson's uncertainty about the eventual fate of those he terms "negroes" should not obscure, therefore, his radically low estimation of their aptitude. He seems more or less convinced that their temperament seems to carry no new idea of its own, and that, on Emerson's view, is evidence of arrest.¹¹

At this point a distinction favored by Paul Taylor (and others) is in order, namely, racialism versus racism.¹² I think we have seen that Emerson is a racialist. He believes that races are real. Not only are they part of nature and thus real in biological sense, they also carry a first-person reality, insofar as they institute temperaments that influence self-relations. (They are also real in a cultural sense in that Emerson believes that racial dispositions hypertrophically manifest themselves as cultural dispositions, e.g., as a tendency toward unbridled commercialism among Anglo-Saxon communities.) I think we have also seen that Emerson is a racist. He believes that certain persons are inferior to others with regard to their overall agential power and because of the race to which they belong. Not that Emerson's racism leads him to defend slavery; it doesn't.¹³ But he predicts vastly different futures for persons of different races and simply because of their respective races.

Like most, I find Emerson's racism deeply objectionable, by which I mean, erroneous in a way that contributes to morally unacceptable conditions. If he had a ridiculous theory of tides, I wouldn't find that deeply objectionable, just ridiculous. But at significant points, Emerson's work with race conducts life in a manner that, though opposed to slavery, remains vicious. By rendering people of African descent "nearer to geology," by terming them "pre Adamite," even in their nineteenth-century present, and by predicting for them a future as fertilizer, Emerson intensifies the dehumanization that enslavement enacted, rhetorically inflecting the emancipation proclamation with tragic irony. (What would political freedom secure for a race unable to harness the currents of its age? As "Fate" suggests, the grass will be greener on the other side, but for reasons other than imagined.) Moreover, in so far as these commitments led Emerson, and through him, his readers, to treat people of African descent as more or less unable to be "co-workers in the kingdom of culture," Emerson's racism rhetorically perpetuates the kind of namelessness that led Orlando Patterson (1982) to regard slavery as a condition of "social death."[14] Why form credence, and through credence, civilization, alongside of and in dialogue with persons trapped in some lost, nearly prehistoric world? The results at best will prove "negro-fine," Emerson's own term for expressions that are not "a new creation out of the soul, out of virtue & truth ... but an imitation ... gaudiness like a negro gay with cast off epaulettes & gold laced hat of his master" (JMN5, 395).[15]

One might take some solace from the moments when Emerson wonders whether his grasp of "negro" potential is adequate. But the very terms of his deliberation are troubled. In his 1844 "Address on the Emancipation," Emerson says of nature:

> It deals with men after the same manner [of animals and insects]. If they are rude and foolish, down they must go. When at last in a race, a new principle appears, an idea;—*that* conserves it; ideas only save races. If the black man is feeble and not important to the existing races not on parity with the best race, the black man must serve, and be exterminated.... I esteem the occasion of this jubilee to be the proud discovery, that the black race can contend with the white; that, in the great anthem which we call history, a piece of many parts and vast compass, after playing a long time a very low and subdued accompaniment, they perceive the time arrived when they can strike in with effect, and take a master's part in the music. The civility of the world has reached that pitch, that their more moral genius is becoming indispensable, and the quality of this race is to be honored for itself. (CW10, 325)

Note first the "must" here is empirical, not moral. The claim is that over time, arrested races will perish, not that humans aware of this arrest should take matters into their own hands. Second, what strikes me here is less the reversal of fortune that "the black man" receives than the persistence of the idea of "a master's part," which suggests that Emerson's racial history is always supremacist, even when Anglo-Saxons need to share the stage. One should thus not be bought off by a wavering estimation of African talent, for it will come at the expense of others, Native Americans, for example. Exploring the meaning of civilization in 1862, Emerson writes: "In the brutes is none: and in mankind, the savage tribes do not advance. The Indians of this country have not learned the white man's work; and in Africa, the negro today is the negro of Herodotus" (CW10, 394). Of course, in time, the white man and his work will be superseded, but that does not change the supremacist terms of Emerson's philosophy of history and the supremacist way in which he conceives his own historical moment.

As I've suggested, I think Emerson's naturalism leads him in part toward these unjust proclamations. He wishes to account for everything in nature's terms, and thus he was ripe for the race discourses of his century. Through temperament, race allowed him to keep mind continuous with nature and to treat nature yet again as an ordered sequence of parts and wholes. As scholars such as Bill Rossi have noted, Emerson was particularly influenced by Robert Chambers's anonymous work, *Vestiges of the Natural History of Creation* (1844).[16] Emerson was drawn to the thought that each species or race is fit for a time and a place but that, over time, its development would slow (or arrest) and give way to others better suited to the evolving moment. What I would add here is that Emerson needs such a view because he believes "the dice of God are always loaded. The world looks like a multiplication-table, or a mathematical equation, which, turn it how you will, balances itself" (CW2, 60). And since different peoples or races seem to suffer different fates, he can combine the notions of race and arrested development to explain why, in a balanced universe, certain peoples seem to thrive at one point only to suffer horribly, even unjustly, at another. I should note that Emerson's early concern with balance is a bit more optimistic than his latter feel for progress, which admits that "Providence has a wild, rough, incalculable road to its end" (CW6, 4). But the commitment to theodicy remains throughout, and it seems to be a driving force in Emerson's conception of race. Much like his spirit-inflected, naturalist metaphysics force him to regard race as biologically real, so too his theodicy leads him to affirm evaluative conceptions of race, which he thinks of in terms of progressive and arrested development.

I note the theodicy and naturalism of Emerson's thought because they are braids within the rhetorical mode in which his racism operates most tenaciously. In both the "Address on the Emancipation," delivered in 1844, and again in 1862, when he stridently defends what would become the Emancipation Proclamation, Emerson, even while addressing his political present, and with the goal of meliorating it, speaks as a philosopher of history. And when he slides into that mode, race seems to work unchecked by self-culture's credence. Gone is the thematic and performative space of contestation that we saw operative in the essay "Race" and staged, forcefully, at the opening of "Fate." And that troubles because, when the first and second person disappear, that is, the author's self-relation and the presumed critical reception of the addressee, third-person events such as racialized temperaments become the sole subject and truth of humanity, a metaphysical substratum expressing itself through "a dozen million of Malays and Mahometans," including "one or two astronomical skulls." Many of Emerson's most racist remarks are frozen and attempt to freeze us in a scene that "Fate" as a whole tries to undermine and displace: "I seemed, in the height of a tempest to see men overboard struggling in the waves and driven about here and there. They glanced intelligently at each other, but 'twas little they could do for one another; 'twas much if each could keep afloat alone. Well, they had a right to their eyebeams, and all the rest was Fate" (CW6, 10–11). This already bleak scene "bleakens" further now that we have seen how race seems locked within the waves of fate named here and how "Fate" swells through race's hypertrophic manifestations. At these moments, then, I insist on drawing Emerson's texts back into the rhetorical site and practice of self-culture, which attunes us to our conduct, to all it conducts, and to the labor of credence, which demands our deliberate or ecstatic commitment.

But doesn't the essay "Fate" already do that? It insists, after all, that thought and the moral sentiment free us from fate, allow us to conspire with and redirect it, and the essay, in resolving itself to address the conduct of life, embodies the process that occasionally allows one to say: "A personal influence towers up in memory only worthy, and we gladly forget numbers, money, climate, gravitation, and the rest of Fate" (CW6, 16). So "Fate" does qualify itself in a way. But its forays into the philosophy of history also undermine personal power, at least for those races with guano in their future—they seem lost, though there may be exceptional individuals. And that is a heavy load to lie on the backs of those readers who, even if they prove to be exceptions, will only prove the rule. It turns a purported talented tenth into an exotic appearance and crushes the dream that they might become, in time, a reconstructive force. In fact, it encourages them to cut their losses and throw in, for the course of their lives, with those facing a genuine future. No MLK,

No Malcolm X, no Ida B. Wells, in short, no point and purpose for the black prophetic tradition that Cornel West has recalled us to again and again, or for his trenchant critique of those forces undermining the self-renewing establishment of black intellectual traditions.[17]

Readers of "Fate" should never forget that it ends with a double consciousness, that mode of thought whereby one sides with divinity against oneself and takes one's suffering as a cosmic benefit even though no such compensation can be seen, or even imagined. Said otherwise, there are times when fate dashes whatever abandon credence can muster, and so, with a double consciousness, credence dissociates in order to "rally on his relation to the Universe, which his ruin benefits" (CW6, 26). Race as well as Emerson's theodicy are the principal forces behind this diremption. The former renders the latter unthinkable and so nature in its beauty, truth, and goodness rises into a process that passes all understanding. Emerson finds himself in this corner when he loses his thought to the philosophy of history. Unchecked, it is a merciless discourse, and there are moments when it threatens to devour his thought.

—V. "AND THE MIND GOES ANTAGONIZING ON." In highlighting Emerson's movements within the philosophy of history, and in exposing their racism and the supremacist form it takes, I do not wish to give the impression that Emerson's conception and exemplification of self-culture, and of credence, more specifically, is ready-made to tackle the challenges that race currently throws our (or threw his) way. Self-culture can only experiment with lines of thought it finds in its way, for example, conceptions of race, nature, God, and friendship. And it can only pursue the work of credence by way of other thoughts with which it settles for the time being, such as conceptions of the self, its sociality, genres such as the essay, etc. Emersonians thus cannot simply abandon Emerson's racist racialism and presume they have sufficient means for confronting the question (and recurring maelstrom) of race. Some other grasp of how race and fate intertwine is needed, particularly one less trapped within a biologically grounded conception of race-based temperament.

And yet, all this is not to say that Emersonian self-culture is somehow intrinsically or essentially racist, as if Emerson's self-conception, as well as his conception of his addressees, could only circle within a mode no larger than "one white man to another." The work of credence, which has been my focus here, is in no way limited to Anglo-Saxons or any race and on Emerson's own terms. Please recall the following from "Experience": "Given such an embryo, such a history must follow" (CW3, 32). The passage continues: "On this platform, one lives in a sty of sensualism, and would soon come to suicide. But it is impossible that the creative power should exclude itself. Into every intelligence there is a door which is never closed through which the creator passes" (CW3, 32). Emerson never wavered from his sense that each individual fate had an incalculable dimension and not just in the epistemic sense. In his view, nature itself is ecstatic, growing and surging, mutating. Later in "Experience," he writes, "Nature hates calculators; her methods are saltatory and impulsive. Man lives by pulses; our organic movements are such; and the chemical and ethereal agents are undulatory and alternate; and the mind goes antagonizing on, and never prospers by fits" (CW3, 39). To say that a door to the creator, in each and every intelligence, always remains open says more, therefore, than "our predictive powers are insufficient to map how human thought unfolds." Thought and nature are saltatory—they dance, proceeding by leaps rather than by gradual transitions, and that wild neurochemistry may emerge and surprise all involved, including the mind whose fit is only now becoming apparent.

I recall us to the turbulent core of Emerson's philosophy of nature, what I have elsewhere termed his "law of metamorphosis," because it underwrites, I believe, his sense of credence and self-culture more generally, for example, his feel for friendship and conversation, his emphases on the mind's originary receptivity, his valorization of youth, real and felt, his commitment to perseverance, his aversion to conformity, his impatience with a foolish consistency, and his insistent observance of the difference between the world we think and the one with which we converse wherever we go. In particular, this law of metamorphorsis orients self-culture toward its own surpassing twists and turns, prepares it for the succession and surprise that are, according to "Experience," lords of life. And given this, no one is intrinsically excluded from Emersonian self-culture, either from the character it demands, the futures it opens, or from its address in those texts signed "Ralph Waldo Emerson." Yes, certain races are marked and denigrated at several points, and this forces those thereby abused to prove themselves exceptions to a rule stated and presumed. But taking oneself as a possible exception to the rule is the core of Emersonian self-culture and its mantra of self-trust, youth, and abandonment. All should strive to prove exceptions to the rules that not only govern our lives, but also to the rules that we, in our conduct, have become, whether as intractable apologists for business as usual or proponents of ill witted conceptions of race frozen in the oppression-bearing speculations of a philosophy of history. Said otherwise, the trope of race in Emerson does not outrun this still radiant commitment from "Circles."

> The life of a man is a self-evolving circle, which, from a ring imperceptibly small, rushes on all sides outwards to new and larger circles, and that without end. The extent to which this generation of circles, wheel without wheel will go, depends on the force or truth of the individual soul. For, it is the inert effort of each thought having formed itself into a wave of circumstance,—as, for instance, an empire, rules of an art, a local usage, a religious rite,—to heap itself on that ridge, to solidify, and hem in the life. But if the soul is quick and strong, it bursts over that boundary on all sides, and expands another orbit on the great deep, which also runs into a high wave, with attempt again to stop and to bind. (CW2, 180–81)

This is a call and a challenge to all who read it, even if that wave of circumstance bears the name "Emerson." But it also calls us to actively receive, acknowledge, and praise such occurrences when we find them, knowing that by doing so, we are getting quicker and stronger. Lecturing on Christmas, 1864, Emerson reportedly said, "There is much in the calamities we have suffered which is disinfecting. We have learned to forget foreign nations. We have grown internally—have begun to feel the strength of our strength. While European genius is symbolized by some majestic Corinne crowned in the capitol at Rome, American genius finds its true type—if I dare tell you—in the poor negro soldier lying in the trenches by the Potomac, with his spelling book in one hand and his musket in another" (Gohdes 1932, 40–41). Now, this should not lead us to forget Emerson's racist racialism, which can be found across his corpus.[18] But it does, I think, embody what is possible within the current of Emersonian self-culture, that life-praxis, which does not aspire to solve the times, but allows them to resolve themselves into questions concerning the conduct of life, questions that cannot be answered ahead of time, questions that might—I happily tell you—draw out replies that can surprise even the one who utters them.

At this point I wish I had more to say, particularly about what might displace Emerson's racialist racist philosophy of history and thus better inform an Emersonian self-culture that wishes to be equal to a moment still conducting racism. And this tempts me to close with a shorthand of names and hopes, phrases and promises. But that would try to earn something on the cheap that can only be accomplished in its concrete execution, and, I would add, in conversation with the full range of those with whom our lives our bound, whether by choice or fate. Let me say instead, therefore, that whatever that task will involve, it will also involve actively inheriting our predecessors, and with regard to the full occasion of their word and deed, particularly when we are convinced that they still offer a glimpse of a future worth pursuing.

NOTES

1. I introduce and use this notion across *Emerson and Self-Culture* (Lysaker 2008, 7–8, 68–70).

2. Not that their hectoring led Emerson to reject the abolitionists' aim. "The professed aim of the abolitionist is to awaken the conscience of the Northern States in the hope thereby to awaken the conscience of the southern states: a hope just & sublime" (JMN12, 153).

3. I should also note that Emerson believed that politics was only capable of reflecting the self-culture of citizens. "But the wise know that . . . the State must follow, and not lead the character and progress of the citizen . . . and that the form of government which prevails is the expression of what cultivation exists in the population which permits it" (CW3, 117–118). I thus do not share Anita Goldman's view that "Emerson's recognition in his early writings that rights do not provide a sound enough basis for thinking about America as a nation simultaneously leads him to develop a concept of race," if only because "thinking about America as a nation" is not his principal concern (1994, 182).

4. I thus partially share Len Gougeon's insistence that we always set Emerson's remarks on race within the dialectic of his thought. As Gougeon notes, these remarks are "elements of a thought process and not a final product" (2014, 200). But, and I think Gougeon underplays this, most are sincerely ventured as holding true for Emerson, if only in a partial manner. Emerson is not merely entertaining them but giving himself to them and letting them take him where they will, although, when the dust settles, he no doubt will allow a new thought to contest wherever he had landed.

5. The work of freedom (and constitutional amending) that Cavell finds exemplified by the essay "Fate" is akin to what I cast as the reforming work of credence. I am not denying, therefore, that the kind of work Cavell locates in "Fate" is operative in Emerson. I think it is, and I have tried to develop it in my own way in chapter 7 of *Emerson and Self-Culture* (2008). But I don't think "Fate" exemplifies this work very well and certainly not as an oblique condemnation of slavery. Moreover, I think taking it in this way, and exclusively so, obscures how "Fate" is racist in disturbing ways.

6. Even more examples can be found in the journals. Here is one from 1853, titled "Race": "I adjourn the question of race, for it is too early. When we have got the names Celt, Saxon, Roman, we are still only using an / arbitrary / idle / & superficial distinction, as if we classified people by the street in which they lived. The foundations of race are not in anatomy, but in metaphysics. Temperament which tyrannizes over family-lines derives from moral & elemental causes, & the existence of individual men as of man himself shrouds the moral laws. There is a profound instinct stirring all the new interest of mankind in race, and which, beginning at the most outward facts, will shed one after the another the covers of the question, until it reaches the spiritual causes." (JMN13, 233–234)

Regarding the races, Emerson often lists several, for example, Egyptian, Carthaginian, Greek, Mahometan, Saxon, and Chinese, and elsewhere, the Nubian, the Negro, the Tartar, the Greek (LL2, 186; JMN7, 90).

7. Eduardo Cadava reads these lines from "Fate" as an ironic exposition of the fate of oppressed groups in systems of global labor (2010). However, he only arrives at this reading after presuming Cavell's unconvincing and unsupported insistence that the essay is a performative

countermand to the place of slavery in American life. His larger goal is to show that a Benjaminian feel for the barbarism of history operates in Emerson. I agree and would offer the "Address of 1844," in its reworking of sugar and cotton, as an example. But I do not think that "Fate" and these lines in particular conduct that sensibility.

8. It appears that Emerson held this view for most of his life. Writing to Horatio Greenough in 1852, he states: "That the negro was pre Adamite, I early discovered, but now that he too reads books, the courtesy to present company seems to require that it be a little parliamentary stated" (CL8, 330).

9. In "American Civilization," Emerson identifies what may lie at the core of this right, namely, a "man's right to his labor" (CW10, 403).

10. "You complain that the negroes are a base class," he writes in journal LN. "Who makes & keeps the jew or the negro base, who but you, who exclude them from the rights which others enjoy?" (JMN16, 55).

11. After recalling a late speech at Howard University, where Emerson delivered a "short disquisition on Self-Reliance," Lawrence Buell believes "we must conclude that Emerson was every bit as willing in January of 1872 as in August of 1844 to grant African Americans the capacity for serious thought. He wasn't about to herd black collegians into the mechanical trades" (2003, 261). I don't want to disagree entirely with this claim, but I would like to qualify it. From the standpoint of the philosophy of history, and given Emerson's statistical bent therein, Emerson seems committed to predicting that audience he addressed in 1872 was the exception not the rule for people of African descent.

12. I have in mind Taylor's *Race: A Philosophical Introduction,* now in its second edition, particularly chapter 1 (2013, 3–26).

13. Len Gougeon seems to take Emerson's antislavery stance as evidence that the charge of racism does not apply to him. In fact, he insists: "For Emerson, equality was not bounded by race or gender" (2013, 202). But equal with regard to what? I agree that Emerson supported formal political equality for blacks and women, but the preponderance of the evidence suggests that he thought those he termed "negroes" were intellectually inferior to those he termed "Anglo-Saxon" and simply because of forces that he categorizes in terms of race. And that is enough to merit the term "racist."

14. The phrase "co-worker in the kingdom of culture" comes from Du Bois's *Souls of Black Folk* (2000).

15. The entry was penned in 1837 and later indexed in Notebook Phi under "American pomp and negro fine" (JMN12, 298). Emerson later uses the phrase as a general category in at least two publications, "To the Public," written in 1847, and "Saadi," written in 1864 (CW10, 342, 440). I first encountered the term "negro-fine" in the "Saadi" essay, where its derisive sense is apparent. Its other occurrences (and origins) in Emerson's texts were located and recorded by Glen Johnson in his notes for volume 10 of *The Collected Works of Ralph Waldo Emerson* (CW10, 703).

16. I have in mind Rossi's "Emerson, Nature, and Natural Science" from Joel Myerson's *A Historical Guide to Ralph Waldo Emerson* (2000, 101–150).

17. I have in mind "The Dilemma of the Black Intellectual" and the recent portraits he assembles through interviews with Christa Buschendorf (West 1993, 67–85; West and Buschendorf 2014).

18. I found this passage in Len Gougeon's contribution to *Ralph Waldo Emerson in Context.* While I have used it in support of a different kind of claim, I am nevertheless happy to note the debt.

REFORMING ETHICAL LIFE

> It seems, reading them [Heidegger and Wittgenstein], ... that some moral claim upon us is levied by the act of philosophizing itself, a claim that no separate subject of ethics would serve to study.... [W]hat needs attention from philosophy, is our life as a whole.
> —*Stanley Cavell*

> What I propose, therefore, is very simple: it is nothing more than to think what we are doing.
> —*Hannah Arendt*

—I. Amazed, curious, angered, or beset by gnawing doubts, philosophy finds itself recoiling even as it relies upon a given. And it does so while borrowing words, images, names; even first philosophies play the role, in part, of commentary. "Where do we find ourselves?" Emerson asks. We find ourselves responding and thus find ourselves in the figure of a response. And that response is far from initial; it responds to a situation already found in some sense or other, or more likely by several senses—for example, one of place, of balance, of history, of kinds of things, of relative welfare, and so on. Where do we find ourselves? Already under way, purposefully positioned, responding and finding, finding and responding (again and again), quoting, conversing.[1]

Turning back into my quoting relations, I find myself not merely addressed and addressing but also among beings whose welfare concerns me; that is, I find myself among beings that have a claim on my attention, my concern, even my life, and in manners both negative and positive. I did not always find myself so claimed. My first self-experiences, to the degree I recall them, were far more modest: being hungry (or was it hangry?), holding a rattle, laughing, guzzling milk, my father singing. And my future may include the erosion of those capacities that such finding requires. But for the time being, I find myself committed to not harming others and to seeing them flourish. And in many cases, I even want to help them do so. In fact, how they fare in the course of their lives matters in a way that determines how I fare in the course of mine. If they suffer, I suffer. If they flourish, I flourish. My fate is bound to theirs. Not that I share psychological states with others. Rather, my sense of (also my feel for) the relative state of my welfare reflects in part my sense of theirs. And that, I take it, indicates a course of life in which other beings have something like *moral standing* (their welfare matters to us, lays a claim on us), which we register in experiences of concern, experiences that English names "conscience."[2]

I have begun something like a phenomenology of ethical life—enmeshment in a world of moral standing is found in responsive events of conscience. But let us not forget the conversation. "Ethics" denotes several phenomena. One is an academic subject. Traditionally the province of philosophy and religion, ethics is now also its own area of inquiry, replete with certificates and undergraduate minors. "Ethics" also denotes the specialization of a class of professional termed "ethicists." One finds them in hospitals and wherever consultants are able to sell their wares. One may even find them in government. In 2005, the Norwegian government hired Henrik Syse to "help run one of the world's largest investment funds. Syse, a former philosophy professor, was hired three months ago as the ethicist for the country's $190 billion Petroleum Fund. He weighs in on thorny questions."[3] "Ethics" also denotes a social-psychological phenomenon, one that anthropologists, psychologists, and sociologists describe and explain, say, in the form of value systems and worldviews or as evolutionary phenomena like sympathy or altruistic behaviors.

What I aim to say has implications for these various senses of "ethics," and I will explicitly articulate the trajectories of some, while others no doubt elude my grasp. But on the whole, this professional landscape is not my principal concern. My focus instead is the conduct of life, where Emerson begins "Fate." Where do we find ourselves? Outstripped by our condition. The unpredictable logic of events, the opacity and multiplicity of human motivation, the innumerable viewpoints and commitments of our peers and predecessors (most of whom we do not know and with whom we can barely converse given the limits of our literacy)—our condition is less a stage than a maelstrom, and while we have our exits and entrances, sound direction is rare. And yet, we conspire. We throw in with one set while resisting several others. Whether in wonder, doubt, or anger (or still some other mood), most of us ask: to what end, and is this the best we can do?

—II. I find myself moving toward certain ends and away from others. And in important ways, the life in question is not merely mine. In fact, if my phenomenological reconstruction of conscience is at all apt, the substance of concern is "life," which includes my welfare and that of others. I underscore this because it suggests that current obsessions with the egoism/altruism opposition are possibly misplaced. If I only thrive when others are thriving, my concern is directed toward myself and others, and I can only satisfy my egoistic interest if the interests of others are satisfied, thus rendering me altruistic. Not that I am secretly interested and only interested in something like the satisfaction that comes with helping others. I'm not, and the nonfalsifiable insistence that I am is cynicism masking as intellect. My interest is that their interests are realized (call this a minimal condition of friendship and love). And with that interest in view, the very distinction between altruism and egoism bucks and sways and begins to return to solution. Not that the distinction never applies, but I think an originary grasp of ethical phenomena finds a kind of conduct whose interests bind together the welfare of self and other.

There is a word for what is an instance of and a concern for the conduct of life—praxis. As a praxis, ethics is a responsive, reflexive activity that, in a self-elaborating manner, seeks, articulates, and pursues a life that is praiseworthy and worthy of pursuit, what many, myself included, are content to call *the good life*.[4] To term ethics "praxis" is to stress that it is something done as opposed to merely believed; that it is a kind of action, a pursuit, or better still, a task because we only discover along the way (if we ever do) whether we have been successful. To find oneself in ethical praxis is thus to find oneself with a job to do.

An activity, then. As such, ethics is irreducible to a system of values to which one would assent if asked or to a range of feelings one might have. Having a belief that X is good is quite different than acting in accord (let alone from) X. To employ a different distinction, "ethics" is not something that one has. Rather, it concerns how one is. (I think this bodes ill for those who would employ surveys to track the "ethics" of a population. The form allotted the ethical, the form in which it presumably appears—I believe, I strongly feel—is off. As we will see, it takes a part for the whole.)

In stressing its active dimension, I am not claiming that "ethics" is practical rather than theoretical. By definition, praxis involves *prohairesis*. As Joe

Sachs notes in his translation of Aristotle's *Nicomachean Ethics*, "An action [*praxis*] is chosen, and presupposes deliberation and forethought" (Aristotle 2002, 103). *Prohairesis*, a kind of "grasping in advance" or forethought, is commonly translated as choice or even intentional choice. But within the praxis of ethics, it is more than a single act of assent: it is a process of reflective, deliberative (and thus deliberate) commitment to a course of action.[5] It names, in part, the labors by which we elect to do something or commit to doing it, labors integral to ethics. On this account, then, the praxis of ethics not only concerns the substance of our commitments but also that we actively form them (and of how we do so)

By taking ethics in the sense of praxis, I am not supporting something called "applied ethics" over and against "normative ethics" or "metaethics." Traditionally, applied ethics champions an ethical theory in a particular sphere. For example, in the domain of animal welfare, Peter Singer uses utilitarianism to institute animal rights, whereas Tom Regan turns to Kant for the same end.[6] Or, like Tom Morris, one might rely on virtue ethics to establish a culture of corporate excellence.[7] In such cases, however, the formation of one's normative (and metaethical) commitments has been left to someone else. But every prevalent theory (e.g., deontology, utilitarianism, care ethics, and virtue ethics) suffers from theoretical weaknesses that are lost on those who simply apply them. In its haste to apply some ethical standard, applied ethics often foregoes a key ethical labor, therefore, one that is necessary to determine whether or not its recommendations are in fact praiseworthy. Now, I will not go so far as to term this omission unethical, but only because that sounds like a categorical condemnation. I will claim, however, that bypassing the labor involved in forming core, ethical commitments is blameworthy.[8]

My second concern with applied ethics lies in the nature of "application." One key to praxis is the *phronesis* with which one applies one's normative commitments. Somewhat ironically, applied ethics often leaves "application" undertheorized, and this threatens to reduce ethics to doctrine as it obscures the complex work of sorting through what is expected of one in any given here and now. But doctrine, or what I would rather call "normative commitment," only proves ethical in its enactment, and applied ethics, or so I fear, leaves us less insightful than we should be about the irreducibly personal trials presented by the task of ethics.[9]

What though of metaethics? To my mind, concerns about the nature, meaning, and proper role of moral feelings, terms, and judgments can distract us from the concrete situations in which we find ourselves—rather than address a pressing concern, we spend the day debating what it might mean to render a "concern" "pressing" in a "morally distinct" manner. And yet, this may be more of a question of when and where than of whether to or not. Metaethics also reflects an ongoing effort to make sense of where we find ourselves with regard to phenomena such as moral feelings and terms. Said otherwise, metaethics, when viewed as a part of ethical praxis, is something of an effort to behave ethically in one's inheritance and perpetuation of those traditions that inform ethical praxis.

Let me provide two very different examples. When Habermas offered discourse ethics as a supplement to social theory, his initial task was to rethink the activity of moral judgment in terms of communicative action.[10] In his view, conscience directs us less toward enduring grounds for judgment (e.g., by way of a natural or formal, moral law) than into conversations about what should be done. His work thus highlights, at the metaethical level, the ways in which our evaluations and prescriptions are intersubjectively ventured speech acts that seek recognition and acceptance from a series of concrete others. Now, one could correctly regard this as a metatheoretical reorientation that may entail a normative claim, namely, the fundamental principle of discourse ethics, which holds (and I paraphrase) that norms are valid if and only if they are or could be approved in genuine, practical discourse by those affected by the actions the norms in question propose to validate (Habermas 1983, 76). But Habermas's metaethical reflections also reorient ethical praxis insofar as they set our evaluations and prescriptions within dialogical contexts, thus exposing conscience to the full, embodied play of intersubjective communication. Habermas's work, right or wrong, is thus continuous with ethical praxis even as it scrutinizes it.

A different kind of praxical metaethics is apparent in Stanley Cavell's ongoing inheritance of Emerson and Thoreau, what he terms, at one point, the "task of endless responsibility for one's own discourse," which one executes by reading and rewriting "the terms of one's condition," for example, the very word "condition" (2003, 46, 70). I call this a kind of metaethics because it continually works and reworks the terms by which we present and justify ourselves to our peers, though without limiting ourselves to some special domain of ethical terms (like "good" and "evil") and operations (like judgment). Instead, insofar as we might meet through any term or phrase, we are responsible for "every term we utter," which implies, Cavell (2003, 72) believes, that as we address one another, every word can count. I thus find, at least in Cavell's hands (and in a different way, in Habermas's hands as well), that metaethics is just a name for the most reflexive dimensions of ethical praxis in its effort to be responsible for the lives our conduct will conduct.

—III. Conversing about where we find ourselves, and finding ourselves committed to treating one another well, I (possibly we) have been exploring the phenomenon of ethics as praxis. Let me continue this line of thought with the claim that as such, ethics presumes a form of life, though I should specify that I am taking "form" from Hegel and not from Wittgenstein, although I leave open whether the two might productively intertwine.

Each chapter of the *Phenomenology* concerns a pattern or form (*Gestalt*) in which self and world interact: namely, consciousness, self-consciousness, reason, and spirit. And each of those contains subpatterns, for example, perception, life and death struggle, observing reason, ethical life, and absolute knowing. What renders Hegel's book a phenomenology is its attempt to immanently articulate the logic organizing each pattern. For example, consciousness presumes a fundamental distinction between subject and object that might prove conjoined in phenomena such as sensation, perception, and explanation via laws.

In this essay, I am proposing that ethical praxis has a form that we might phenomenologically specify along Hegelian lines; that is, we might articulate its various elements (e.g., some normative measure) and the principle(s) of their integration (e.g., *prohairesis*). But such an analysis needs to take Hegel's thought of form quite seriously. Hegel introduces the notion, and "form" is precisely the term he uses, in his discussion of lordship and bondage. Form is what, through labor, the bondsman (or functionary) draws out of the order of nature, thus encountering an objectification of his or her own self-consciousness. For example, if I assemble a chair from a tree I have found in the forest, that chair, qua concrete form, discloses that my activity is a *formiriende Thun*, a formative activity, thus allowing me to encounter part of the truth of my self-conscious nature, a part deformed and obscured by social relations of bondage. In other words, form in this Hegelian sense is a manifestation of the way in which human activity inhabits and transforms the world in which it finds itself.[11]

I recall this thought (in what is, admittedly, a hasty and schematic manner) because it binds *forms* to the course of life (as opposed to pure idealities or natural kinds), and that is precisely how I wish to think of the form of life underwriting ethical praxis. Its history is part and parcel (and contributor to) the ecosocial history of human beings, from our affective dispositions to cognitive developments in the history of conscience, say in the nuanced ways in which jurists and activists have tried to think of responsibility in terms of various action-intensities, from cause-in-effect to proximate causality to whatever responsibility we might have for global economic orders on the basis of our labor and consumption. Is the custodian who cleans bathrooms in a Nike office or a construction worker who helped build that office responsible in some meaningful sense for blameworthy labor practices overseas?[12] Is someone who buys Nike shoes? And if "yes" in any of these cases, to what degree? Or is it all or nothing? We still have to think our way through these questions. Regardless, the general point is that, qua praxis, ethics emerges out of the very life-activity it informs, as I more or less already claimed when I said that ethics is a responsive, reflexive activity that, in a self-elaborating manner, seeks, articulates, and pursues a praiseworthy life. And this is why part of the task of ethics involves configuring, as best it can, what that praxis entails, hence my admiration for metaethics, understood in the manner outlined herein.

I suppose another stress is in order, this one directed toward the figure "life." Earlier I suggested that conscience concerns the conduct of *life*. I have just argued not only that conscience is part of a praxis but also that ethical praxis presumes a form of *life*. But I fear that my earlier stress of "conduct" might suggest that the principal concern is the life that is mine. But that would not do justice to the ways in which I find myself. As I suggested at the outset, the life that is mine inevitably quotes and converses with what it is not, to employ a Hegelian register. Moreover, I rarely, if ever, conduct what is simply my fate; in the least, I am preparing a world for those who might follow me, either in time or by example. To say, then, that ethical praxis concerns the conduct of life is to say that it is concerned with the kind of world it would find around the corner, the kind of world it would sponsor, whether through action or inaction, commission or omission.[13]

——IV. Let me further schematize the form of ethical praxis. The concerns of conscience, which do not begin in wonder, call for action. A formal facet of the praxis thus arises in the question: "What is to be done in this situation in which I find myself?" If that description is apt, ethical praxis requires actors who, to the best of their abilities, render any and all motivations, even urges, renewed *possibilities for* action. I say "renewed" because, in an originary sense, what befalls an agent is already a possibility. What befalls an agent is open to further interpretation and response. Someone hurts your feelings. This is not just some state of affairs but something for you to address. Having one's feelings hurt occurs within the course of a life and thus it transpires within a field of possibility—that is its actuality, in fact. And that is the scene that ethics enters. Confronted by a possibility, we consider how best to respond, which is already a response. We think it through. Should you feel hurt? If so, should you let it pass? If not, how should your reply? Should you return the hurt? Ethics takes the possibilities that arise on the course of our lives and renders them determinate. That is the deed with which this form begins.

Ethics, then, concerns the course of a life in its possibilities, or better still, given all one conducts, its copossibilities. Interrelated as we are, my course of action stages, in part, a course of life for others, and so too theirs for mine. And that is the scene in which I would like to inherit one of Aristotle's claims in the *Nicomachean Ethics* (1109b30–1109b35), in order to further specify the concerns of conscience. Ethics concerns voluntary actions. First, actions become voluntary as a result of a process accomplished (which is not to say initiated) by the actor: desires are renewed as possibilities to which we might commit following a process of reflective deliberation. Should that process of reflective deliberation be *impossible* (and note that "reflective, deliberative action" does not exhaust the field of response open to humans), the action cannot be described as voluntary. Second, the claim is not that ethical habits are inadmissible but that they become "ethical" only after one commits to and cultivates them by way of a practice of reflective deliberation. A very young child with good habits has not yet acquired the form of life, "ethical praxis," though he or she may be off to a good start.[14]

In claiming that ethical praxis addresses a course of action as a *possible* course of action, I am not forgetting the role that normativity plays in an ethical form of life. Regardless of one's metaethics, I think it undeniable that ethical praxis is normative; that is, it seeks to bring the possible in line with some measure that functions like a moral compass, though I want to leave open, for the moment, how the measure operates. For now, allow me to present a different matter: a life that does not distinguish between what is desirable and what is right or virtuous is amoral in my view and in principle.

One finds oneself in a situation, begins to respond (again), and, in some way or other, considers the worthiness of that response. Now, one may act on that initial response, but it only becomes formally ethical insofar as it undergoes some process of evaluation. For example, a friend may ask for a loan, and I may want to comply, but in ethical praxis, my wanting to comply must be evaluated with reference to something other than my wanting to comply, for example, with reference to some conception of friendship and/or principles for managing money. Again, this process of evaluation may run through habits that have been cultivated, and thus the "evaluation" need not be an explicitly self-conscious activity. Nevertheless, explicit evaluation must remain a formal possibility. Even when habits run the show, they can stand in for explicit evaluation insofar as they have been affirmed because of their tendency to produce praiseworthy outcomes.

Allow me to say a bit more about "normativity." By invoking the term, I am not, in any metaethical sense, favoring deontological rules, a virtue-grounded *êthos*, moral feeling, a conception of care, or a consequentialist calculator. At the formal level, these all function in more or less the same way. Presuming that the situation involves some kind of moral conflict, a measure, in a process of reflective, deliberative commitment, is brought to bear on a possibility in order to determine whether one should commit to the course of action specified (or underspecified, as we shall see). But I am claiming that an ethics without normativity is not worthy of the name. Said otherwise, I see no future in a purported ethics that does not concretely help me with the following question: How should I proceed? I see no future because without any measure, ethical praxis collapses back into amoral acts derived from the positivity of desire or intuition or habit or whatever it is that informs action, including responses to those in need.

A felt need for concrete directives leaves me somewhat dissatisfied with my earlier forays into ethical theory. In two very different books, I tried to present what I took to be the ethical import of the events I was essaying: the poetry of Charles Simic when read through Heidegger's conception of poetic building and dwelling, and Emerson's praxis of self-culture. (Complementary ventures were also presented through readings of Jean-Luc Nancy.)[15] In a way, I was offering an *ethics of the future* (or of possibility), one concerned to preserve the future by remaining open to the incalculable character of its arrival. I was developing an *êthos* based on an experience of the birth of sense as an event of possibility, of what *might* be (or rather, be again), should we commit to it. In *You Must Change Your Life*, the goal, which I termed *preserving the possible*, was to facilitate an experience of any and all meanings that would prevent them from congealing into the real deal, into the appearance of a necessity transparently known as such. One could call this my attempt to resist totalitarianism as a discursive-political phenomenon. In *Emerson and Self-Culture*, my concern was fanaticism as a personal phenomenon. There I offered what I termed an *êthos of the moment*, a doubled double consciousness, one that (1) essayed genuine commitments even as it proactively anticipated, even sought, the self-overcoming of those explanatory and normative orders through which commitments are essayed, and one that (2) essayed each side of that initial double consciousness as an offer of exemplarity to another with whom one was bound in ethical friendship, even as one attended to and graciously received his or her conduct in kind. My thought was (and is) that such an existential bearing renders us better than we might otherwise be by keeping us, even in our most heartfelt commitments, living, fluid, responsive to error, and capable of change. Said otherwise, I have been trying to imagine a self-transcending form of character nevertheless oriented in and toward a determinate world in which one lives in a manner that embodies all that one finds best.

I suspect that you can see or, rather, feel the rub. As writerly projects, as offers to those whom I have called, following Emerson, "unknown friends," most if not all of my previous efforts move within the kind of form I have here been terming ethical praxis. And as such, they revolve around some conception of the good that leads me to (1) resist totalitarian social orders and fanatical attachments and (2) praise fluidity, responsiveness, and growth. Yes, that conception of the good may be incalculably given—it may be fluid and open to revision or even sudden redirection—but without such a conception, without some conception of the good, neither my criticisms nor my recommendations, neither my provocations nor my exhortations, make a lick of sense as *commitments* (as opposed to outcroppings of nature, objective spirit, culture, etc.).

I also feel the rub when I consider what we might term "implicit commitments." In order to pursue the projects just mentioned (or practice deconstruction or pursue a critical theory or write *Totality and Infinity* or lecture in Bremen), one relies on a host of sociohistorical forces, what I regard as "enabling conditions"—for example, ecological, governmental, educational, and economic orders, and so forth. In fact, any would-be ethical praxis will find itself enabled (or frustrated) by conditions upon which it depends. And to the degree to which it avails itself of these conditions, it, in a sense, commits to them, that is, deems them either (1) not worth resisting here and now or (2) worth maintaining for the time being. The point bears repeating (and I am far from the first to present it) because should one take ethical praxis to concern the conduct of life, then one's concern should include those ecosocial orders one's conduct conducts, even when they are not the principal concern of one's action.

——V. What I have just been offering, in brief, is an argument for not abandoning one metaethical orientation or trajectory (consider Hegel, Marx, and Jane Addams) in favor of another (consider late Heidegger, late Adorno, and deconstruction). Because the former conspires with present possibilities, invests in them, it cannot help but proceed with insufficient care and reflection regarding all that its ventures will bring about and occlude; it risks what Derrida terms "the madness of decision" (Cornell et al. 1992). But that is true of all actions, as Derrida well knows, including the actions by which one proposes interruptions of reconstructive praxis. It thus seems essential that ethical praxis account for its explicit and implicit commitments, and in normatively thick terms; that is, we should explain why we incline toward or away from democracy; toward or away from global capitalism; toward or away from friends, lovers, kinds of work, and so on. More generally, if we would not be left with theoretically poor interventions and engagements, ethical praxis should refuse philosophical offers that leave us unable to say anything concrete about where we find ourselves and where we should head.

I also have a more particular conversation in mind, and it concerns the work of Emmanuel Levinas. In general, I am frustrated by the trajectories that Levinas's thought opens, taking "frustration" to name a mood wherein a more sustained engagement proves impossible. One finds oneself turned away and so, seeks other interlocutors. That said, the onset of such a mood does not, I believe, relieve one of the obligation to account for why one has ceased reading, ceased conversing in any overt, sustained fashion. What follows is thus an accounting along those lines.

Levinas's thought revolves around an insight into the transcendental, temporal logic of intentional consciousness, irrespective of whether the awareness so named is self-conscious or prereflectively operative. As I understand it, the claim is that intentional consciousness is always already situated among others to whom it has responded, such that intentional consciousness is a second response to those others and such that the other is a condition for the possibility of intentional consciousness. In the language of *Otherwise than Being*, Levinas claims, "The knot tied in subjectivity [its being always already bound to an other to whom it has always already responded], . . . signifies an allegiance of the same [the presentations through which intentional consciousness re-presents the world to itself] to the other, imposed before any exhibition of the other, preliminary to all consciousness" (1998, 25). Or as he says several pages later, "The subject is affected without the source of the affection becoming a theme of representation" (101). Playing with Hegelian language, Levinas thus insists that being-for-itself is in fact, initially, being-for-another: "Subjectivity is not for itself; it is, once again, initially for another" (1985, 96).[16] Or to employ the idiom of the Hebrew Bible, intentional consciousness, as it arises, takes shape as a response that says, "Here I am," as if it were Abraham responding to the call of God, who proceeds to command him to bind Isaac (Genesis 22:1–2).

According to Levinas, this event, this knot, marks an allegiance between self and other that is best thought of in terms of a responsibility for the other who makes one's own self-relation possible. As Levinas tells Philippe Nemo, "The tie with the Other is knotted only as responsibility, this moreover, whether acknowledged or refused, whether knowing or not knowing how to assume it, whether able or unable to do something concrete for the Other" (1985, 97). Or in the language of *Otherwise than Being*, "this allegiance will be described as a responsibility of the same for the other, as a response to his proximity before any question," for example, Who are you? What are my obligations here? How does this responsibility compare with my other obligations? and so on (1998, 25–26). Of note, it is not our deeds, voluntary or involuntary, for which we must assume responsibility but, rather, the other: "I understand responsibility as responsibility for the Other, thus as responsibility for what is not my deed" (Levinas 1985, 95).

I have no deep quarrel with this account of intentional consciousness. What gives me pause, however, what frustrates me (and yes, I realize that this is the intended effect, to impede, even halt, my praxis) is the invocation of the language of responsibility.[17] At the most basic level, I find it arbitrary. Why does some kind of responsibility follow from the fact that intentional consciousness is inextricably entwined with alterity? Now, it might seem to follow given Levinas's use of the category of "the other," which suggests an argument like: we only live through others and are thereby indebted to them in a manner than can be repaid only by taking responsibility for them again and again, that is, infinitely, given that each time we respond we only fall further into debt; they are, after all, the condition of the possibility of each response.[18] But this only seems to follow given the connotations carried by the phrase "the other." If one brackets that term, it seems that Levinas's concept of "the knot" recounts the impersonal entwinement of intentional consciousness with the world. I say "impersonal" not just because, as Levinas himself claims, our being-in-the-world is not the accomplishment of intentional consciousness (hence my language of "entwinement") but also because that to which intentional consciousness is a response is not principally another subject or person, let alone her or his voluntary acts or labor or anything that is somehow diminished or exploited by my very being. Rather, it is an unthematizable field of events that affect and propel intentional consciousness. I thus submit that the language of "the other" anthropomorphizes that to which our conscious lives are a response, thus allowing Levinas to trade on an intuition that one should pay one's debts whenever one makes use of another. But one is not making use of another here, for neither "one" nor an "other" has yet to congeal in the events that Levinas recounts. And once this is apparent, I find Levinas's ethical language to effect the actual imposition, one that redescribes how the course of a life is fundamentally relational and dependent, which is how I would prefer to account for the knots of subjectivity.

It is not just the arbitrariness of Levinas's language of the ethical that frustrates me. Because its principal concerns are (1) events that are not the work of any agent, let alone voluntary, and (2) events that concern persons before they are persons who can be harmed or helped, Levinas's thought fails to shed light on what it might mean to behave more or less responsibly with regard to the other. But if that is the case, Levinas's thought asks us to assume responsibility for the other without providing us with any sense of what an adequate response would be. I thus cannot find any kind of determinate future awaiting me should I allow Levinas's thought into my ethical praxis.[19]

Another conversation is unfolding, and this one concerns my insistence that conceptions of the good life are the chief measures within ethical praxis. In particular, I am thinking of Alain Badiou, for whom the good is subordinate to the true. He writes, "Mathematics holds something of the secret of thinking. It is that mathematics, while not the most important, is something which makes more transparent, or takes us closer to, this secret of thinking. This is the first point. I think I hold a fidelity to this idea, but, at the same time, the heart of the most radical experience is politics. Politics itself, in a sense, is also a thinking through forms. It is not the thought of arrangements or the thought of contracts or the good life. No. It is a thinking of form" (2007, 102–103).[20] This conversation is actually quite broad and complex, beginning with "form," but for the time being, I will keep to the good. Also, politics and ethics mark distinct registers, but in each case, Badiou's beliefs about the good are more or less the same, and precisely because, in both cases, the principle issue is truth, or rather, the event of a truth procedure, such as politics, but also art, in which phenomena acquire sense. Badiou advocates an infinite responsibility to the true, both as it operates within a given truth procedure and with regard to the truth of procedures per se, procedures that become salient once one thinks through forms. The result is something like a firm resolve to be true to the procedure within which one finds oneself, say as a Pauline Christian, even to the point of remaining open to the incalculable arrival of a new regime, a possibility that can never be preemptively foreclosed. "A complete truth is a fiction," he says, "because a truth is never complete, never finishes," in part because it cannot completely account for itself (2002).

I term Badiou's commitment a "firm resolve" because Badiou presents it as an imperative: *Keep going*! "This ethics combines," he writes, "under the imperative to 'Keep going!,' resources of discernment (do not fall for simulacra), of courage (do not give up), and of moderation [*reserve*] (do not get carried away to the extremes of Totality)" (2001, 91). Because, for Badiou, ethics concerns our being in and of truth-procedures, I can see why he denies the centrality of the good; the good is possible only within a truth procedure. Badiou writes, "What provokes the emergence of the Good—and, by simple consequence, Evil—exclusively concerns the rare existence of truth-processes" (60). And, more generally, "Ethical questions, for me, are questions in the field of truth" (2002). Said otherwise, one can pursue and realize a good only within a procedure wherein that good is a possibility, and from the standpoint of a kind of subjectivity that is also a possibility within the selfsame truth procedure. (For Badiou, truth is infinite, whereas the positioning of a subjectivity is always finite.)

And yet, what leads Badiou to commit to the grammar of an imperative, and a categorical one at that, and to this imperative in particular? From what do these commitments follow? I ask because the call for moderation seems to arise in reply to Badiou's belief that all representational systems are riddled by incompleteness, which exposes them, in principle, to interruption by a new event. But why choose to respond to the incompleteness of all representational systems in this way? Why not become fanatics? Why not become a last man and rest with simulacra? (Why not take the blue pill?) Why continue to be "this 'some-one,' a human animal among others, which nevertheless finds itself *seized* and *displaced* by the eventual process of truth?" (ibid.). The incompleteness of any set does not mandate one response over another.

I underscore the arbitrariness of Badiou's commitments in order to uncover what underlies them. In particular, they seem driven by particular aversions, such as to our animality, which Badiou regards as *beneath* good and evil, and which he describes in terms of the "cruel innocence of life" (2001, 59–60). I'm not sure what cruelty means in this context, but it carries clear connotations of aversion, and thus an operative sense of what is bad or base, one that carries over, as a constitutive outside, into proclamations like: "The real content of humanity for me is creation and invention of truths" (2002). It is also impossible for me not to hear affirmations operating in Badiou's assertion that the event of a truth-procedure addresses us with imperatives that demand what he calls "fidelity." The event of a truth-procedure may claim us, and like Paul, we may find ourselves converted, that is, turned around, and to the point that we have become someone else. And there may be, as Badiou claims, a "joyful or enthusiastic clarity of the seizing" in finding ourselves so claimed. But nothing in the finding qua finding requires the grammar of an imperative (2001, 60). This imposition of the imperative on a far more variable, syntactic scene alerts my nose to the presence of a longing, which I take to bear traces of a conception of the good, one built around the wish to be an exclusively rational animal. Now, to the degree that Badiou's aversions and longings persist and propel his thought, and precisely at those points where his language proves arbitrary, something like a conception of the good still operates. And if it does, then even as we think through forms, we remain bound to continue formulating and experimenting with conceptions of the good life.

——VI. While I more or less have stressed the reflective dimensions of ethical praxis, I do not mean to do so at the expense of affect. In book 6 of his *Nicomachean Ethics*, Aristotle states that "choice is either intellect fused with desire or desire fused with thinking" (1139b). Or in Charles Chamberlain's words, "When both parts of Aristotle's bipartite soul—*dianoia* and *orexis*—function in harmony, the result is *prohairesis*," ethical commitment (1984, 152).[21]

I think this nexus of desire, evaluation, and commitment, so much a part of the past of ethical theory and, more importantly, so integral to ethical praxis, must also focus their future. For example, the question remains: How much influence do reflective deliberation and commitment wield in the conduct of life? Note, I am not asking: How much control does reason exercise over the passions? That way of framing the question seems outmoded, though it no doubt still captures particular struggles, for example, *really* wanting to tell someone off while believing that no good will come from doing so. But as a way of thinking human praxis, it fails. It now seems clear that reflective life is suffused by feeling, from our holistic grasp of situations (I think here of Damasio's work on background emotions [1999, 50–53]) to our sense of having found a successful way of essaying that situation (I think here of Dewey's account of choice in *Human Nature and Conduct* [1983, 134–138]). Taking ethics as praxis thus need not involve subordinating affect to reason. In fact, given the findings of empirical psychology, it seems misleading to speak of a nexus of reflection and affect, although, at present, a suitably reconstructed language of deliberation and commitment is wanting.

At this point, we could look at some recent claims from philosophical psychology, social psychology, and/or neuroscience and try to parse their implications for ethical praxis, for example, the possible universality of five domains of moral concern (suffering, reciprocity, hierarchy, purity, and group boundaries) or the affective basis of ethical evaluation, which initiates in the limbic as opposed to the higher cortical areas of the brain.[22] But I would rather make some more general points, the first of which concerns whether one should distinguish, in principle, philosophical from psychological inquiries into ethical praxis. My thought is no, not in any strong, categorical sense. In fact, scientific inquiry into desire, motivation, judgment, and so on is formally indistinct from philosophical taxonomies of the same phenomena. In *Nicomachean Ethics*, for example, terms such as *hexis*, *energeia*, *prohairesis*, and *orexis* do not represent the intrusion of psychological inquiry into ethical theory. Rather, that taxonomy is a part of the very ethical theory and, more importantly, the praxis that *Nicomachean Ethics* is.

But I would say even more than "do not fear the play of psychological research in ethical praxis": *ethical praxis requires psychological research*. A reflective, deliberative pursuit of the good that does not study the conduct it aims to direct is neither reflective nor deliberative. In fact, in its shortsightedness, its likelihood of finding and realizing the good is haphazard at best, and that seems to be a vice. My point is not Daniel Dennett's claim that the "only meaning of life worth caring about is one that can withstand our best efforts to examine it" (1995, 22). I am not championing "truth" as a value that trumps all others. Rather, my point concerns power. We will not get very far if we do not know what we face. In Dewey's words, "What cannot be understood cannot be managed intelligently" (1983, 5). The consummation of ethical praxis is conduct conforming to a measure that finds such conduct proper and praiseworthy. That result follows on the heels of a complex process, however. And without much knowledge of the dynamics of that process, for example, of the conflicts that prevent us from doing what we think best, or of the forces that obscure the direct and/or indirect consequences of our behavior, or of the values that lie hidden in our inherited conceptions of gender, race, and class (or of the brain or the genome), we are more likely to act in ways that, in retrospect, we will regard as less praiseworthy than they might have been.

Because I am admitting into ethical praxis third-person explanatory and predictive discourse, I want to clarify the terms of admission. In his initial foray into the history of sexuality, Foucault (1978) recalls us to various *ars erotica*, discourses of sex more interested in pleasure than in what sex really is. Such arts do not ignore matters of truth, however. It is vital whether position A, whisper Y, or caress 65 produces pleasure. Without such knowledge, everyone (and everyone's parts) would be worse for wear. In other words, third-person explanatory discourse is being admitted into ethical praxis in order to empower pursuits of the good.

But what about the good itself? Might an explanatory discourse discover goods that would orient ethical praxis? My answer depends on whether we situate that discourse within the form of ethical praxis or whether we replace ethical commitments with the conclusions of third-person inquiry. If we pursue the latter strategy (which would involve deferring to the authority of third-person inquiry with regard to what goods should be pursued), then we have lost the form of ethical praxis altogether, which thoroughly rejects positivism. For example, it may be true that most, if not all human societies distinguish between an in-group and out-group and preferentially treat, without apparent hypocrisy, in-group members. But that fact alone does not commit me to doing likewise (and not just because truths about groups are not necessarily applicable to every member of the group). Instead, ethical praxis regards the generalization as a possibility for being, which transforms the fact into a question: Should *I* pursue certain in-group distinctions in order to refine my world of moral concern?

That said, such generalizations might prove instructive. In fact, third-person discourses such as psychology and anthropology can play the same role that tradition plays for Aristotelian virtue ethics—they can detail portraits of the qualities, requirements, and consequences of lives oriented toward various goods. And those brushstrokes may be preferable in certain ways to what we gain from more local ways of recording exemplarity—more traditions will be included, and our feel for what such lives require and conduct will have greater predictive power.[23]

"Aha," you might be thinking: "But they cannot tell us whether we *should* pursue such lives." I suppose everything hinges on how one hears *should*. As Owen Flanagan (2007, 52) observes, empirical observations can provide persuasive grounds for hypothetical imperatives. For example, one could imagine a psychologist claiming on the basis of multiple, longitudinal studies that if one wants a life of rich self-realization, one should develop one's character in an integrated fashion by attending to various enabling conditions like a good diet, plenty of intellectual stimulation, and a varied social life that includes friendship and intimacy. The suggestion might be: I have interviewed thousands of people more or less like you, and these steps met with excellent results; both the agents and those who knew them regarded the lives in question as richly self-realized. Or, with even more focus on the end in question, one might think: humans, for centuries and from all kinds of cultures, have abandoned lives devoted to carnal pleasure because such lives grow stale and usually hurt one's conquests; I think, therefore, that I should follow their lead—a life of carnal pleasure will more than likely prove harmful and meaningless.

Of course, such imperatives draw their weight from the consequences they predict in light of some allegiance to ends that render those consequences persuasive. Hypothetical imperatives are thus more or less hypotheses, as Dewey suggests: they predict that doing or not doing X will produce a certain kind of life, or better yet, world, since one's life is almost always part and parcel of the lives of others.[24]

But what accounts for those ends that render certain hypotheses hypothetical imperatives? At issue is the meaning of something being an end in itself. In *Nicomachean Ethics* (1097a15–1097b8), the notion more or less names an end, *eudaemonia*, which many, even most, seek for its own sake; that is, it is that for the sake of which other actions are done, and thus it is complete in itself. But this is just an empirical claim about the status of that end in a historical community, and Aristotle's argument rests, in large measure, upon the ability of that status to persuade his interlocutors. Yes, he adds that *eudaemonia* is self-sufficient, but that seems to be nothing more than a claim about what it is like to find oneself in such a life—it lacks nothing (*Nicomachean Ethics*, 1097b10–1097b20). The language of "end in itself" thus seems descriptive through and through. One slice makes use of a historically extended consensus, whereas another makes a prediction: live in this manner, and purposive action will have to look no further for a sense of self-sufficiency and completeness.

Permit me to step back. My claim is that third-person discourses are quite useful for ethical praxis. They help us navigate the seas of self and world and improve our chances of reaching port. More than that, they can help us decide what ports to seek by recounting what others have said and done about getting there and what one is likely to encounter on arrival. In that sense, then, third-person discourses can give us insight into the means and ends that might orient a life in pursuit of the good, including phenomena that seem good in themselves, that is, pursuable for their own sake. But such discourses cannot ultimately settle the matter for us without breaking the form of ethical praxis. Commitment—like enactment—is a personal phenomenon, requiring activities that no one can do for us.

"But discourses like psychology simply cannot tell us what we *should* do!" I think I understand the objection even though I will not accept the terms in which it is presented. For some, *should* means "duty" in the sense of "unconditional obligation," and a hypothetical imperative nor an empirical description nor a prediction can obligate us in that way. We may not seek the end in question (or find it worthy of being sought), and as Hume made plain, some evaluative statement is needed to tie an empirical premise to a normative conclusion.

I want to resist conceiving of ethical praxis along these lines. First, this metaethical interpretation of conscience inhabits a figurative landscape ruled by an imperative-dispensing commander to whom some kind of unconditional allegiance is owed. But in ethical praxis, no voice or feeling or rule or proposal merits unconditional allegiance. I say this formally but also with a view toward the kind of life such an interpretation conducts. Every prescription risks a future that may conduct life in a manner that we, with good reason, will later regret. I thus resist taking *should* in any sense that seriously weakens my ability to imagine or reevaluate what it prescribes. And since committing to that ability (which is really the ability to commit in an ethical manner) renders conditional my allegiance to any directive, I cannot find a future for ethical praxis in the continued insistence that ethical obligations compel and deserve a kind of unconditional allegiance.

Second, ethical commitments individuate us in profound ways, indicating how we have conspired with and thus conducted a world that exceeds, wildly, our grasp and control. Because I would not free anyone from the burden of that responsibility, I would rather turn our consciences away from imperatives and toward commitments that compel our allegiance as we find them in our way, to come back to one more Emersonian phrase.

I am drawn to Emerson's phrase at precisely this juncture in which ethical praxis finds itself normatively directed because it describes how ethical praxis comes upon normatively endorsed futures that provide the substance of its commitments—*we find them in our way*. I take the phrase to name a process that blurs the distinction between discovering and inventing. Given the degree to which our affective and cognitive inheritances inform processes of deliberative commitment, one does not simply discover what should be done. Rather, we are tugged to-and-fro by a multiplicity of affects, imaginative anticipations, internalized expectations, and so forth. Ethical commitment, like all actions, is thus a result whose full set of antecedent conditions verges on a kind of mathematical sublimity. In such a context, *discover* simply says too much. But this is not to say that we simply invent what we think we should do, as if some calculating ego were master of this house. Instead, our sense of what should be done in each case is found, as it were, and in our way, which is to say according to our manner of being but also as possible obstacles to our initial responses to whatever situation has claimed us.[25]

I have been elaborating a form for ethical praxis and, in the last part of this essay, defending the idea that third-person inquiries are germane, even necessary, for its pursuit. Let me close by locating one other point where third-person inquiry and ethical praxis might, even should, intertwine. I have claimed that ethical praxis needs a conception of the good in order to answer the question, What *should* I do? But how do I know *what* I am about to do or *what* I have done? When I prepare to commit, how do I apprehend the substance of the commitment I am about to evaluate? Let me return to Hegel for another foothold. In *Philosophy of Right*, part 2, particularly sections 118 and 120, Hegel suggests that the truth of one's subjective purposes lies in the consequences of one's actions and that a mature moral agent understands his or her intentions through consequences. As he writes in the *Nürnberger Propädeutik*: "In general it is important to think about the consequences of an action because in this way one does not stop with the immediate standpoint but goes beyond it. Through a many-sided consideration of the action, one will be led to the nature of the action" (1991, 421).

If Hegel is right, then knowing what is to be done only arises within ongoing engagements. Ethical knowledge is thus dependent on the very praxis it would orient; for only through praxis does one discover "the *what*" of what ought to be done. But how do we apprehend such matters? One rich approach lies with social theory, the attempt to think human action and institutions in terms of interacting social forces, including persons and the social forms in which they meet one another. Given the interconnectedness of things and the multiple effects of every action on a wide range of beings (karma, for short), we need to track what we are doing when we go to the store, lend money, vote from the standpoint of conscience as opposed to consequence, ignore chronic poverty in various urban and rural communities, and so on. In other words, if we wish to know the substance of our commitments, ethics cannot proceed without the aid of social theory. Note that my point is not simply that we need to know the consequences of X in order to know whether we should commit to it. Rather, without social theory, in many cases, we will not know what X is. As John Stuhr has it: "think and live forward. Think and live prospectively instead of retrospectively" (2003, 9).

Finally, if ethical praxis must interpret experience in order to know the substance of its commitments and thus whether to maintain them, the future of ethics rests not only with concrete conceptions of the good but with their active pursuit, for it is only in pursuing certain goods that we come to know their nature. In other words, the future of ethics cannot be contained within the bounds of philosophy if philosophy continues to understand itself as distinct from concrete praxis. My claim is not quite that of thesis 11, however. Instead, I am claiming that one cannot even ethically interpret the world except in an effort to change it.

NOTES

1. Note that *conversation* also carries a plainer meaning, namely, "to live with," which *Webster's* traces to *conversari*, though one might also look to *converso*, meaning "to interact or pass time with," since *converso* is the root for *conversatio*, meaning both a "way or life" and a "conversation." I am particularly drawn to the last sense given that I find the course of life bound to conversations, most of which I never began and some I will not live to conclude.

2. As Dewey observes in his 1942 article, "How Is the Mind to Be Known?," "conscience" has roots in *conscire*, which gives a literal sense of knowing-with. This suggests an awareness of some state of affairs, for example, one's conduct, which is not merely private but part and parcel of a kind of sociality (see 1989, 28). I should stress that I do not offer these etymological reflections as evidence for some social ontology. I do not believe that the history of a human language offers the authoritative expressions of a primal mind that our present discourse has lost. But etymologies do help me tune the terms I employ—they give them a sense I would have you recall over and against other senses.

3. Chuck Salter, "Job Title of the Future: Corporate Ethicist" (2005).

4. For the purposes of this article, I will not take up the distinction between those things that are praised and those that are honored that Aristotle offers in chapter 12, book 1, of *Nicomachean Ethics* (1101b10–1102a4 [see 2002]).

5. This discussion has benefited from Charles Chamberlain's "The Meaning of *Prohairesis* in Aristotle's Ethics" (1984).

6. I have in mind Peter Singer's *Animal Liberation* (2002) and Tom Reagan's *The Case for Animal Rights* (1985).

7. See Tom Morris's *If Aristotle Ran General Motors* (1997).

8. If one chooses one's theory because it furthers one's initial commitments, the blame only grows. One of the powers of ethical theorizing lies in its ability to test our commitments and possibly transform them. If one only chooses theories that support one's commitments, one transforms ethical inquiry into rationalization and replaces deliberative commitment with the kind of formal fanaticism one finds in de Beauvoir's portrait of the serious man (1976, 45–52).

9. Following *Emerson and Self-Culture* (2008), I use "personal" to name those labors that no one can accomplish for us, for example, understanding, persevering, committing, etc. I call attention to these efforts because they individuate persons—and thus allow us to describe character, that is, how folk enact or perform their lives—without instituting an atomistic social theory. With regard to applied ethics, I am suggesting that the field loses sight of "the personal," which is unfortunate, since it forms the crux of "application," a process I have been exploring in terms of commitment, which I offer as a way of quoting Aristotle.

10. Habermas's mature social theory can be found in both volumes of his *Theory of Communicative Action* (1985), and his most explicit metaethical reflections can be found in *Moral Consciousness and Communicative Action* (1983) and *Elucidations of Discourse Ethics*, which appeared in English as *Justification and Application* (1993).

11. This line of thought is not unique to the *Phenomenology*, where it occurs in paragraphs 190–196 (see Hegel 1977). It also can be found in *Philosophy of Right*, sections 54–58 (see Hegel 1991). It is precisely because Hegel ties "form" to labor that I am invoking these discussions and not the phrase *Gestalt des Lebens*, which he employs in the penultimate paragraph of the preface to *Philosophy of Right*.

12. I regard Nike's labor practices as blameworthy because they (1) favor overseas production in countries hostile to organized labor, (2) evidence greed in the profit margins they seek, and (3) are party to the scam of subcontracted labor for the explicit purpose of benefiting from labor conditions that would be impossible to institute and enforce in the United States. See the Global Exchange website for a clear-headed discussion of Nike's practices, http://www.globalexchange.org/sweatfree/nike/faq (accessed October 18, 2016).

13. My thanks go to Cindy Willett for highlighting the need for this emphasis.

14. What about those who fail to deliberate? They can, and they could have in this instance, but they did not. Admittedly, the phenomenon is somewhat paradoxical. If they could have but did not, did they voluntarily elect not to deliberate, which is to ask: did they deliberately

not deliberate? To be clear, this is neither impossible nor, on my view uncommon. People give themselves moral holidays, which I take to involve limiting one's deliberation to whether or not to deliberate any further about the matter. I say "any further" because so-called moral holidays are usually cases of license. One gives oneself license to indulge in what one would normally forgo and without any mitigating circumstances. To the degree this captures "those who fail to deliberate," it places the phenomenon well within the form of ethical praxis. But no doubt other examples could be enumerated, including ones that blur the line between voluntary and involuntary courses of action. But that is to be expected if ethical praxis, as a form, emerges from the course of life as it occurs in ecosocial history.

15. In particular, see chapter 7, "Preserving the Possible," and chapter 5, "On the Edges of Our Souls," in my *You Must Change Your Life* (2002) and *Emerson and Self-Culture* (2008), respectively. My Nancy essays are "Lenin, Nancy, and the Politics of Total War" (1999a) and "On What Is to Be Done with What Is Always Already Arriving" (1999b).

16. This claim is also made in an extended footnote in chapter 2 of *Otherwise than Being* (Levinas 1998, 189–190).

17. In *Otherwise than Being*, Levinas writes, "The subjectivity as *the other in the same*, as an inspiration, is the putting into question of all affirmation for-oneself, all egoism born again in this very recurrence" (1998, 111).

18. Levinas writes in *Totality and Infinity*: "*The infinity of responsibility denotes not its actual immensity, but a responsibility increasing in the measure that it is assumed*; duties become greater in the measure that they are accomplished. The better I accomplish my duty the fewer rights I have; the more I am just the more guilty I am" (1969, 244; emphasis in original).

19. I suppose I can see one determinate future for a life that takes to heart Levinas's interpretation of our being-in-common. Immediately following the lines from *Totality and Infinity* quoted in note 19, we find: "The I, which we have seen arise in enjoyment as a separated being having apart, in itself, the center around which its existence gravitates, is confirmed in its singularity by purging itself of this gravitation, purges itself interminably, and is confirmed precisely in this incessant effort to purge itself. This is termed goodness" (1969, 244–245). This is a future of asceticism that, ironically enough, infinitely negates itself in the name of an infinite responsibility.

20. I first encountered this passage in Paul Livingston's *The Politics of Logic* (2011, 9).

21. I have stressed the reflective, deliberative dimension of ethical praxis for an ethical reason. Our national habits are corrupt. Many value money above all, and even more demonstrate open contempt for intellectual virtues. I thus think that the future of ethical praxis requires us to cultivate the kind of reflective, deliberative skills that genuine commitment entails. My point is not Habermasian in any technical manner: I do not think that communicative action is the fundamental form of our being-in-the-world such that we are obligated to present ourselves to ourselves and one another via a categorically arranged set of validity claims. Rather, my claim reflects the challenges of the present: we are not equal to the occasion of our own ethical dilemmas, and thus a renewed emphasis on humanist reflection is in order, one that involves virtues such as honest self-objectification; concentration; a historically rich self-understanding; the courage to speak and change one's mind; an ability to reckon with the likely and possible consequences of our pursuits; the proactive construction and exploration of possible alternatives; active, literate, and charitable listening; etc.

22. Both views have been advocated by Jonathan Haidt and various colleagues (e.g., Haidt and Bjorklund 2008).

23. This is more or less the project of eudaemonics that Owen Flanagan advances in *The Really Hard Problem* (2007).

24. In *Human Nature and Conduct*, Dewey says things like, "Principles exist as hypotheses with which to experiment," and "all principles are empirical generalizations from the ways in which previous judgments of conduct have practically worked out" (1983, 164–165).

25. My feel for the complexity of ethical praxis and commitment leaves me frustrated with discussions that center around Hume's claim that one cannot derive what should be done solely from what is the case. In my view, ethical commitments are not "derived" in any strict sense, let alone in a process of judgment that draws conclusions from well-formed premises. Not that moral reasoning is mere rationalization. But it is affect-laden (which is Hume's deeper point in that part of the *Treatise*) and a part of a larger process that I have been trying to articulate in terms of ethical praxis.

EMERSON AND THE CASE OF PHILOSOPHY

I will have no covenants but proximities.
—*Ralph Waldo Emerson*

I have the ambition to be a practical preacher (of philosophy).
—*Ralph Waldo Emerson*

—I. No Word of Welcome: Philosophy is an unsettled affair. Even after a century of professionalization, it houses and draws outsiders.[1] Like Hume, some have worked beyond the confines of established academies, whereas others, say Nietzsche, also forsook established modes of writing. And if we expand the philosophical canon to include philosophers from historically marginalized groups, outsiders swell to an imposing rank, including the likes of Elizabeth of Bohemia, Sor Juana, and W. E. B. Du Bois.

Philosophy has also spawned heralds, even proponents of its own demise. Wittgenstein and Heidegger (insiders trying to work their way out) convinced themselves (and several others) that philosophy had reached its limits. Not that philosophy had realized itself. Rather, its radical reflexivity unleashed, philosophy found itself unable to complete the tasks that had settled into subdisciplines such as metaphysics, epistemology, and ethics. And yet, rather than close the book on philosophy, Wittgenstein and Heidegger gave rise to vital traditions of thought, from ordinary language philosophy to hermeneutics and deconstruction—the move outside turned out to be the swift currents of an inception.

Philosophy is thus an evolving, manifold affair, a constellation lit by multiple stars, rising or setting depending on the angle your satellite affords. Or, to work from a different metaphor, philosophy admits of many cases, as if it were a mutating virus, replicating in a string of hosts whose lineages reach back into several ancient cultures. However, even given this breadth (and turbulence), Emerson's place remains marginal. He is rarely taught in Philosophy departments, and a dissertation on Emerson risks professional suicide. Interestingly, Nietzsche's case has been affirmatively settled, but Emerson, despite his profound influence on Nietzsche, remains suspect.

Not that philosophers and scholars haven't championed Emerson's cause in various ways, particularly in recent years. Van Leer's *Emerson's Epistemology* (1986) and Van Cromphout's *Emerson's Ethics* (1999) locate Emerson within established philosophical fields. Is Emerson a philosopher? We will know, they say, when we test his contributions to philosophical subdisciplines. Similarly, Goodman's *American Philosophy and the Romantic Tradition* (1990) ties Emerson's case to philosophical topics, such as freedom and idealism, as does Lawrence Buell, whose *Emerson* (2003) explores, among other things, Emerson's intersection with virtue ethics.

Another tack connects Emerson to figures/traditions whose philosophical standing is secure. West's *American Evasion of Philosophy* (1989) sets Emerson at the origins of American pragmatism, whereas Cavell, across several essays (1981–2003), takes Emerson to inaugurate a line of moral perfectionism that includes Thoreau, Nietzsche, Heidegger, the later Wittgenstein, and Austin, and that contests the modernity of folk such as Descartes and Kant, often at the level of phrasing. Goodman, in his recent *American Philosophy before Pragmatism* (2015), takes a similar tack in reading Emerson relative to well and less established figures, namely Plato and Neoplatonism, Kant (in part through de Staël), as well as Hume and Montaigne, though not Hegel and Schelling.

In the wake of West and Cavell's gestures of inclusion, some have debated which of these approaches should prevail. Anderson (2006) and Albrecht (2012) argue against Cavell's historiography and for more continuity with pragmatism. Saito (2005) tries to weave together (rather than split) the difference, working between Emerson and Dewey in a Cavellian vein. No doubt Emerson also could and should be read for his readings of and relations to classical Indian and Greek philosophy, as was more common fifty years ago, for example, Dale Riepe's "Emerson and Indian Philosophy" (1967) and Ray Benoit's "Emerson on Plato: the Fire's Center," which begins: "The idealists dismiss Emerson as a pragmatist and the pragmatists dismiss him as an idealist. It is safe to say that one is wrong, but it is safer to say that both are right" (1963, 487).

And yet, throughout these apologia, (each, in its own way, of value), few mention how often Emerson explicitly *distanced* himself from philosophy. In discussing nature, for example, he insists: "It will not be dissected, nor unraveled, nor shown. Away profane philosopher! . . . Known it will not be, but gladly beloved and enjoyed" (CW1, 125). Similarly, in defending involuntary perceptions as the "last fact behind which analysis cannot go," Emerson asserts, "If we ask whence this comes, if we seek to pry into the soul that causes, all philosophy is at fault" (CW2, 37). Finally, at the close of "Nominalist and Realist," after refusing to resolve that dilemma, Emerson confesses that he has "no word of welcome for them," namely, a pair of philosophers who had come to visit (CW3, 145).

Emerson's relation to philosophy is thus an active one. More specifically, it is bound to an assessment of philosophy, which I now aim to examine. Where and why does Emerson contest philosophy, and with what terms? And is that contestation carried out in the name of philosophy, or is something else on offer, and if so, what is it?

—II. The Poet in Prose: Writing to Lydian Jackson in 1835, Emerson declares: "I am a born poet, of a low class without doubt yet a poet. That is my nature & vocation. My singing be sure is very 'husky,' & is for the most part in prose" (CL1, 435). According to Emerson, a poet is a "perceiver" and "dear lover of the harmonies that are in the soul & in matter, & specially of the correspondences between these & those" (ibid.). The scene concerns self and world, how each is well ordered (harmonious rather than cacophonous or dissonant), and what their accord entails. Emerson's perceptions thus concern not only how things are, but also how they are when they are as they should be. Not that his concern is prescriptive. He does not report a grasp of imperatives, normative principles, or regulative ideals, though such things might lie within the harmonies he hears. Rather, Emerson claims to apprehend moments when values are immanently evident within facts, that is, when self and world are in harmony with themselves and one another.

As a kind of shorthand, we might say that Emerson takes himself to perceive patterns of order or, more briefly still, thoughts. For example, he might identify elemental activities of the soul such as doing, thinking, and saying, as he does in "The Poet." Or, he might realize how matter cooperates organically, for example, when trees generate hydrocarbons and discharge oxygen with the help of sunlight and ground water. Or, he might analogize matter and soul, finding common ground in how they "grow." Or, focusing on soul harmonies, Emerson might perceive himself to be a poet in husky prose, that is, his soul has an order (his principal activity is a kind of saying) and a purpose (the conversion of experience into imagistic signification). And if we take that twofold realization as a whole, a vocation emerges, itself a pattern of order fit for a life.

What though is the character of such perceptions? Keeping to his letter, we find that Emerson aligns it with love, precisely what "The Method of Nature" demands from those who would fathom nature, its method, and no doubt the essay as well. The accords that Emerson perceives are thus not simply intellectual but affective and affirmative. Such perceptions claim him as the beloved claims the lover; he falls for them. I take this to mean that Emerson does not assemble the harmonies he perceives, say in synthetic judgments directed toward simpler parts analytically distinguished and convened. Rather, he is struck by the harmonies as harmonies, that is the prima facie character of their occurrence. One realizes one's vocation and only later analyzes its call, as I did in the previous paragraph.

Emerson's letter to Lydian indicates, at least in his case, how thought—that is, a pattern of order—occurs, namely, as an affective and semiotically rich reception. The *case* of Emerson thus partially comes to pass in the dative—his work is the indirect object of affective disclosures. He is a poet not simply because he has made himself one but because that is what he has been given to be, it is where he finds himself—called to a poetry in prose.

Affective reception is not the whole of the tale, however. In a letter to Henry Ware Jr., dated 1838, he says: "For I do not know, I confess, what arguments mean in reference to any expression of a thought. I delight in telling what I think but if you ask me how I dare say so or why it is so I am the most helpless of mortal men; I see not even that either of these questions admit of an answer" (CL2, 167). Here the activity concerns how a thought or pattern of order is expressed. And that provides us with something like a pattern within which to think of Emerson's relation to philosophy. How does it stand with regard to reception on the one hand, expression on the other? As he writes in "Intellect," "to genius must always go two gifts, the thought and the publication" (CW2, 198).

But "pattern" isn't quite right. What is at stake is a kind (or kinds of action). Relying on an Emersonian term, I would rather say that being a poet or a philosopher is a question of "manner," which involves an effort to "facilitate life, to get rid of impediments, and bring the man pure to energize" (CW3, 75).[2] In terms of philosophy then (or poetry), energizing one or the other, at least in part, revolves around how one undergoes the event of thought in its occurrence and transmission.

But let us return to expression in particular and with regard to argumentation. After his Divinity School Address, Emerson defensively informs Ware that he eschews prototypical justification when expressing himself, remaining instead with the thought that has gripped him, concentrating on the what as opposed to the why. And this means that he is averse, as a rule (which means there will be exceptions), to demonstrating how his commitment follows inferentially from some other, distinct thought. Moreover, and this adds a new facet to argumentation (while reinforcing what I just mentioned), Emerson does not labor to "make-good his thesis against all comers" (ibid.). But this is already evident in the address itself. "Truly speaking," he writes, "it is not instruction, but provocation, that I can receive from another soul. What he announces, I must find true in me, or wholly reject, and on his word, or as his second, be he who he may, I can accept nothing" (CW1, 80). While this passage iterates the common, Emersonian theme of self-reliance, it further suggests that "expression" also concerns how best to address another. "Expression" not only names a subjective labor, therefore, but also an intersubjective one, and as we explore it, we should keep both dimensions in mind.[3]

Emerson identifies as a poet in prose who aims to receive and express patterns of order without engaging in prototypical practices of justification or contestation. For many, this closes the case of his relation to philosophy. By expressing thoughts without establishing linear chains of inference, without affirming the conclusion after (and only after) an ordered presentation of premises, Emerson seems to set himself outside what most take philosophy to entail, at least as a necessary condition. Yes, Emerson might address issues also addressed by philosophers, such as freedom and knowledge, and his replies might echo, at the level of content, dominant philosophical positions, for example, idealism in metaphysics, but his path toward to these questions and views has a decisively unphilosophical manner. This is a cogent reading. No reliable reader of Emerson should find the preceding assessment simply false. And yet, I remain struck by the fact that Emerson doesn't simply fall outside philosophy and into some other class, say literature. Instead, he *sets* himself outside what many take philosophy to entail and elects to tarry there, work there. And that setting is worth exploring.

—III. A Philosophy of Constants: Predictably, Emerson's conception of philosophy evolves, but some generalizations are possible. Early on, Emerson aligns philosophy with a kind of corrosive skepticism. After declaring in 1825 that the "best good that is reaped, is the glorious congregation of final causes," which "bring of obedience & honor to Deity," he asserts, "the examination of a single idea with the eye of exact philosophy leads to atheism & to universal doubt" (JMN3, 54).[4] Then in August of 1834, reflecting on "our mood of pyrrhonism," he states, "If there were many philosophers, the world would go to pieces presently, all sand, no lime" (JMN4, 310). I find the image of limeless mortar quite exact, and it marks a concern to which we'll return. The charge is that philosophy proves unable to fashion material that binds, that allows stacked stone to ascend and stand together. Keeping to the image (which recalls the lime mortar supporting the buildings of Greece and Rome), the charge is that philosophy is unable to secure livable structures. Something in either its reception or expression enables negation but not affirmation.

By 1836, however, Emerson also evidences a more affirmative stance toward philosophy. In particular, he aligns it with an idealizing vision not only more compatible with religious insight but even superior to its popular tenets. "Religion does for the uncultivated which philosophy does for Hume, Berkeley, & Viasa; —makes the mountain dance & smoke & disappear before the steadfast of Reason" (JMN5, 123).[5] And it does so by apprehending the laws that underwrite and guide nature in its dynamic unfolding. Referring to Bacon in a lecture of 1835, he says, "No single mind since Plato has enriched his fellowmen with so many of those truths which by their dignity and extent of application we incline to call laws" (EL1, 187). And speaking a year later about history, Emerson finds "philosophy the announcement of its laws," concluding, "Therefore is philosophy the only true historian, and the only true prophet" (EL2, 12).[6]

Emerson's appreciation for philosophy grows as he increasingly appreciates the power of its idealizations. Idealizations enable us to settle the world with some basic terms. "Unity or Identity, & Variety," jots Emerson in an entry from 1845. "The poles of philosophy. It makes haste to develop these two" (JMN9, 303–304). Returning to the language we drew from Emerson's letter to Lydian, we might say that philosophical idealizing apprehends harmonies in the soul, in nature, and in their relation. As he remarks in a notebook from 1860: "The world, the galaxy, is a scrap before the metaphysical power" (TN3, 313). For example, ascertaining the reliance of persons on temperament (something Emerson consistently affirms), gives some unity to a diverse life of actions. Or, "Motion and Rest," to pull terms from "Nature" (1844), allow us to think of particular objects as individuals (nature at rest), without thinking that their emergence and decomposition mark discontinuities in the whole; both are moments in a differentiating unity. "Compound it how she will," Emerson insists, "star, sand, fire, water, tree, man, it is still one stuff, and betrays the same properties" (CW3, 105). Or, and most generally, the thought that Atman is Brahman binds mind to matter and matter to mind, part to whole, and gods to the morass they purport to rule. (This explains why Emerson places the fabled author of the *Vedas*, Viasa, among the philosophers.)

Philosophy does not simply find such patterns, however. It also specifies them, purifies them of accidental traits. Valorizing Plato in *Representative Men* (1850), Emerson says: "This defining is philosophy. Philosophy is the account which the human mind gives to itself of the constitution of the world. Two cardinal facts lie forever at the base; the One; and the two. 1. Unity or Identity; and, 2. Variety. We unite all things by perceiving the law that pervades them, by perceiving the superficial differences and the profound resemblances. But every mental act,—this very perception of identity or oneness, recognizes the difference of things. Oneness and Otherness. It is impossible to speak, or to think without embracing both" (CW4, 28). This is why Emerson favors philosophy over the anthropomorphic and miraculous tenets of popular Christian faith. They prove too particular, too attached to one variety, or in the case of the divine, one luminous example. And so they also incline toward dogmatism, at least in manner. But philosophy frees the idealizing trajectory already at work in all symbolization and drives it toward the limits of generalization, which has salutary effects. Lecturing in 1845, Emerson claims, "Philosophy overlooks no appearance as trifling" (LL1, 90).[7] Its eye on the ideal, philosophy finds each occurrence the oblique facet of a larger crystalline structure—it indicates larger patterns and concretizes what would otherwise be an amorphous flurry. Moreover, "philosophy teaches how to be personal without being unparliamentary" (JMN7, 192). In its openness to all appearances, philosophy can prove parliamentary—everything has its say. And yet, it remains personal insofar as it takes its idealizations to be representative.[8]

I have been tarrying with passages primarily from the mid-to-late 1840s, though some from the turn of the decade. They convey, I think, something characteristic of Emerson's affirmative sense of the task of philosophy—to inventory and thus order all appearances, hence the cosmos, through an ongoing, revisionist process of basic categorization.[9] Set within nature's diversity, categories disclose underlying patterns of order and thus prove akin to laws—they govern how things come to pass. And when set into an ordered system, these law-like categories provide a typography of the world in its diversity.

This conception of philosophy—call it surveying the cosmos—persists for the remainder of Emerson's writing life. It recurs in the 1850s and 1860s, and is in full bloom in his lectures on the *Natural Method of Mental Philoso-*

phy (1858) and across the pages of at least three topical notebooks: *IT* (middle 1850s), *PH* (1860–1870), and *ML* (1865–1869).[10]

In *PH*, Emerson states: "Philosophy seeks to find a foundation in thought for everything that exists in fact," which entails a "true science of the mind" (TN2, 334, 339), And in *IT*, he ventures just that, a "New Metaphysics" that requires him to "write a collection of Accepted Ideas, a Table of Constants" (TN1, 134). Several topics are broached in these notebooks and the lecture series, such as intellect, genius, art, conversation, subjectiveness, and identity, each of which recurs in the published essays, sometimes as their principal, titular concern, other times as essential factors. For example, "Intellect" and "Art" appear in *Essays: First Series*, and conversation proves integral to "Friendship." In *Essays: Second Series*, subjectiveness is a key facet of "Experience" and Emerson uses "identity" as his pole star in navigating the debate between nominalists and realists—"You are one thing, but nature is *one thing and the other thing*, in the same moment" (CW3, 139). While we might consider the relative essentiality of each constant as well as what Emerson makes of it (*ML* lists six "laws of mind," *IT* treats twenty-six candidates), I am more intrigued by what they purport to name, and by Emerson's choice of the term "constant."

"Natural Method of Mental Philosophy" contains six lectures that Emerson delivered in the spring of 1858, with four repeated in a later, unnamed November series. Across these texts, a *constant* indicates an idealized site of continuous order within and between mind and matter. This is consistent with what we have seen. What proves more conspicuous in these lectures is the genesis of constants, which Emerson ties to the discovery of an analogical or homological figure, for example, breath. "The air that we breathe is an exhalation of all the solid material of the globe," Emerson announces. "We might say, the Rock of Ages dissolves himself into the mineral air to build up this constitution of man's mind and body" (LL2, 53).[11] As an analogue between mind and nature, breath becomes a universal figure, applying to physiological and mental states as well as to the circulating wind and atmosphere. But it does not function as a universal type instanced in particulars. Nor is it a necessary condition, as if it were an elemental simple in more complex phenomena. Rather, as an analogue it focuses on and magnifies aspects of the cosmos, namely, that all things seem to circulate and assume new shapes as they do so. Thinking in terms of a constant like "breath" does not allow one to sufficiently define a particular, therefore. Rather, it gives one a facet of things that in turn allows one to move between part and whole, at least with regard to that characteristic. I take in the wind, and it leaves me as a shout along a street. Both are in the order of breath, and yet knowing that does not define what either is. In fact, "breath" is a weak image if my shout is full of longing, though it may carry more if my mood is blustery. (And once we leave the expressive power of speech, does the analogy hold at all? Could the wind pose a question, issue a command, or make a promise?) Regardless, the analogue does not gather its referents in any manner approaching sufficiency. But it does link what it gathers along a differentiating line, and that provides something like continuity if not identity.

Because it is an analogue, a constant keeps one moving down the line of continuity that it establishes. While an abstraction, a constant does not pretend to bring the whole of the world along with it. The "like" of analogy keeps open a difference that requires alertness to how far the analogy holds. How similar are these intakes and outtakes of breath that we call wind and speech? And is that all there is to these, or are they similar and/or different in other ways that might call for other constants? Finally, the figural power of the analogy is suggestive in its own right. Start with speech and wind and you may have the makings of an image of the soul, as one sees with words such as psyche and spirit. Tie breath and life and you may come to think that trees produce hydrocarbons through a kind of breathing, taking in carbon dioxide, water, and sunlight and releasing oxygen. Or, to return to the human, tie breath and life and you may find images for circumstances that undermine or suffocate us. Analogies have an inventive, semantic power with which one can work in thinking about the soul, matter, or the relation between them. Whereas necessary and sufficient conditions offer a closed set, apprehending a good analogical constant is just the beginning.

According to Emerson, the location of such analogies and homologies is simply mind at work. "All thought is analogizing," he notes in *IT*. But not just in our case: "A physiologist told me, when he was at a loss in his study of embryos, he would go and talk with astronomers about the nebular theory, and what occurred in such and such conditions of the forming planet; and presently he got the analogic hint he wanted. Homology is the great gain of modern science. And it reaches much wider, not only through matter, but through mind. He who enunciates a law of nature, enunciates a law of mind" (LL2, 87). Our concern at this point is not whether this is true but the "new metaphysics" it conveys. Thought in terms of constants, philosophy is a matter of locating idealized figures concrete enough to convene the multiplicity of things within a continuous operation. Each constant is a specie of mind, but equally of nature, and each strives to orient us in the world without dislocating us from it, even in its own figuration. And yes, "mind" or "spirit" as well as "nature" are constants. Each is a bold generalization that gathers, for example, how perceiving and willing travel. And where; how a sprout ascends or a star explodes and why. And do not forget that each has analogic roots. Mind takes its leave from memory, nature from birth, spirit and psyche (and the soul) stem from breath, although "roots" drifts into another analogy that Emerson favors. "Intellect; 'Tis a finer vegetation." And, just a paragraph later in "The Natural Method of Mental Philosophy": "Nature works after the same method as the human Imagination" (LL2, 87).[12]

When considering the analogical origins of constants, we should not forget another aspect of their genesis. "Constant" only becomes a figure of thought by way of contrast. Thinking of the one and the many, we turn to "constants" because change is ubiquitous. "The Universe is only in transit," he observes, "or, we behold it shooting the gulf from past to future. And this the mind shares. Transition is the attitude of power, and the essential act of life" (LL2, 91). And so on down into everything. "An individual body is the arrest or momentary fixation of certain atoms, which, after performing compulsory duty to this enchanted state are released again to flow in currents of the world" (LL2, 119).[13] While these remarks introduce a new constant, metamorphosis, note also the stage on which a philosophy of constants arises: continuous change, that is, history. Philosophy is inevitably the philosophy of history according to Emerson. History is its most proper subject matter and its source. Yes, Emerson is a resolute naturalist, but this is nature on the move, protean in character. We thus might speak of ecosocial history as the principle scene out of which philosophy arises and to which it returns. Regardless, I am unsurprised that *Essays: First Series* commences with "History," for history is also where thought first finds itself. "No man can antedate his experience," Emerson writes, "or guess what faculty or feeling a new object shall unlock, any more than he can draw to-day the face of a person whom he shall see to-morrow for the first time" (CW2, 21).

This passing glance at "History" brings a different question to the fore. Is it the case that Emerson's affirmative stance toward a philosophy of constants was a discrete experiment in the 1850s and 1860s, one that filled a few notebooks and occupied a few lectures, but never found its way into his most incisive and memorable work, the essays? I don't think so, and knowing why clarifies how constants function in Emerson. As noted, topoi-like constants appear in both series of *Essays* and not just as the occasional title. Emerson's essayistic ventures and experiments travel a topography settled, in part, by recurring figures. Turning toward *Essays: First Series*, we find (1) the *one* and the *many*, (2) the former *metamorphosing* into the latter, (3) a movement that, in the soul, doubles into *voluntary* and *involuntary* movements, with (4) the whole morass through mud and toil governed by a law of *compensation* that works in the draw of *polarities* (which in turn explains how error arises—through one-sided thinking). In short, constants stage and to a certain degree generate some of the problematics that Emerson performs and essays, such as negotiating perspectivalism in "Circles" (given the constant of metamorphosis). Or, in "Self-Reliance," the one and the many help establish a distinction between involuntary and voluntary perceptions. And while the former have a will of their own, Emerson exhorts us to defer to them given their relative proximity to the living "one" whose expression we are.

To be clear, I am not claiming that essays such as "Circles" and "Self-Reliance" amount to Emerson's "new metaphysics" in disguise, or that they are premature attempts to express what later came to fruition. I am claiming however, that that the formal substance of his philosophy of constants is already operative in *Essays*.[14] Let me try to make this a bit more concrete. One way to read certain essays is to treat them as studies in particular orientations toward the world. While this is evident in *Representative Men*, where we encounter orientations like the mystic, skeptic, and the man of the world, one finds similar portraits in earlier collections. In *Essays: First Series*, for example, the "man of the world" is cast in terms of prudence and heroism. Consider the scene that requires such virtues. Thinking just of "Prudence," the essay is staged by unruly material conditions that require management and the threat posed by an unbridled ethos of management. And Emerson's response is something like an exhortation—be prudent but only within a teleological orientation funded by wisdom. The staging is predictable, but if we look a bit closer, we see that "prudence" only becomes a topic for Emerson because he finds us oriented toward two poles that he associates with the one and the many. Whereas philosophy and poetry (and religion) pursue the one, prudence makes do with the many, what becomes "appearance" once we think the one in terms of expression and metamorphosis. In fact, prudence "is the science of appearances," it "moves matter after laws of matter" (CW2, 131).[15] And it is something we need: "Scorn not thou the love of parts" (CW2, 130). Because we live among parts and as a part ourselves, prudence has a claim on us. And yet, prudence should not be left to its own devices according to Emerson. Rather it must be oriented (not supplemented) by thoughts that push past appearance into the one and work back from its center: "a true prudence or law of shows recognizes the co-presence of other laws, and knows that its own office is subaltern, knows that it is surface and not centre where it works. Prudence is false when detached" (CW2, 131–132). "Prudence" thus unfolds on a stage of constants. From the problems it poses to the exhortation it advances, it circulates among the many even as it pulls back from their glitter and glow in favor of idealizing thoughts drawn to (and from) the one.

—IV. Running into Poetry: In an ongoing process of idealization that refuses to halt at the parochial symbols of ritualized religion (or extant culture), philosophy articulates constants that arise out of and aim to order ecosocial history in the full diversity of its becoming. Second, it does so through a kind of analogical thinking that gathers mind and body, thought and nature along a differentiating continuum, and it invites us to measure the perspicacity of the figures it employs and to follow out their autosuggestion. Third, its pursuit is, ideally, expansive—nothing is beneath its attempts. Finally, Emerson is drawn to philosophy not only because it bundles and binds protean nature, but also because it provides a topography upon which one can pursue the activities of scholar, preacher, citizen, lover, friend, hero, and prudential reckoner, to name some of his cardinal characters.

And yet, even given this proximity to and apparent use of philosophy, Emerson does not settle with its terms. An entry from *PH* shows his approbation and withdrawal in miniature. "Metaphysics, the true science of the mind, is reckoned arid. There can be no greater mistake. Tis full of paradoxes: it is always new: tis perpetually running into poetry" (TN2, 335). Far from lifeless, constants convene the cosmos and thus function as orienting figures according to Emerson—at least insofar as they run into poetry. "I think that Philosophy is still rude & elementary," he records several pages later. "It will one day be taught by poets. The instinct that led Heraclitus & Parmenides & Lucretius to write in verse, was just, however imperfect their result" (TN2, 349). Qua preference the declaration is unsurprising. "The Poet," which stages a revision of Plato's *Republic*, favors the sayer over knowers and doers.[16] But the suggestion that poetry and philosophy move along a continuum is intriguing, as is the claim that the former better realizes tendencies constitutive of philosophy.[17]

Another passage in *PH* notes, "I think that not by analytic inspection, but by sympathy & piety, we correct our metaphysics" (TN2, 364). I am drawn to this line because "correct" offers a reading of "running into," in the sense of "flows." Addressing *the one* as "nature," Emerson says, in a passage we have already visited: "It will not be dissected, nor unraveled, nor shown. Away profane philosopher! seekest thou in nature the cause? This refers to that, and that to the next, and the next to a third, and everything refers. Thou must ask in another mood, thou must feel and love it, thou must behold it in a spirit as grand as that which it exists, ere thou canst know the law.

Known it will not be, but gladly beloved and enjoyed" (CW1, 125). This is a dizzying scene. Phenomena are bound to others in myriad ways, which is why natural history is always ecosocial in a certain sense. Each part indicates a larger web of relations, but that web (or series, or network, or pattern—choose your figure) is not itself among the things that ceaselessly turn us toward yet another. Rather, we posit wholes amid experiences of connection and dependence, or what Emerson terms "quotation."[18]

In medias res, we find analogies amid the fray, miniatures for larger patterns of order, say mind in memory, life in breath, nature in birth, metamorphosis in quotation. And that finding calls for something other than philosophy, according to Emerson. The goal (a law, a constant) is proximate to what philosophy seeks, but philosophy's mood and manner are out of synch, its love not quite the right kind of love. Rather than receive and affirm the disclosive power of a term or figure such as breath, philosophy interrogates it. Philosophy might deploy examples that test the scope of the constant being proposed—this "too" is "breath"? Or, it might pare away qualities derived from our initially confused perception—I need air to hear you but your exhalation said "hello" (not "goodbye") and that difference seems unconnected to the air, which would have borne either to my ear. Or, it might try to uncover, by way of transcendental critique, the origin of the term on offer. As an analogy of nature's circulations, "breath" may use a more originary category of quantity, namely totality, and set it to work alongside categories of relation, either substance/accident or causality, though at least one. Or, one might find "breath" too opaque to account for the activity of metaphorizing and insist that we dig deeper into the comparative cognition that posited, linked, and traveled between source and target domains. These are not unfair questions. Analysis may purify our terminology and thus concretize our operative terms—"This defining is philosophy," you might recall. But it will not generate those terms or replace them. For that to happen, philosophy must run into poetry, in other words, become poetry, or, encounter it (as one can "run into" friends). "Whoever discredits analogy," Emerson announces in *English Traits*, "and requires heaps of facts, before any theories can be attempted, has no poetic power, and nothing original or beautiful will be produced by him" (CW5, 135).

Let's refine this argument. Very early (1824, in fact), Emerson records the following: "Metaphysicians are mortified to find how entirely the whole materials of understanding are derived from sense" (JMN2, 224).[19] One might expect this to lead to a sense-data theory of ideation. But like Nietzsche after him, Emerson takes the thought in a different direction. "A mourner will try in vain to explain the extent of his bereavement better than to say a *chasm* is opened in society. I fear the progress of Metaphysical philosophy may be found to consist in nothing else than the progressive introduction of apposite metaphors" (JMN2, 224). Emerson is thinking of images like Plato's cave or Locke's blank slate, but a more general point is also present.

Few distinctions are as foundational to philosophy as "appearance" and "reality." Without this opposition, without the scene it convenes (and the continuity it presumes), the problems of epistemology and metaphysics do not arise, which is why Hegel insists that the object of knowledge is always twofold. But what do these terms name? "Real," for example, seems to go back to *res*, hence thing, but that is one sort of reality metaphorized into the whole, much like mind, through the German *Minne* and the Latin *mentio*, has roots in memory. And "appearance," with roots in *pareo*, is bound to the visible, to being seen, which again is *a* way of being, and how that way occurs for another being, namely one with eyes. To be sure, this need not render the terms "false." They are, in a way, apposite. But they are apposite metaphors and thus analogical, and that is Emerson's deeper point. "The etymologist finds the deadest word to have one been a brilliant picture," he writes in "The Poet." "Language is fossil poetry. As the limestone of the continent consists of infinite masses of the shells of animalcules, so language is made up of images, or tropes, which now, in their secondary use, have long ceased to remind us of their poetic origin" (CW3, 13). To the degree this is right, philosophers are running into poetry with almost every turn of phrase, particularly if thought works through quotation.

I am exploring Emerson's claim that philosophy runs into poetry, which I have read as "flow into" and "encounter." In order to generate terms that might function as constants (and set the conditions from which further problems arise), figures are needed, and that turns on a metaphorical venture that Emerson regards as poetic. Let us probe deeper still, focusing on the reception of figures. Because basic figures arise in analogical movements, their apposition must be taken on faith, that is, trusted, and this gives the event a lyric quality, the now of its occurrence haunted by a fickle muse. "Man is a stream whose source is hidden," Emerson writes in "The Over-Soul," adding, "Our being is descending into us from we know not whence" (CW2, 159). Unable to follow out the analytical question "whence it came," philosophical interrogation gives way, abandons itself to (runs into) the movement of figures. Thought must allow itself to be carried away, as it were, by the term or phrase or dyad's power of figuration. "The Universe," Emerson writes in 1845, "& the individual perpetually act & react on each other," recalling the scene from "Method of Nature." "Thus all philosophy begins from Nox & Chaos, the Ground or Abyss which Schelling so celebrates. And in every man we require a bit of night, of chaos, of *Abgrund*, as the spring of a watch turns best on a diamond. In every individual we require a *pièce de resistance*, a certain reliance & fortitude" (JMN9, 223).

This "bit of night," which every individual presumably requires, democratizes what Keats finds in every "Man of Achievement," namely, negative capability, lyric poetry's chief virtue. In the thick (or thin) of its occurrence, philosophy too must prove able to bear "uncertainties, Mysteries, doubts, without any irritable reaching after fact & reason" (Colvin 1825, 47). The onset of constants, of any founding, orienting figure, demands a receptive concentration, a readiness to recognize a term or phrase or dyad that might inaugurate a day or more of thinking, for example, *Aufhebung*, the color line, *ambiguïté*, *Sprachspiel*, etc. No doubt this involves a kind of patience. "We cannot force the truth as suits our needs or timing," Edward Mooney writes, thinking of Henry Bugbee (in the company of Emerson and Thoreau). But a kind of abandon is also required, one that can and will, without irritation, move with the actions and reactions that suffuse life unfolding, events that include reaching after reasons, sounding out words and phrases like experience, the ordinary, *natura naturans*, and *tò kalón*.[20]

If thought, in its originary occurrence, is lyrical, is its presentation also poetic? ("I conceive a man as always spoken to from behind," Emerson says [CW1, 129].) Here is "Intellect" on expression: "The thought of genius is spontaneous; but the power of expression, in the most enriched and flowing nature, implies a mixture of will, a certain control over the spontaneous states, without which no production is possible. It is a conversion of all nature into the rhetoric of thought, under the eye of judgment, with a strenuous exercise of choice. And yet the imaginative vocabulary seems to be spontaneous also. It does not flow from experience only or mainly, but from a richer source" (CW2, 199). Say, like Heidegger, we are taken by the thought that we do not exit the mind in order to enter the world of things and others. Instead, all share something like a world. But how to say this? We might begin to rethink how we are *in* the world, inflecting temporality into our spatiality and various relations with things, situations, one another, and ourselves. But our *being-in* is not itself a thing, and so Heidegger has to root around to get at what he wants to say (and us to think). On the one hand, we need to negate presumptions about our *in*, namely, that the world is a container in which we, part *res extensa*, do what we do. And we need to be careful not to trap time in our spatial imaginary. (For example, number lines and time lines keep the past, present, and future at a discrete distance from one another.) On the reconstructive side, our *in* needs to not only carry interanimating temporal dimensions (or ecstasies), but their ontic emissaries as well, namely memory, purposiveness, attention, mood, speech, etc., and without saddling the latter with a conception of the cogito that pulls them back out of the world, thus rendering our materiality once again mere thingyness and discursivity a flurry of idiotic (because completely private) ideality.

Expression entails, in part, these negative and reconstructive developments. And while we expect them to cohere as a whole (at least insofar as they seem to cohere), that whole propagates itself through somewhat tangled expansions, the fate of which may rest upon a turn of phrase or word, which is more or less what happens to "in" in Heidegger (if it is "in" Heidegger). If, through purposive ventures, we are both here and somewhere else, and in a way that bears the past, conspires with the present, and anticipates the future, and all at the *same time* (whatever that means), then saying something like "I am *in* the world" seems a whirl of a thought, one so at odds with what we ordinarily take "in" to mean that the phrase positively aches as it moves from its source domain into a target domain that still proves elusive, despite the current ubiquity of the phrase "being-in-the-world."

My brief recollection of *Being and Time* indicates, I think, that developing a philosophical account of some range of phenomena requires us to conspire with found terms and develop, from (and contrary to) their suggestiveness, what we hope to say. And this requires the thinker to inhabit language (and the phenomena to which she or he is responding) with the exquisite care that we also associate with poetry; that is, with a supple feel for the suggestive nuances and implications of vexing words such as "in." Why poetry? Our care manifests itself as more than an obsession over radiant chains of inference, and the terms that most grab us usually do just that—*they* grab us, sometimes despite their familiarity. Look at all we do to say it just so. We rely on graphemes such as scare quotes and italics; we negate what we do not mean to mean; we invoke suggestive examples, real and counterfactual; and we work and rework our metaphors, for example, *Geworfenheit*, which takes Emerson's thought of "man as always spoken to from behind, and unable to turn his head and see the speaker," and extends it to include all that befalls us, which leaves us thoroughly "thrown," *geworfen* (CW1, 159).[21] Much more than inferences from premises order the expression of positions as rich and influential as *Being and Time*.

One might think that dependence on poetic figures at such a fundamental level condemns philosophy (and thought more generally) to apologetics on behalf of a mystic vision. But recall that Emerson regards analogical figures as expansive in their autosuggestion. To abandon oneself to a term or phrase in its occurrence is thus also to open oneself to where it might lead (or not lead, given the "like" of an analogy does not preclude the appearance of incongruity). "Analysis, too, is legitimate to a poetic soul," Emerson suggests in *PH*. "I find analysis not less poetical than synthesis; but it must be analysis into elements, & not mechanical division. If I can detect nature converting water into hydrogen & oxygen, two beautiful and perfect wholes, I see not that it is less grand than when she recomposes water, a new whole. Mechanical analysis picks the lock: right analysis produces the key" (TN2, 347). Within a whole, parts are luminous, according to Emerson. (I take it that mechanical analysis simply decomposes the whole into parts, and, over time, proves corrosive with regard to the very notion of wholes and even the question of their integrity.) If "nature converting" is kept in mind, aggregations and disintegrations become variations on a theme. But we can say more than this. Analysis is not only legitimate; it is also essential. Abstractions aligned with unity must find fitting, concrete counterparts. "The universal does not attract us until housed in an individual" (CW1, 127). As philosophy runs into poetry, therefore, it also runs into those eddies and currents that allow figures like "stream" to continue to work in the course of experience.

Emerson's fabled revisionism is no less part and parcel of his poetic feel for philosophy's first steps. "The first questions are still to be asked," Emerson writes in "The Senses of the Soul." "Let any man bestow a thought on himself how he came hither, and whither he tends, and he will find that all the literature, all the philosophy that is on record, have done little to dull the edge of inquiry" (CW10, 154). The heart of this line lies with the edge of inquiry, its sharpness relative to what has passed as literature and philosophy. But inquiry comes to pass only relative to determinate regions of epistemic concern, here marked as "whence" and "whither," as first and final causes (unsurprisingly). The poetic character of Emerson's founding tropes is thus not opposed to inquiry but a condition of its possibility, particularly since each figure only gathers phenomena with analogues such as breath, tempests, spatial locations, waves, and streams, each of which underscores the difference between the world thereby thought and the conversation in which that thought arose. Not that running into poetry at such originary sites somehow mandates, on pain of contradiction, a radically revisionist theory of knowledge. Depending on one's goals, several responses seem possible for those stopped short by the opacity of our *where-from* and *whither*, including irrational affirmation, tenacious loyalty and defensiveness, relativistic tolerance, aesthetic experimentation, etc. But deferring to poetry in one's reception and expression of constants is quite compatible with a revisionist approach to the inquiry those figures enable. Of course, should one's constants include something like "metamorphosis," something like radical revisionism will be on order. "For all symbols are fluxional," Emerson writes, "all language is vehicular and transitive, and is good, as ferries and horses are, for conveyance, not as farms and houses are, for homestead" (CW3, 20). But that order comes from the autosuggestion of a figure that, on its own terms, might have been otherwise.

—V. A PHILOSOPHY OF FLUXION: We should be wary of deferring, entirely, to Euro-modernity's insistent, epistemic bias, as if we were knowers before doers, as if life's first step were observational rather than erotic. (In the beginning, there was a deed because there also was a need.) If one recalls that we not only think, in part, with constants, but also live, in part, through the scenes they help establish, philosophy's immanent encounter with poetry not only signals an epistemic limit, but the onset of various tasks, some of which we have just surveyed with regard to expression. But that was in the rather narrow context of philosophizing. If one expects to live with and through a set of founding constants, something like the ongoing expression of their indications will prove all the more necessary, particularly given a constant like metamorphosis, which, through time, sets ontological variability into the partiality of analogical insight.

Two journal entries from 1845 concretize the matter: "The philosophy we want is one of fluxions & mobility; not a house, but a ship in these billows we inhabit. Any angular dogmatic theory would be rent to chips & splinters in this storm of many elements. No, it must be tight & fit the form of man, to live at all; as a shell is architecture of a house founded on the sea. The form of man, the soul of man must be the type of our Scheme, just as the body of man is the type after which a dwelling house is built" (JMN9, 223).[22] Note the displacement of an earlier image. In 1834, Emerson worried that philosophy was unable to secure mortar for habitable venues—its analysis proved too granular; the result was all sand, no lime. But by the time *Essays: Second Series* appears, the very notion of standing walls has been displaced in favor of a ship able to navigate the metamorphoses that Emerson often expresses in terms of the sea, whether addressing thought as waves of circumstance or casting history as a tempest (CW2, 180–181; CW6, 10–11). Figures of "fluxions & mobility" are needed to maintain continuity through the changes that surround and beset us, inside and out as it were. "If anything could stand still, it would be crushed and dissipated by the torrent it resisted, and if it were a mind, would be crazed; as insane persons are those who hold fast to one thought, and do not flow with the course of nature" (CW1, 124).

Emerson contrasts figures of fluxion with "angular" theories, those that force us into corners, where a kind of single-mindedness rules. This helps explain, I think, Emerson's resistance to philosophy at the close of "Nominalist and Realist." Recall that as the essay closes, Emerson remembers a visit from "a pair of philosophers." He recalls thinking: "Could they at once understand, that I loved to know that they existed, and heartily wished them Godspeed, yet, out of my poverty of life and thought had no word of welcome for them when they came to see me" (CW3, 145). The passage is remarkable. "Nominalist and Realist" is the rhetorical close of *Essays: Second Series*; "New England Reformers" was added late in the game because the "printers told him that 'it was not large enough for the shape' he wanted" (CW3, xxix). This refusal of philosophy is thus something like the last word on the various experiments and ventures that precede it. Second, the refusal hints at what is at issue between the parties—a two-faced thought that professes love but does not welcome it. I take this as a hint because philosophers presumably want to know Emerson's angle on the debate between nominalists and realists. Which is he? But he refuses the question and its effort to corner him, having written a few paragraphs earlier: "All the universe over, there is but one thing, this old Two-face, creator-creature, mind-matter, right-wrong, of which any proposition may be affirmed or denied" (CW3, 144). However, this is not to say he rejects the distinction between nominalist and realist, or deploys it ironically. Rather, he uses both terms (and those just listed) as pole stars that enable navigation of nature's dynamic, interconnections, which are only ever particular—dogs, no "dog"—even as, among the shifting plurality, one always finds a path lain by predecessors quoted at every turn. "We fancy men are individuals," he writes; "so are pumpkins, but every pumpkin in the field, goes through every point of pumpkin history" (CW3, 144).[23]

Let me state the point in more general terms. In Emerson's hands, cardinal oppositions function as constants designed to enable one to find one's way through nature, allowing each pole to function like a magnet that gathers up a part of the world. For example, one might think through matter by way of causality and thereby acquire predictive control of multiple forces and occasions, which might lead to other constants, say "temperament," which, on "its own level, or in the view of nature . . . is final" (CW3, 32). But as we work with matter, Emerson also keeps mind in mind, particularly the interruptive and redressing draw of its spontaneity, which he figures as a "whisper" at various points in "Experience" (CW3, 32, 39). But as one becomes immersed in the ventures initiated by what can only be understood as "casual" (as opposed to "causal"), matter should maintain its draw, say in the form of enabling conditions, from nutrition to neurons, even as we say I, me, you, and we, promise, love, want, believe. Of course, tensions run along the line thereby established, incongruities even. For example, the people we address do not appear in any given, spatiotemporal event, nor can they if their being is at all diachronic. How then does one think the self by way of "matter" (or phenomena that are also synchronic, e.g., an ecosystem)? But Emerson affirms matter *and* mind nonetheless, and that "yes" proves unphilosophical in its suspension of unanswered questions on the basis of an unearned sense of apposition. But so much the worse for philosophy, he thinks. "Philosophy also takes an inventory of her possessions; and an inventory is of pride; it is the negative state. But Poetry is always affirmative, & Prayer is affirmative" (JMN8, 74). This entry is admittedly oblique. However, the charge that philosophy's manner, here pride, leads away from affirmation is consistent with what we have seen. And it calls to mind the belief that one's (say Kant's) inventory is complete, and that, taken as a whole, its consistency is more important than whether it proves apposite with regard to "these billows we inhabit." As the famous line reads: "A foolish consistency is the hobgoblin of little minds, adored by little statesmen and philosophers and divines" (CW2, 33).

This ability to move affirmatively and concretely between opposed constants, or rather, within a constant's polarity, brings about a something like a power of navigation. Recall our discussion of "Prudence." Even within the term, a kind of movement is solicited, that between management and a higher idealism, say one that can remind us of what makes wealth valuable. Our movement within prudence, however, is also forced to move between these concerns and those of "Heroism," which willingly rejects the concessional terms of the world. "Toward all this external evil, the man within the breast assumes a warlike attitude, and affirms his ability to cope single-handed with the infinite army of enemies. To this military attitude of the soul, we give the name Heroism" (CW2, 148). But then, that pair of general social action, focused on things and causes, is contrasted with a more intimate sphere of persons, namely, "Friendship" and "Love." One pair is thus a whole to be contrasted with another pair, which creates a four-term whole mapping social life, from quickening heartbeats to balancing checkbooks. Social life is not all that billows, and so Emerson sets that quartet alongside the contrasting and slower pulses that resound through the more impersonal registers that he explores in "History," "Spiritual Laws," "The Over-Soul," and "Compensation," what we earlier cast in terms of first and final causes. Yet even these views, cast from everywhere and oriented toward the operation of universal forces, face their own contrasting quartet. Like every thought, each is also a personal event and as such, it involves tasks such as self-trust, abandoning what once proved apposite, conspiring with inspiration, and staying true to the imagination's expansions, phenomena plumbed and affirmed in "Self-Reliance," "Circles," "Intellect," and "Art." As an expression of thought, therefore, as a "conversion of all nature into *the rhetoric of thought*, under the eye of judgment, with a strenuous exercise of choice," *Essays: First Series* navigates all manner of topics with the sense that each is a star in a larger constellation suffused by forces only yet announcing themselves.

As I'm presenting it, *Essays: First Series* embodies (or performs) and thus images the kind of fluxion and movement that Emerson seeks. It has clear elements, marked by titles, but none splinter off into realms of their own. Moreover, those elements, again as a whole, are "tight & fit the form of man"; that is, they mark out and explore recognizable dimensions of human life, at once personal, interpersonal, and impersonal, which is to say, they employ and refine constants that can claim a kind of apposition—one will have to mind such matters in the course of a life. And if we take all that is affirmed by this whole, both sides of the nominalist/realist debate are affirmed as well; that is, *Essays: First Series* performatively affirms what Emerson thematically asserts in *Essays: Second Series*: "every man is a partialist" and "every man is a universalist also" (CW3, 144). For instance, he affirms the universality of "partiality" (everyone is partial) as well as the partiality of the universals that he posits, whether we think in terms of the topoi he elects or the generalizations he ventures on their behalf. The more general point though is that *Essays: First Series*, as a rhetorical whole, images thought in and as fluxion, and concretely, that is, (1) with topics responsive to life's cardinal tasks, (2) with an epistemic self-regard that is lyrical in its self-trust, and (3) in its expression, which relies upon a dramatic interplay of essays (i) with one another, (ii) among pairs, (iii) in three offsetting quartets, and thus (iv) across the volume, which turns the whole into a drama of sorts, perhaps that of "Man thinking" in knots, to recall the subject of "The American Scholar."

The drama of Emerson's first *Essays* is forecast in a journal entry that also invokes "fluxion": "As the musician avails himself of the concert, so the philosopher avails himself of the drama, the epic, the novel, & becomes a poet; for these complex forms allow the utterance of his knowledge of life by *indirections* as well as in the didactic way, & can therefore express the fluxional qualities & values which the thesis or dissertation could never give. This is the courage of the cabinet as of the field. There is the courage of painting & of poetry as well as of siege & stake" (JMN7, 190). Here is the point we have circled several times, albeit at varying heights. Given the billowing nature of its subject, knowledge of life needs to receive and express "fluxional qualities and values" that more rigid, angular modes of thought mishandle, which leads philosophy into poetry. Permit me one more example.

"Experience" is something of an epic. It begins in exile from a more or less forgotten homeland: "Ghostlike we glide through nature, and should not know our place again" (CW3, 27). It does not rest content with this state of affairs, however, but poses and pursues its opening question—"where do we find ourselves?" And it does so by way of an inventory, which the essay figures as "lords of life" who, not unlike Greek gods, interact and thereby stage the human condition. But that inventory seems undone by what it names, for example, succession, and so Emerson is unable to bring the lords of life to order. Not only does he say as much, but also, the poem prefacing the essay is amended at the essay's close. Use, surprise, surface, dream, succession and spectral wrong, temperament, and the inventor of the game become illusion, temperament, succession, surface, surprise, reality, and subjectiveness. Not that Emerson therefore abandons the task of navigating life on the terms given by such lords, rather, if anything, the journey, like any good epic, ends in a transformative realization: "I dare not assume to give their order, but I name them as I find them in my way" (CW3, 47). And that is something of a homecoming, that is, it counts as an answer to the essay's opening question: "Where do we find ourselves?" In naming what we find in *our way* (thereby naming obstructions according to our manner of finding), we find ourselves finding ourselves, naming and renaming our world in ascending generalities (e.g., pattern of order, lord, law, constant) and descending particularities (e.g., race, temperament, native genius or talent), and navigating the world within (or is it against?) the horizons they open. As a whole, then, the essay, moving across demarcated sections, epically images "finding" and "naming." And it does so with the kind of courage aligned with trust, that is, by venturing claims and images, and by maintaining trenchant tensions among them, say between temperament and "the creative power," or between the surfaces that Emerson would skate and the "subterranean and invisible tunnels and channels of life" that force us to dance when they call—"Nature hates calculators; her methods are salutatory and impulsive" (CW3, 32, 39).

I have been working my way through Emerson's suggestion that philosophy runs into poetry, exploring its why and how, and focusing on moments of reception and expression that are part and parcel of the life of thought. More recently, though, I have turned to rhetorical wholes and how they stand as images of thought, particularly in their movements.[24] After recalling Plato, Shakespeare, and Milton and thinking that each proved exceptional through self-trust, Emerson concludes, punning, "Then I dare; I also will essay to be" (CW1, 102–103). Hearing *esse* in "essay," the suggestion is that he will exist in and through his essays. Their activity will be his activity, their navigations of the human condition his own. But given that "essay" connotes venture and experiment, the image on hand is in transition, emerging from a found world and testing its "knowledge of life" against what is found, which exceeds it. Through indirection, Emerson gives us that commitment and its results, performing it, thus imaging it, as a tragedy is the image of an action (or possibly two) according to Aristotle.

—VI. Evasion or Transfiguration? If Emerson is right to think that philosophy runs into poetry, is it also true that Emerson runs from philosophy? In setting Emerson at the birth of what later became pragmatism, Cornel West finds what he terms an "evasion" of philosophy, by which he means Emerson abandons the quest for certainty and the search for foundations (1989, 36). West's view seems right insofar as Emerson, despite his evolving sense of the value of philosophy, never commits to the self-grounding, inferential justifications characteristic of many philosophical projects. We can see this in three ways. "Sensibility is all," he records in *PH*, adding a sentence or so later: "The Conduct of Intellect must respect nothing so much as preserving the sensibility" (TN2, 342). Emerson maintains this commitment because he regards sensibility as a prediscursive apprehension of those harmonies of soul and matter that we noted at the outset. "I define genius," he says, "to be a sensibility to all the impressions of the outerworld,—a sensibility so equal, that it retains accurately all impressions, so that it can truly report them without excess or loss, as it received them" (TN2, 352). In organizing one's thought, therefore, our prime directive is to trust in our reception and then labor to express it appropriately. And in that process, establishing valid or even sound patterns of inference is not essential. "The mind is true," Emerson insists, "though the premises are false, the conclusions are right" (TN3, 254).

Suppose, however, that one's expression meets with resistance from another? Emerson again defers to something like sensibility and what it apprehends. "I will not be chidden out of my most trivial native habit by your dictate, O philosopher, by your preference for somewhat else. If Rhetoric has no charm for you, it has for me" (JMN7, 402). Strikingly, Emerson takes argument to involve an agon of conclusions, a "dictate" from one side, a "native habit" on the other (which I take as a marker of sensibility). And if we try to tie dictates to reasons offered on their behalf, we run into "chidden," which connotes scolding and, intransitively, angry quarreling. This suggests that Emerson does not regard argument as a mode of thinking in its truest form. Rather, it is an assemblage of excuses offered on behalf of real thought, namely concrete, condensed perceptions, which are then essayed in an experimental, figurative manner, say in puns, startling sentences, across and between essays, even in (and as) whole volumes. "The cunning & discoursing of our philosophers is not willful, but an inevitable resort of weakness" (JMN9, 271).

We have already noted Emerson's preference for provocation. And this leads him to favor poetry. Considering the addressee, he finds poetic language more provocative and stimulating, writing, for example: "An image doth wonderfully persuade" (TN1, 157). Emerson also fears, however, that arguments can colonize. The force with which they lead to a conclusion may render the addressee a mere follower. And this is why, at least in part, he stresses the experimental quality of his essays: "But lest I should mislead any when I have my own head, and obey my whims, let me remind the reader that I am only an experimenter. Do not set the least value on what I do, or the least discredit on what I do not, as I pretend to settle anything as true or false. I unsettle all things. No facts are to me sacred; none are profane; I simply experiment, an endless seeker, no Past at my back" (CW2, 188). Yes, "mislead" applies to the determinate results of his essays, for example, the prospects he considers at the close of "Self-Reliance," and no doubt he was gun shy in the wake of his "Divinity School Address" and the ire it provoked. But it also reflects a more general concern. Leading another may mislead him or her away from what is paramount for Emerson, the claim of genius and the tasks of reception and expression that it sets. "Experimenter" proves a powerful term in this context, therefore. It invites corroboration, which embodies the "cardinal virtue of a teacher to protect the pupil from his own influence" (JMN10, 471).[25]

To be sure, Emerson was not uninterested in changing his mind if a better thought or manner appeared. But we need to ask how a better thought demonstrates its superiority, and for Emerson, argument does not win the day. Lecturing in 1848, Emerson asked: "Why should I give up my thought because I cannot answer an objection to it?" His reply is something of maxim. "Consider only whether it remains in my life the same it was" (LL1, 176). In other words, take the thought thereby expressed and let it wander the corridors of one's sensibility and conduct. Does it realign one's outlook or call for a change in manner? Does it evidence that one's conduct bears currents that one finds anathema? If so, adjust, change, and be thankful. "As soon as he sides with his critic," Emerson writes, "against himself, with joy, he is a cultivated man" (CW6, 84). But, he believes, this turn of affairs is mandated at depths that rarely if ever fully appear in chains of inferential reasoning.

Emerson's broad refusal to affirm only what can be vindicated through inferential reasoning (as well as the criterialess self-trust he champions), draws his writings away from much of what philosophers do and have done. But I think that "evasion" overstates how Emerson measures his relation to philosophy. I say this in part because Emerson's "poetry in prose," to return to his letter to Lydian, is philosophically fueled.

Emerson is something of a perspectivalist, though I prefer to think of his view as partialism. For the most part, he thinks that what we know derives from our temperamental fit with nature, which gives us access to some facets while obscuring others. The view is apparent in "The Uses of Great Men." "Each man is by secret liking, connected with district of nature whose agent and interpreter he is, as Linnaeus, of plants; Huber, of bees; . . . Euclid of lines; Newton of fluxions" (CW4, 6). Or, to put the point more generally: "We are tendencies, or rather symptoms, and none of us complete" (CW4, 11). Each take on the world is thus only part of the story, particularly since the comings and goings of our moods, some of which are contradictory, also shade our conceptions. Not that one can know precisely what one does not or cannot know—that would require a self-refuting knowledge of one's ignorance and, more broadly, of each perspective, its roots, and the differences among perspectives—what I would term the view from everywhere. Emerson thus more or less avoids the exaggerated figure of "worldview" and its many heirs, from paradigm to vocabulary. But careful attention to knowing in its occurrence suggests that all accounts are one-sided with regard to the whole of the present and what the future holds. "I cannot tell what I would know; but I have observed there are persons who, in their character and actions, answer questions which I have not the skill to put" (CW4, 5). The point is rather deft, beginning with the confession, in the subjunctive, that he cannot tell what he would know. It isn't just that some people discover particular facts that we do not. Rather, they think in reply to a question we never thought to raise, which indicates that they are more responsive to a whole range of phenomena, not just to particular facets of shared phenomena.

It is worth stressing, however, that Emerson's partialism is not a version of the prison house of consciousness (or language), though such a thought knocks from time to time. Nor is it a full-throttled skepticism, though systematic fluxion means that radical doubt may always seize us, as Cavell rightly insists. Rather, Emerson thinks himself a part that cannot grasp its whole. Having found his finding, and having pushed against its limits, Emerson concludes that he can name the lords of life only as he finds them in his way. But he also insists: "I know better than to claim any completeness for my picture. I am a fragment, and this is a fragment of me" (CW3, 47). Nearing the close of "Experience," Emerson has learned something; he knows better than to lay claim to the whole. This is not a skeptical stance, therefore, though neither is it Socratic ignorance. One something, anything really, can only be a fragment if it is a part of a larger whole, if it too refers to something larger and other than itself, to recall us to the synchronic and diachronic frenzies charted in "The Method of Nature." Emerson thus knows more than the bends where his knowledge collapses. And this is why I favor terming Emerson a partialist—the part-whole logic of his metaphysics informs his epistemology which, in turn, recoils upon his epistemology at a practical level. "I know better that the world I converse with in the city and in the farms, is not the world I think. I observe that difference and shall observe it" (CW3, 48).[26] The difference that Emerson observes, and his decision to attend to that difference, perpetually ("I shall observe" renders something like a promise), recalls me to the differences at play in analogical figuration. And this thickens our feel for Emerson's epistemic praxis. It commits to a recursive movement between the world it finds and the world it thinks, and not just from one vantage point, but from every outlook (every fragment of me) afforded by a philosophy of fluxion navigating the world according to figurative constants. In short, to think oneself a part is to play and yet remain a part, which requires the very fluxions we charted in *Essays: First Series* and "Experience."

There is more to be said on this score, particularly since the world is one of metamorphosis, which renders our partialities increasingly partial. Not only do phenomena evolve, our own essays add complexity to the whole they would navigate. But let us turn instead to a second facet of what we now might term Emerson's philosophical resistance to philosophy. Emerson also holds that the grounds of mind and nature never appear as phenomena of mind and nature, that is, as a thought or a spatiotemporal object. He develops this position, which we have already noted at points, through a protophenomenological inquiry. Anticipating William James (and creatively quoting Heraclitus), he terms the mind a stream whose source is hidden (CW2, 159). And turning to nature with the same figure, he finds a world that "will not stop to be observed. We can never surprise nature in a corner; never find the end of the thread; never tell where to set the first stone" (CW1, 124).

Keeping to the evidence of *Sinn*, the sense from which reflective thought reconstructs its grounds and posits as well as pursues ends, Emerson finds a surfeit of codependent emergences in which "this refers to that, and that to the next, and the next to the third, and everything refers" (CW1, 125). Yes, one might reconstruct the whole from a seamless series of emerging references, but Emerson finds qualitative leaps or ecstasies in metamorphosing nature, phenomena comparable only in imaginative, analogical acts. "What baulks all language is the broad, radiating, immensely distributive action of nature and of mind. If it were linear, it if were successive, step by step, jet by jet, like a small human agency, we could follow with language, but it mocks us by its ubiquity and omnipotence" (LL2, 74). Turning toward our origins, we only find their issue, therefore, and no selfsame current beneath them, at least not one that even approaches the full range of publications that surround us. And looking toward our ends, we only encounter patterns giving way to new patterns. Originary thinking is thus turned away when it pursues those "first questions" we considered a few pages back.

I am not claiming that Emerson's views are correct (though I have tried to present them in a way that shows their force).[27] But I do take them to suggest that Emerson resists philosophy with philosophy even as he remains averse to expressing himself through strictly inferential reasoning. Rather than simply evading it, Emerson thus distances himself from philosophy with help from its own interrogations. As Buell suggests, some of philosophy's characteristic negativity still flows through Emerson's writings (2003, 237). But does this leave Emerson with a studied suspicion of metanarratives and little else, at least insofar as philosophy is concerned?

My resistance to the language of "evasion" has other roots as well. The term suggests Emerson is just changing the subject, to use a phrase associated with Richard Rorty's deflationary stance in epistemology and the philosophy of mind.[28] Instead of philosophy, which he evades, Emerson, at least on this view, turns toward literature or criticism. But this obscures the ways in which philosophy, as we have just seen, is challenged in the course of Emerson's writings. Moreover, it obscures the continuity that Emerson finds between philosophy and the poetry into which it runs, one marked by constants that allow us to navigate the world as we find it in our way. And if we combine that continuity with the challenges posed, something more than a protopostmodernism may be on the move. By pushing philosophy to some of its limits, and by preserving the task of finding orienting idealities in the differential dynamism of natural history, Emerson may push philosophy toward its own metamorphosis. We might even say, his philosophy of fluxion allows fluxions within philosophy itself, and that is a prospect I would not foreclose at the outset.

As we've seen, Emerson conceives of philosophy's interrogative stance (or manner) in terms of questions regarding first and final causes, and he seems to maintain this line of questioning throughout his work, and irrespective of whether he is approaching the soul or matter in its profligacy. But when those questions reach their limit, they, at least in Emerson's hands, abandon the interrogative for the receptive. "My belief in the use of the course on Philosophy," we find in *PH*, "is, that the student who comes to it shall learn to appreciate the Miracle of the Mind; shall learn its subtle but immense power; shall come to know, that, in it, in no tradition, he must find what truth is. . . . When he has once known the oracle, he will need no priest" (TN2, 349–350). I am drawn to this passage because it preserves philosophy's self-possession, its sense of being accountable to itself in its occurrence (say through dialogue, meditation, or critique, whether transcendental, immanent, or genealogical), rather than to ritualistic religion and tradition. But it also converts the potential arrogance of philosophical interrogation—what we earlier saw as philosophy's pride in its inventory— and dilates it even further until it can behold what Emerson terms a "Miracle," namely, the flash of genius, inspiration, and/or insight, which defies rational explanation and sets self-consciousness at the declarative feet of an oracle. And yes, this leads into poetry, the constants of figuration, but it is a poetry that pursues a path cleared in part, even radicalized by philosophy: to name the lords of life as we find them in our way. Philosophical interrogations of origins thus seem to play a constructive, preparatory role in admitted deference to poetry.[29]

You might find this emphasis on reception troubling. Let me amplify the concern before trying to allay it. Reflecting on *Essays: First Series*, specifically its limits, Emerson is fearful that the tree of life held back a "drop or two of sap, and so dwarfed all my florets and drupes" (CEC, 304). But he is not bowed and happily tells Carlyle, "My whole philosophy—which is very real—teaches acquiescence and optimism" (ibid.). And in a journal entry from the same year, 1841, he records: "Acquiescence, patience have a large part to play. The plenty of the poorest place is too great,—the harvest cannot be gathered. The thought that I think excludes me from all other thoughts. Culture is to cherish a great susceptibility, to turn the man into eyes, but as the eye can see only that which is eye-form or of its own state, we tumble on our walls in every part of the universe, & must take such luck as we find, & be thankful. Let us deserve to see" (JMN8, 79). Rather than bemoan the inaccessibility of things in themselves, Emerson labors to be worthy of the part given him to play. This is the mood that avails itself of the low and the common, to recall the "The American Scholar." With nothing mean in nature, each thread is a thicket in the right hands (or before the right eyes, or to the right ears, or beneath the press of the right finger tips).[30] But derived from the Latin *acquiescere*, "to be quiet," acquiescence may indicate a kind of fatalistic quietism. What though of the maxim "let us deserve to see"? Such a charge has no place among those fully committed to *amor fati*. Instead, it suggests that even as we receive what our eye-form provides, even as we embrace our partialities, we must take them and play them, and in a manner that evidences desert.

We have already seen that manner in Emerson's essays. When philosophy is turned away at the origins, it finds itself amid figures and phenomena, their referrals and autosuggestions. But recall that philosophy's interrogations not only concern *whence* but also *whereto*, and that orientation toward final causes persists, if transfigured, when philosophy runs into poetry (or when poetry comes to pass in prose). If we are attentive to what arrives as an oracular miracle, we will find previews (and referrals to what we do not see) and those indications (and what they in turn indicate) will propel our expression. The work of "deserving to see" is thus not merely receptive but also experimental, inhabiting lines of thought in order to express and test where they lead. Philosophy not only prepares the way for the poetry into which it runs, therefore, it also chases after it, conspiringly. The attentive, responsive finding that Emerson valorizes also involves experimental revisions of what we find in our way, say lines from scripture, images from Plato, or the genre of Montaigne and Bacon; also the suggestiveness of "polarity" and of a given one, say friendship and love (or more obliquely, politics and love); and so too a felt unease with domestic servitude or the haunting referrals of products to their scenes of production, say sugar or cotton, which in turn problematizes our senses before such distant presences.[31] Or, more generally, an Emersonian essay follows out the ends toward which our affirmations lead, attentive to the fluxions that greet it along the way, a practice clearly marked in some of his most canonical works, namely, "The American Scholar" and "Self-Reliance," which devote several pages to the prospects awaiting one who will not spend the day in explanation but abandon him- or herself to what a given set of figures enables. In short, in Emerson's hands, philosophical interrogation frees one for poetry by leading one back to originary sites and becomes prospective in the wake of what poetry offers.

These lines of thought, whose birth is tied to philosophy's interrogative stance, seem to call for a kind of inceptual thinking, a phrase that revises a remark made in "Men of Thought," which Emerson delivered in 1848—"The human faculty warrants only inceptions" (LL1, 178). By this I mean less that Emerson recurrently thinks and figures the scene of inception (thought and nature in their originary occurrence), though he does, and often: involuntary perceptions (1840), emanations of emanations (1841), finding oneself on a stair (1844), as the self-evolving power of spirit (1850), as "an affair of race or of meta-chemistry" (1856), even as a riddle (1860): "All is a riddle, and the key to the riddle is another riddle."³² Rather, I have in mind a certain manner of taking thought in its occurrence, whether at the moment of reception or in the course and current of its expression. Such a manner becomes explicit as a goal when Emerson exhorts us again and again to be ready for and equal to inceptions, say by warning us of foolish consistencies or by instructing us to "cherish a great susceptibility." Second, he seems to treat every conception as the inception of another. "I grow, I grow," he hears nature say, and, in his own voice, asserts: "In nature, every moment is new" (CW1, 126; CW2, 189). And reflecting on his own moments of clarity, he writes, "But that characterizes every insight that is vouchsafed me from this realm of thought that it is felt as initial, that it promises a sequel" (JMN8, 237). And finally, in every case, he refuses to allow any conception to have the final say, which leads him to find limits in each of his representative men and to venture maxims that court their own undoing. "Yet within the limits of human education and agency, we may say, great men exist that there may be greater men. The destiny of organized nature is amelioration, and who can tell its limits?" (CW4, 20).

I have briefly sketched the contours of "inceptual thinking"—how it conducts itself, one could say—because it marks a third way in which philosophy, here as a sensibility, appears transfigured by Emerson's writings.³³ And this intensifies my aversion to the thought that Emerson evaded philosophy and changed the subject. Then again, by transformatively conspiring with certain lines of philosophical thought, his writings do change the subject, but in its nominative as opposed to its accusative case. Freed from the compulsory weight of tradition, and abandoned to autofiguration (emergent and sedimented), whoever thinks by way of first and final causes, inventorying his or her condition, runs into and after poetry. And so struck, she or he begins to conspire and experiment, thinking all the way, "What we have, therefore, to say of life, is rather description, or, if you please, celebration, than available rules" (CW6, 131).

—VII. CONVERTING AVERSIONS: Emerson's essay on Plato circulates through most of the concerns that have arisen: "Every man who would do anything well, must come to it from a higher ground; a philosopher must be more than a philosopher. Plato is clothed with the powers of a poet; stands upon the highest place of the power; and, (though I doubt he wanted the decisive gift of lyric expression,) mainly is not a poet, because he chose to use it the poetic gift to an ulterior purpose" (CW4, 25).³⁴ It is this "more" I have been unpacking as well as what happens to philosophy when it welcomes that influx. And, at least with regard to philosophy, it is this more upon which Emerson's case stands (and that it is more, and also, how it is more). With Emerson, philosophy undergoes a metamorphosis in which certain lines of questioning as well as an overall sensibility is transfigured, and precisely through an embrace of figuration, a poetry into which it always seems to run, one it must trust if it is to proceed at all. What follows is writing highly attuned to its own moments of reception and expression and thoroughly responsive to the world that it finds it in its way—a writing that "overlooks no appearance as trifling" (LL1, 90). And while this is a world appearing in and as language, it also appears in and as, among other things, friendships, economic relationships, political institutions, and immensely dense ecohistorical webs of dependency. In the full range of its performances, therefore, which include its commitments, Emerson's writing images the pursuit of self-knowledge oriented toward the good, though neither end escapes the fluxions he embraces.

Emerson does not transfigure other aspects of philosophy, however, in particular its effort to express and test, inferentially, the thoughts upon which other thoughts seem to rest, what we might term its argumentative stance. He prefers provocations, which do not settle with conclusions and thereby leave room for the reader to continue working. He also holds that nonlinear presentations are surpassingly generative, whether through images, puns, concentrated sentences, or rhetorical interplays. On the affirmative side, I recognize the gains afforded such a catholic embrace of rhetorical operations, having tried to show what they bring to Emerson's thought, from orienting figurations to exemplary performances. But I am troubled by Emerson's lack of welcome for philosophy at the end of "Nominalist and Realist." Perhaps his poverty of life and thought is such that no terms of conversation could be found. I have no qualms with either claim, if left in the affirmative. And I take that to be a serious matter, epistemically and practically. Some parts are so clearly not our own that we find ourselves at a loss when pressed to converse with them. And because even the richest life includes a scarcity of time, wasted hours are genuine losses. But given our part is just a part, visitors less than unknown friends will arrive. Not that Emerson simply refuses the philosophers who knock. He wants them to know that he "loved to know that they existed," thus affirming their part in the whole even while preserving the distinctness of his, a gesture that hints at the more than interpersonal love that, he hoped, might inaugurate a different politics.[35] But at least with regard to philosophy's argumentative stance, which, admittedly, risks a day of explanation, I find Emerson's aversion misplaced. Chains of inferences also have a place in the fluxions Emerson would navigate and run into poetry.

Inferential reasoning, by leading a reader toward a conclusion, need not turn him or her into a follower any more than figurative presentations necessarily overwhelm the rational soul by unleashing the affects. Recall the distance immanent to analogies, which call for a thinking fluxion between sign and signified. A different kind of distance opens between speaker and addressee that no speech act can close without erasing what allows a given remark (or thought) to be an address. All modes of speech and writing admit of a reply. Even in the case of appropriately sanctioned imperatives, one can always disobey (or question the authority of the speaker). Moreover, argumentative prose overtly seeks a reply. The conclusion of an argument is accompanied by an implicit question—"Don't you think?" That's what makes it a conclusion and not a simple assertion. It is presented as following from a set of premises, which are as much for the benefit of the addressee as the speaker. They clarify thought for the latter and offer contestable reasons to the former. In short, no one is required to cease thinking once a "therefore" has its day. In a condensed way, my claim is that inferential argument has its own performativity, one that publicizes currents that lead to various affirmations. And while those publications may strike some differently than more indirect provocations, and while both have undercurrents, why categorically embrace one and exclude the other? The answer cannot be that one is performative, the other not.

Emerson's aversion seems all the less welcome when I realize I can approach inferential reasoning with an experimental sensibility, and in two directions. One might ask, reading Rorty: Really, vocabularies are not truth-functional? Yes, I can see that evidence of the usual sort only occurs relative to a vocabulary—facts about persons only arise in an arena of agencies that includes persons, and thus such facts do not prove the reality of persons. But maybe there is evidence of another sort that comes into play when thought entertains the kind of constants that provide vocabularies with their contours? Or, one might be compelled by John Rawls's claim that utilitarianism does not sufficiently appreciate differences among persons. In presuming that all will take the same phenomena to count as pleasures (or as increases in wealth), utilitarianism presumes a univocal subject of valuation, which few after Nietzsche are likely to find plausible, or after Emerson, for that matter: "Society everywhere is in conspiracy against the manhood of every one of its members," and in part because it "is a wave. The wave moves onward, but the water of which it is composed, does not.... Its unity is phenomenal" (CW2, 29, 49). And yet, policy decisions, at least for large populations, seem destined to suffer a similar fate. Everyone will not receive an individuated tax code. In other words, a conclusion can be an inception as well and a line of thought that neither speaker nor the addressee has anticipated.

In a late essay, "Inspiration," Emerson terms conversation the "true school of philosophy" (CW8, 163). He continues, "A wise man goes to this game to play upon others, and to be played upon, and at least as curious to know what can be drawn from himself as what can be drawn from them" (ibid.). And, or so he claims in *Conduct of Life*, conversation moves us in ways that solitary thought cannot (CW6, 144). But exchanging lines of inferential reasoning also has, or can have, this kind of energy. Among well-suited and disposed interlocutors, whether contesting claims or working together, genuine invention can occur. And surprising results can even prove likely when one anticipates objections and pursues examples and counter-examples. Inferential reasoning need not reduce to self-preserving plea-making, therefore. Yes, some only argue to win, but vanity can plague any mode of address when it runs into something other than applause.

I think Emerson remains blithe in his aversion to argument because he never abandons his theodicy. If we return to "The Natural Method of Philosophy," from 1858, and to a line we have partially considered, we find: "The mind is always true. Though the premises are false, the conclusions are right. And the self-reliance which belongs to every healthy human being is proof of it; proof that not he, but the soul of the world is in him; and in proportion as it penetrates his crust of partiality, saith, 'Here I am; here is the whole'" (LL2, 90). Note the leap. In clinging to a belief despite one's lack of justification, one may turn out to have been right. No doubt. But Emerson takes this to also indicate the presence of a theological underwriter, and that is what returns and emboldens him. Later, in "Self-Possession," which is part of the same series, he says: "Whilst he draws on his own, he cannot be overshadowed or supplanted. He may trust the wisdom of the Creator to bring out his virtue" (LL2, 120). Certain that his affirmations are in some way God's way, Emerson can remain unmoved by disagreement or doubts raised in the course of inferential self-scrutiny and dialogue. And he more or less says so in a journal entry from 1840, where he stages a world of differences and disagreements, but with the following in mind: "Go, dear soul, and scales & a sword, an accusation and a terror, a Day of doom & a Future to the world lying in wickedness" (JMN8, 407). What fires that confidence? Emerson invokes a theological virtue, "Height." I term it "theological" because it sets one above the rest, closer to the divine, and because Emerson is quick to cast that elevation in a theodical manner, insisting, "one man or a company of men plastic & permeable to principles, by the law of nature must overpower & ride all cities, nations, kings, rich men, poets, who are not" (ibid.). He thus sees no reason to enter the fray, which he presents as the "fat & easy & conceited world, the cultivated and intellectual world" (ibid.). Instead, the entry records at its close: "Why should I use a means? Why should I not rush grandly to ends?" (ibid.). For myself, lacking all sense that any god is on any side, I wish to preserve, among other bearings, an inferential manner. Finding myself among means to ends I shall never see, and perplexed and vexed by disagreements among the insightful and sincere, I aim to experiment with whatever I find in my way, including ends and inferential argument.

To be clear, my return to inferential reasoning is not intended to contest the kind of metamorphosis that "first questions" undergo in Emerson's writings, as the contentions I just phrased indicate. I believe that thought is perpetually turned away when it recoils upon its origins, and I know, as far as I know anything, that our ends outrun our ability to anticipate the kind of lives we plan to (or actually) conduct. I thus have in mind an inferential reasoning aware of its own limits (and dependencies), which embraces the experimental kind of thinking that Emerson exemplifies and provokes. Take, for example, Nietzsche's occasional forays into swift argumentation. In section 19 of *Beyond Good and Evil*, for example, he claims that "will" "is a unit only as a word," and in less than two pages, offers four reasons on behalf of his insistence, although two are complex and thus invite an even finer accounting (1966, 25–26). Imagining himself willing in the sense of committing to an action, he observes: (1) whether choosing from aversion or attraction, various physiological sensations are operative and prereflective, such as hair bristling in the heat of an enacted desire; (2) such sensations are accompanied by some thought or thoughts, such as "wow, this is amazing," which unfolds in a manner quite different from sensation; (3) an affect also enters the event, say a rush of joy, but also incredulity; and (4) in willing, we both command and obey, and each moment has a different feel to it.

Convinced that thought will never resolve itself into a fully transparent system, one might turn to traditional modes of philosophical argument as *a* way to express (that is, develop, test, even evaluate, i.e., demonstrate, in the sense of show) the thought one finds. Remarking on the brevity of his discussion, Nietzsche writes, "For I approach deep problems like cold baths; quickly into them and quickly out" (1974, 343). Not that his approach is shallow, or so he insists. "That one does not get to the depths that way, not deep enough down, is the superstition of those afraid of the water, the enemies of cold water; they speak without experience" (1974, 343–344). What is it these enemies of the cold miss? The way swift argumentation braces thought, possibly catching another unawares. And the way in which brevity forces one to concentrate the most motivating moments, moments lost when thought takes too scholarly a turn. In other words, brief, concentrated arguments can free one from certain commitments and to emerging thoughts if one keeps to the character of their emergence, which need not be limited to conclusions shorn of premises.

If a conclusion can be unsettling even as it settles, I am unsure that much distinguishes instruction from provocation, at least not if we allow our thought to be transformed when it recounts its alpha and omega. Regarded as a pattern of mind, inferential reasoning, no less than the interplay of "The Poet" and "Experience," exemplifies a manner even as it defends a thesis, that is, direct expression also carries its own indirection. So, even if we agree that the "hint of the dialectic is more valuable than the dialectic," the hint is no less carried by an exuberant execution (JMN9, 214; repeated in *Platonia*: JMN10, 479). Moreover, as we have seen, Emerson's rhetorical ventures are fueled in part by his own terms of instruction, namely the constants that recur and evolve through his essays and lectures alike. Said otherwise, his performances reflect his commitments, and were his commitments otherwise, his performances likely would be as well. And to repeat, arguments, at least among the earnest, can provoke new thoughts and startling changes. In a journal of 1850, Emerson recalls his reading to date and asks, "What does he add? and What is the state of mind he leaves me in?" (JMN11, 273). Fair, powerful questions, but each is as applicable to inferential reasoning as it is to thought that affirmatively runs into poetry.

Among those averse to instruction or doctrine in any form, the following line often comes to mind: "People wish to be settled: only insofar as they are unsettled, is there any hope for them" (CW2, 189). I find "settle" a powerful pun in this context. It connotes stilled fluxion, but also a wish to be led, to be settled by others like land is settled. And unsettling connotes stirring up the latent silt even as it names decolonization and a return to fluxion. But all movement, like abandonment, which is also valorized in "Circles," require a "wherefrom" and a "whereto," and both prepositions are terms of settlement, at least for the time being. "Circles" also declares, "In nature, every moment is new; the past is always swallowed and forgotten; the coming is only sacred" (CW2, 189). The past, the new, what is forgotten, what is arriving, the sacred (and its contrary pole, the profane), each is a term whose settlements (or constancy) make the following sentence possible: "Nothing is secure but life, transition, the energizing spirit" (ibid.). I thus find no contradiction when I also read, "Books are worth reading that settle a principle as lectures are: All others are tickings of clocks & we have so much less to live, the robbers!" (JMN10, 474–475).

NOTES

1. The American Philosophical Association was founded in 1900. Currently, it "promotes the discipline and profession of philosophy, both within the academy and in the public arena. The APA supports the professional development of philosophers at all levels and works to foster greater understanding and appreciation of the value of philosophical inquiry." Taken from the American Philosophical Association's website, http://www.apaonline.org (accessed October 18, 2016).

2. The opening sentence of "Behavior" says much the same, albeit sixteen years later. "The soul which animates Nature is not less significantly published in the figure, movement, and gesture of animated bodies, than in its last vehicle of articulate speech. This silent and subtle language is manners; not *what*, but *how*. Life expresses" (CW6, 89).

3. Strictly speaking, it could be the case that while he can only receive provocation, others can receive instruction. But Emerson takes himself (and charges his readers to themselves) as representative, and thus I take his remark about provocation to apply to all souls.

4. Sometime in the mid-1820s, Emerson copied the following from Peter Bayle, who likened philosophy to a medicine "so very corrosive" that it would eat through wound, flesh, and marrow alike. "Philosophy is proper at first to confute errors, but if she be not stopped there, she attacks truth itself, and when she has her full scope she generally goes so far as that she loses herself & knows not where to stop" (JMN6, 9).

5. This journal entry appears in a revised manner in *Nature*, suggesting that Emerson found it particularly on point (CW1, 35). In an entry from 1839, Emerson is even less charitable to popular religion. Because it postpones the realization of final causes to the afterlife, "popular Christianity is far below in its tone of teaching the poorest moral philosophy that has been originally taught" (JMN7, 182).

6. It is worth noting that this thought was already germinating when Emerson was accusing philosophy of inevitable atheism. "Few things need more philosophy than the study of history" (JMN3, 54).

7. In *PH*, Emerson develops this thought under the heading "Philosophy." "The attraction of the subject for me is, that its grasp is immense. There is nothing that does not belong to it; not a science, not a trade, not a word of man, speech of orator, prayer of priest, witticism at table, but this sets us on the analysis to find wherein the power wisdom worth or fun lies,—no anecdote, no act of earnest or of play" (TN2, 349).

8. Not that proving representative comes easily. "It is a delicate matter—this offering to stand [representative] deputy for the human race, & writing all one's secret history colossally out as philosophy. Very agreeable is it in those who succeed: odious in all others" (JMN7, 387).

9. Read from a disciplinary standpoint, it appears that Emerson takes philosophy, first and foremost, to be metaphysics and/or ontology. Not that Emerson accepts clear distinctions between metaphysics and epistemology, ethics, or even aesthetics. As my opening paragraphs indicated, facts and values blur in Emerson, as do philosophy's cardinal norms, namely, the true, the good, and the beautiful. But that is a matter for another time.

10. I am relying on dates provided by the editors of *The Topical Notebooks of Ralph Waldo Emerson*, namely, Susan Smith, Ron Bosco, and Glen Johnson. In using them, I am also following a path suggested by Bosco and Joel Myerson in their "Series Headnote" to the "Natural Method of Mental Philosophy" lectures (LL2, 46).

11. A journal entry from 1852 underscores the importance that Emerson attributes to analogies. "The great words of the world such as *Analogy*;—what a step when Plato first spoke that word! Analogy is identity of ration, & what civilization, what mounting from savage

beginnings does it not require! the primary & secondary senses, the several planes or platforms on which the same truth is repeated. So the word of ambition, the proud word of modern science is *homology*" (JMN13, 5).

12. If we were to interrogate the cogency of Emerson's "new metaphysics," we would have to explore how well he handles the riddles that accompany any monism. Synchronic and diachronic differentiation is the cardinal issue, but it gives rise to others, for example, growth, freedom, and error. But it is worth noting the ferocity of his commitment.

> 'Tis indifferent whether you say, All is matter, or, All is Spirit, and tis plain, there is a tendency in the times toward an identity philosophy. Once, we were timorous at allowing dignity to matter.... You do not degrade man by saying, Spirit is only finer body; nor exalt him by saying, Matter is phenomenal merely; all rests on the affection of the theorist, on the question of whether his aim is noble. You will observe that it makes no difference herein whether you call yourself materialist or spiritualist. If there be but one substance or reality, and that is body, and it has the quality of creating the sublime astronomy, of converting itself into brain, and geometry, and reason; if it can reason in Newton, and sing in Homer and Shakspeare, and love and serve as saints and angels, then I have no objection to transfer to body all my wonder and allegiance. (LL2, 97–98)

13. The thought that nature is thoroughly temporal recurs in Emerson. A journal entry from December 1823 stresses identity but only because of insistent change: "The world changes its masters, but keeps its own identity" (JMN2, 187). In "The Method of Nature" (1841), the power of change is accentuated, though still relative to a methodical center: "The method of nature: who could ever analyze it? That rushing stream will not stop to be observed.... Its permanence is a perpetual inchoation" (CW1, 124). And then in 1857, the interplay of identity and change become explicit laws of thought: "My philosophy holds to few laws. 1. *Identity*, whence comes the fact that *metaphysical faculties & facts are the transcendence of physical.* 2. Flowing, or transition, or shooting the gulf, the perpetual striving to ascend to a higher platform, the same thing in new & higher forms" (JMN14, 191–192).

14. With a bit more space, I would argue that a similar reliance on constants underwrites the turn to the low and the common that Emerson demands from the American Scholar. Emerson embraces the low because he believes that nothing in nature is mean and a prereflectively operative vitality burns hotter and truer in the common than in the wizened postures of formal intellectual life.

15. Emerson writes, "Prudence does not go behind nature, and ask whence it is," which is precisely what philosophy does (CW2, 133). And because its power lies in an exact literality, it involves a "theme no poet gladly sung," or so the opening verse informs us (CW2, 130).

16. This quarrel carries over into "Experience," which follows "The Poet" in *Essays: Second Series*. "Experience," and its opening question, "where do we find ourselves?," comes to pass after we have presumably drunk the Lethe "that we may tell no tales," thus after the journey recounted in the myth of Er, which more and less closes the *Republic* (10.614–10.621).

17. Apparently, Emerson discussed the matter with Thoreau. Journal Y, filled with entries from 1845 and 1846, states, "H.D.T. says 'that philosophers are broken down poets'; and 'that universal assertions should never allow any remarks of the individual to stand in their neighborhood, for the broadest philosophy is narrower than the worst poetry.' But truly philosophers are *poètes manqués*, or neutral or imperfect poets" (JMN9, 269). The judgment is even harsher in *Letters and Social Aims*: "The critic, the philosopher, is a failed poet" (CW8, 30).

18. According to my reading, quotation is a constant according to Emerson, a term that marks continuity in metamorphosis. "But the inventor only knows how to borrow," he writes, "and society is glad to forget the innumerable laborers who ministered to this architect, and reserve all its gratitude for him. When we are praising Plato it seems we are praising quotations from Solon, and Sophron, and Philolaus. Be it so. Every book is a quotation; and every house is

a quotation out of all forests, and mines, and stone quarries; and every man is a quotation from all his ancestors" (CW4, 24). I explore Emerson's conception of quotation in *Emerson and Self-Culture* (2008, 35–37).

19. In May 1835, Emerson also recorded: "Anschauung. Truth first. Genius seems to consist merely in trueness of sight in using words as show that the man was an eye-witness and not a repeater of what was told. Thus the girl who said 'the earth was a—gee;' Lord Bacon when he speaks of exploding gunpowder as a 'fiery wind blowing with that expansive force, &c'—these are poets. Aristotle" (JMN5, 37).

20. In "A Lyric of Place," Mooney brings patience and passion into what he too regards as a lyric philosophy, though he opts to identify vices that one should shun (e.g., dryness and impatience) rather than virtues to enact. Regardless, the result resonates with what I have found in Emerson, though in the end, my own predilections will have more to say in favor of linear inference than either Mooney or Emerson can muster (Mooney 2009, 31–52).

21. I am not suggesting that Heidegger has Emerson in mind when he introduces the thought of throwness (1962, 174). It is more likely that Heidegger has Rilke in mind, and that he is detheologizing late, uncollected lines that figure human existence as a matter of catching and returning what is thrown our way, lines that Gadamer later uses as an epigraph for *Truth and Method* (Rilke 1996, 138–139; Gadamer 1992, v). But the proximity of their thought (and their difference) is intriguing, and I wanted to show that, in both cases, metaphors pull the chariot. That said, Rilke did read Emerson. He even used a line from "Considerations by the Way" as an epigraph for his book on Rodin (Mason 2011, 37). Interestingly, Baudelaire quotes the same line: "The hero is he who is immovably centered" (Arsic 2010, 78; CW6, 147). And given that figures such as Nietzsche, Musil, and Maeterlinck also read Emerson, we should not forget that Emerson was part and parcel of European letters in the latter half of the nineteenth century and into the twentieth (Thiher 2009, 20; Maeterlinck 1912, 9).

22. The opening line recurs in Emerson reflections on Montaigne: "The philosophy we want is one of fluxions and mobility" (CW4, 91).

23. Joseph Urbas (2013) offers a nuanced reading of "Nominalist and Realist" that counters those interpretations that overemphasize the skeptical, nominalist motifs one also finds in Emerson. As he reads Emerson, the goal is to "embrace both sides of the opposition" between nominalism and realism, and in a way that leads to a synthesis (86). I agree that Emerson wishes to grasp the whole, but that requires philosophy to run into poetry and thus to exceed what can be grasped conceptually, particularly with terms such as "nominalism" and "realism." Second, as I will now suggest, Emerson less wants to synthesize the opposition than to embrace it as an opposition that keeps thought movingly attuned to how the cosmos wheels and deals.

24. Cavell's musical training and ear have given his readings a musical cast, evidenced most directly by the title, *Emerson's Transcendental Etudes* (2003). Given his focus on phrasing, particularly in the sentence, the notion of etudes is particularly apt, as if, with every sentence (perhaps even word by word), Emerson is studying and practicing the art of thought. As a differential complement to that focus, I have been engaging Emerson along more orchestral lines, stressing how larger units of thought work with and through each other to produce a whole larger than the sum of its parts.

25. For a thorough, insightful, and critical discussion of this side of Emerson, see "Emerson as Anti-Mentor" in Lawrence Buell's *Emerson* (2003, 288–334).

26. The epistemic bearing condensed in these startling sentences is expanded at length and amended in part in chapter 5 of my *Emerson and Self-Culture*, "On the Edges of Our Souls" (2008, 119–140).

27. My own account of where originary thinking issues can be found in *You Must Change Your Life: Poetry, Philosophy, and the Birth of Sense* (2002).

28. Rorty's position evolves over three key texts: *Philosophy and the Mirror of Nature* (1979), *The Consequences of Pragmatism* (1982), and *Contingency, Irony, and Solidarity* (1989). Using language we found in Emerson, Rorty's position is that a set of constants is not truth-functional and thus favoring one or another is more a matter of changing the subject than of demonstrating on the basis of reasons the superiority of either.

29. One can almost see this transformation at play in a journal entry from 1845. Writing of the scholar, Emerson asks, "Can he uncover the living ligaments, concealed from all but poets, which attach the dull men & things we converse with, to the splendor of the First Cause?" (JMN9, 187).

30. Emerson's use and delimitation of philosophy is both Kantian and not Kantian. On the one hand, Emerson, like Kant, follows out philosophy's pursuit of the unconditioned, a pursuit he too finds inevitable (TN2, 370). And like Kant, he believes theoretical reason (or what Emerson contracts into the "understanding") will never find its prey (TN1, 183). But Emerson does not then draw a line that we cannot cross in our efforts to fathom nature's sublime mechanics. Rather, Emerson returns philosophy to its praxical bearings and readies it to rework the world that it finds in its way, ever poised for a bolder generalization. This undoes, however, any categorical distinction between theoretical and practical reason. Moreover, given the prevalence of poetry in this emergent activity, the true, the good, and the beautiful enter into a kind of a proximity that normally eludes the critical self-regard of modernity.

31. As my examples suggest—each from Emerson's own inheritances—rethinking the thought of final causes can reorient us historically as well; that is, the future that such work anticipates may concern a past one thought one knew. "Every new thought modifies, interprets old problems," Emerson writes in "Men of Thought." "What is written in invisible ink the fire of thought will bring out and explain. The retrospective value of new thought is immense" (LL2, 78).

32. Each of these scenes is taken from a major essay and/or volume: "Self-Reliance," "The Method of Nature," "Experience," "Plato, or the Philosopher," "Literature," and Illusions," with the quoted texts coming from "Literature" and "Illusions" (CW5, 134–135; CW6, 167).

33. This is the Emerson that Cavell has found and championed. (I think it is also the writer that Lukács aimed to be in *Soul and Form* and that Benjamin was in *One Way Street* [Lukács 2010; Benjamin 1996].) Taking what we too often flatly term "style," Cavell casts Emerson's prose as a deliberate way to inhabit ordinary language, one executed word by word. As Emerson notes in blotting book III: "To the same purpose I find at this date in Guesses at Truth—'In good prose (says Schlegel) every word should be underlined.' 'no italics in Plato.'—In good writing every word means something" (JMN3, 271). Cavell presents an Emerson for whom giving an account of oneself is both exquisitely self-involved, perfectionist even, and deeply responsive to the sense of others, without whom the project would be meaningless. Plainly, I take such accounting to be only part of the drama, but it is a crucial part.

34. The line first appears in journal Y: "Every man who would do anything well, must come to it from a higher ground, and a philosopher must be more than a philosopher. Plato is a poet" (JMN9, 304). Emerson finds Plato an enduring icon because his dialogues remain attentive to either side of the divided line, and so they have fluxion, even the lime that Emerson thought philosophy lacked. Plato is thus the exemplar of a style that "at once decides the high quality of the man. It flows like the river Amazon. . . . No sand without lime, no short, chippy, indigent epigrammatist or proverbialist with docked sentences but an exhaustless affluence" (JMN8, 290). That said, for Emerson, images are insurmountable. "I had rather

have a good symbol of my thought, or a good analogy than the suffrage of Kant or Plato" (JMN10, 307).

35. Earlier in *Essays: Second Series*, in "Politics," Emerson writes, "What is strange too, there never was in any man sufficient faith in the power of rectitude, to inspire him with the broad design of renovating the State on the principle of right and love" (CW3, 128).

ABBREVIATIONS FOR EMERSON'S WORKS

CE1–12   *The Complete Works of Ralph Waldo Emerson.* Edited by Edward Waldo Emerson. Centenary edition. 12 vols. Boston: Houghton Mifflin, 1903–1904.
CEC   *The Correspondence of Emerson and Carlyle.* Edited by Joseph Slater. New York: Columbia University Press, 1964.
CL1–10   *The Letters of Ralph Waldo Emerson.* Edited by Ralph L. Rusk et al. 10 vols. New York: Columbia University Press, 1939–1995.
CS1–4   *Complete Sermons of Ralph Waldo Emerson.* Edited by Albert J. von Frank et al. 4 vols. Columbia: University of Missouri Press, 1989–1992.
CW1–10   *The Collected Works of Ralph Waldo Emerson.* Edited by Robert E. Spiller et al. 6 vols. to date. Cambridge: Harvard University Press, 1971–2013.
EAW   *Emerson's Antislavery Writings.* Edited by Len Gougeon et al. New Haven: Yale University Press, 1995.
EL1–3   *The Early Lectures of Ralph Waldo Emerson.* Edited by Stephen E. Whicher et al. Cambridge: Harvard University Press, 1959–1972.
JMN1–16   *The Journals and Miscellaneous Notebooks of Ralph Waldo Emerson.* Edited by William H. Gillman et al. Cambridge: Harvard University Press, 1960–1982.
LL1–2   *The Later Lectures of Ralph Waldo Emerson.* Edited by Don Bosco et al. 2 vols. Athens: University of Georgia Press, 2001.
MMF1–2   *The Memoirs of Margaret Fuller Ossoli.* Edited by Ralph Waldo Emerson, James Freeman Clarke, and W. H. Channing. Boston: Phillips, Sampson, 1852.
P   *Parnassus.* Edited by Ralph Waldo Emerson. Boston: James R. Osgood and Company, 1875.

PN	*The Poetry Notebooks of Ralph Waldo Emerson.* Edited by Ralph H. Orth et al. Columbia: University of Missouri Press, 1986
TN1–3	*The Topical Notebooks of Ralph Waldo Emerson.* Edited by Ralph Orth et al. 3 vols. Columbia: University of Missouri Press, 1990–1994.
UL	*The Uncollected Lectures.* Edited by Clarence Gohdes. New York: William Edwin Rudge, 1932.

BIBLIOGRAPHY

Addams, Jane. 1964. *Democracy and Social Ethics*. Edited by Anne Firor Scott. Cambridge, MA: Harvard University Press.
Adorno, Theodor W. 1974. *Minima Moralia: Reflections on a Damaged Life*. London: New Left Books.
Albrecht, James. 2012. *Reconstructing Individualism: A Pragmatic Tradition from Emerson to Ellison*. New York: Fordham University Press.
Amnesty International. "US Military Aid to Colombia." https://www.amnestyusa.org/our-work/countries/americas/colombia/us-policy-in-colombia (accessed 10/19/2016).
Anderson, Douglas. 2006. *Philosophy Americana*. New York: Fordham University Press.
Aristotle. 2002. *Nicomachean Ethics*. Translated by Joe Sachs. Newburyport, MA: Focus.
Arsic, Branka. 2010. *On Leaving: A Reading in Emerson*. Cambridge, MA: Harvard University Press.
Ashbery, John. 1991. *Flow Chart*. New York: Knopf.
———. 2008. *Collected Poems 1956–1987*. New York: The Library of America.
Badiou, Alain. 2001. *Ethics: An Essay on the Understanding of Evil*. London: Verso.
———. 2002. "On the Truth Process." http://www.egs.edu/faculty/alain-badiou/articles/on-the-truth-process/.
———. 2007. *The Concept of the Model: An Introduction to the Materialist Epistemology of Mathematics*. Translated by Zachary Luke Fraser and Tzuchien Tho. Melbourne: re.press.
Baudrillard, Jean. 1988. *America*. London: Verso.
Benjamin, Walter. 1996. *Selected Writings: Volume 1: 1913–1926*. Edited by Marcus Bullock and Michael W. Jennings. Cambridge, MA: Harvard University Press.
———. 2003. *Selected Writings: Volume 4: 1938–1940*. Edited by Howard Eiland and Michael W. Jennings. Cambridge, MA: Harvard University Press.
Benoit, Ray. 1963. "Emerson on Plato: The Fire's Center." *American Literature* 34, no. 4: 487–498.
Buell, Lawrence. 1993. *Ralph Waldo Emerson: A Collection of Critical Essays*. Englewood Cliffs, NJ: Prentice-Hall.
———. 2003. *Emerson*. Cambridge, MA: Harvard University Press.
Cadava, Eduardo. 2010. "The Guano of History." In *Emerson for the Twenty-First Century*. Edited by Barry Tharaud. Newark: University of Delaware Press.

Cavell, Stanley. 1988. *In Quest of the Ordinary: Lines of Skepticism and Romanticism.* Chicago: University of Chicago Press.

———. 1989. *The New yet Unapproachable America: Lectures after Emerson after Wittgenstein.* Chicago: University of Chicago Press.

———. 1990. *Conditions Handsome and Unhandsome.* Chicago: University of Chicago Press.

———. 1995. *Philosophical Passages: Wittgenstein, Emerson, Austin, Derrida.* Cambridge, MA: Blackwell.

———. 2003. *Emerson's Transcendental Etudes.* Stanford, CA: Stanford University Press.

Celan, Paul. *Breathturn.* Translated by Pierre Joris. Los Angeles: Sun and Moon Press.

Chamberlain, Charles. 1984. "The Meaning of *Prohairesis* in Aristotle's Ethics." *Transactions of the American Philological Association* 114: 147–157.

Colvin, Sidney, ed. 1825. *Letters of John Keats to His Family and Friends.* London: Macmillan.

Cornell, Drucila, Michel Rosenfeld, and David Gray Carlso, eds. 1992. *Deconstruction and the Possibility of Justice.* New York: Routledge.

Damasio. Antonio. 1999. *The Feeling of What Happens: Body and Emotion in the Making of Consciousness.* Orlando: Harcourt Publishers.

de Beauvoir, Simone. 1976. *Ethics of Ambiguity.* Translated by Bernard Frechtman. New York: Citadel Press.

———. 2011. *The Second Sex.* Translated by Constance Borde. New York: Vintage Press.

Deming, Richard. 2007. *Listening on All Sides: Toward an Emersonian Ethics of Reading.* Stanford, CA: Stanford University Press.

Dennett, Daniel. 1995. *Darwin's Dangerous Idea: Evolution and the Meanings of Life.* New York: Simon and Schuster.

Descartes, René. 1984. *The Philosophical Writings of René Descartes.* Translated by John Cottingham. Vol. 2. Cambridge: Cambridge University Press.

Dewey, John. 1972. *The Early Works, 1882–1898.* Edited by Jo Ann Boydston. Carbondale: Southern Illinois University Press.

———. 1981. *The Later Works 1925–1953.* Edited by Jo Ann Boydston. Carbondale: Southern Illinois University Press.

———. 1983. *The Middle Works: 1899–1924.* Edited by Jo Ann Boydston. Carbondale: Southern Illinois University Press.

———.1989. *The Later Works 1942–1948.* Edited by Jo Ann Boydston. Carbondale: Southern Illinois University Press.

Du Bois, W. E. B. 2007. *The Oxford W.E.B. Du Bois: The Souls of Black Folk.* Oxford: Oxford University Press.

Edelman, Gerald. 2005. *Wider than the Sky: The Phenomenal Gift of Consciousness.* New Haven, CT: Yale University Press.

Flanagan, Owen. 2007. *The Really Hard Problem: Meaning in a Material World.* Cambridge, MA: MIT University Press.

Foucault, Michel. 1978. *The History of Sexuality.* Translated by Robert Hurley. New York: Random House.

———. 1997. *Ethics: Subjectivity and Truth.* Vol. 1 of *The Essential Works of Michel Foucault.* Edited by Paul Rainbow. New York: New Press.

———.2000. *Power.* Vol. 3 of *The Essential Works of Michel Foucault.* New York: New Press.

Fowler, Alistair, ed. 1991. *The New Oxford Book of Seventeenth Century Verse.* Oxford: Oxford University Press.

Gadamer, Hans-Georg. 1992. *Truth and Method.* New York: Crossroad Publishing Company.

Gill, Lesley. 2007. "Right There with You: Coca-Cola, Labor Restructuring and Political Violence in Colombia." *Critique of Anthropology* 27, no. 3: 235–260.

Gohdes, Clarence. 1932. *Uncollected Letters by Ralph Waldo Emerson*. New York: William Edwin Rudge.
Goldman, Anita. 1994. "Negotiating Claims of Race and Rights: Du Bois, Emerson, and the Critique of Liberal Nationalism." *Massachusetts Review* 35, no. 2. (Summer): 169–201
Gómez-Peña, Guillermo. 1996. *The New World Border: Prophecies, Poems, and Loqueras for the End of the Century*. San Francisco: City Lights.
Goodman, Russell. 1990. *American Philosophy and the Romantic Tradition*. New York: Cambridge University Press.
———. 2015. *American Philosophy before Pragmatism*. Oxford: Oxford University Press.
Gougeon, Len. 2014. "Race." In *Ralph Waldo Emerson in Context*. Edited by Wesley T. Mott. Cambridge: Cambridge University Press.
Green, Andy. 2015. "Tom Petty on Past Confederate Flag Use: 'It Was Downright Stupid.'" *Rolling Stone*. July 14. http://www.rollingstone.com/music/news/tom-petty-on-past-confederate-flag-use-it-was-downright-stupid-20150714.
Grimmett, Richard F. year. "Instances of Use of United State Armed Forces Abroad, 1798–2004." Congressional Research Service Report RL30172. http://www.au.af.mil/au/awc/awcgate/crs/r130172.htm (accessed October 5, 2004).
Habermas, Jurgen. 1983. *Moral Consciousness and Communicative Action*. Translated by Christian Lenhardt and Shierry Weber Nicholsen. Cambridge, MA: MIT University Press.
———. 1985. *Theory of Communicative Action*. Translated by Thomas McCarthy. Boston: Beacon Press.
———. 1993. *Justification and Application: Remarks on Discourse Ethics*. Cambridge, MA: MIT University Press.
Haddock Seigfried, Charlene. 1988. "Advancing American Philosophy." *Transactions of the Charles S. Pierce Society* 34, no. 4: 807–839.
Haidt, Jonathan and Bjorklund, Fredrik. 2008. "Social Intuitionists Answer Six Questions About Morality." *Moral Psychology*. Edited Walter Sinnott-Armstrong. Cambridge: MIT University Press. 181–217.
Hardt, Michael, and Antonio Negri. 2000. *Empire*. Cambridge, MA: Harvard University Press.
Hass, Robert. 1989. *Human Wishes*. New York: Ecco Press.
Hegel, G. W. F. 1977. *The Phenomenology of Spirit*. Foreword by J. N. Findlay. Translated by A. V. Miller. New York: Oxford University Press.
———. 1990. *Lectures on the History of Philosophy*. Edited by Robert F. Brown. Berkeley: University of California Press.
———. 1991. *Philosophy of Right*. Translated by H. B. Nisbet. Edited by Allen W. Wood. Cambridge: Cambridge University Press.
Heidegger, Martin. 1962. *Being and Time*. Translated by John Macquarrie and Edward Robinson. New York: Harper Perennial.
Hobsbawm, Eric. 1989. *Politics for a Rational Left: Political Writing, 1977–1988*. New York: Verso.
Hume, David. 1964. *A Treatise of Human Nature*. London: Oxford University Press.
James, William. 1983. *The Principles of Psychology*. Cambridge, MA: Harvard University Press.
Johnson, Denis. 1982. *The Incognito Lounge*. New York: Random House.
Kant, Immanuel. 1999. *Practical Philosophy*. Edited by Mary Gregor. Cambridge: Cambridge University Press.
Kirkby Times. 2003. "Coca Cola—The Real Thing?" July 22. http://www.kirkbytimes.co.uk/news_items/2003_news/boycott_coca_cola.html.
Kovalainen, Heikki. 2010. *Self as World: The New Emerson*. Tampere, Finland: Tampere University Press.

Levinas, Emmanuel. 1969. *Totality and Infinity*. Translated by Aphonso Lingis. Pittsburgh: Duquesne University Press.

———. 1985. *Ethics and Infinity Conversations with Phillipe Nemo*. Translated by Richard A. Cohen. Pittsburgh, PA: Duquesne University Press.

———. 1998. *Otherwise than Being: Or beyond Essence*. Translated by Alphonso Lingis. Pittsburgh, PA: Duquesne University Press.

Levine, Alan. 2011. "Skeptical Triangle? A Comparison of the Political Thought of Emerson, Nietzsche, and Montaigne." In *A Political Companion to Ralph Waldo Emerson*, edited by Alan Levine and Daniel Malachuck, 223–264. Lexington: University of Kentucky Press.

Livingston, Paul. 2011. *The Politics of Logic: Badiou, Wittgenstein, and the Consequences of Fatalism*. London: Routledge.

Lopez. Michael, ed. 1997. "Emerson and Nietzsche." *ESQ: A Journal of the American Renaissance*. 43, no. 1–4.

Lukács, György. 2010. *Soul and Form*. New York: Columbia University Press.

Lysaker, John. 1999a. "Lenin, Nancy, and the Politics of Total War." *Philosophy Today* 43, no. 4: 186–195.

———. 1999b. "On What Is to Be Done with What Is Always Already Arriving." *Studies in Practical Philosophy* 1, no. 1: 86–113.

———. 2002. *You Must Change Your Life*. University Park, PA: Penn State Press.

———. 2004. "Taking Emerson Personally." *Georgia Review* 58, no. 4: 832–850.

———. 2006. "I Am Not What I Seem to Be." *International Journal for Dialogical Science* 1, no. 1: 41–45.

———. 2007. "Extoling Art in an Intolerable World." *Journal of Speculative Philosophy* 21, no. 1: 44–60.

———. 2008. *Emerson and Self-Culture*. Bloomington: Indiana University Press.

Lysaker, John, and Paul Lysaker. 2005. "Being Interrupted: The Self and Schizophrenia." *Journal of Speculative Philosophy* 19, no. 1: 1–40.

———. 2008. *Schizophrenia and the Fate of the Self*. Oxford: Oxford University Press.

———. 2016. "Metacognition and the Prospect of Enhancing Self-management in Schizophrenia Spectrum Disorders." *Philosophy, Psychiatry, & Psychology*, in press.

Lysaker, John, Jason K. Johannesen, and Paul Lysaker. 2006. "Schizophrenia and the Experience of Intersubjectivity as Threat." *Phenomenology and the Cognitive Sciences* 4, no. 3: 335–352.

Maeternlinck, Maurice. 1912. *On Emerson, and Other Essays*. Translated by M. J. Moses. New York: Dodd, Mead.

Mason, Eudo C. 2011. *Rilke, Europe, and the English-Speaking World*. Cambridge: Cambridge University Press.

McDermott, John Joseph. 1986. *Streams of Experience*. Amherst: University of Massachusetts Press.

———. 2007. *The Drama of Possibility: Experience as Philosophy of Culture*. Edited by Douglas R. Anderson. New York: Fordham University Press.

McKenna, Erin, and Pratt, Scott. 2015. *American Philosophy: From Wounded Knee to the Present*. London: Bloomsbury.

Mikics, David. 2003. *The Romance of Individualism in Emerson and Nietzsche*. Athens: Ohio University Press.

Mooney, Edward. 2009. *Lost Intimacy in American Thought: Recovering Personal Philosophy from Thoreau to Cavell*. New York: Continuum.

Morris, Tom. 1997. *If Aristotle Ran General Motors*. New York: Henry Holt.

Neisser, Ulrich. 1988. "Five Kinds of Self-Knowledge." *Philosophical Psychology* 1, no. 1: 35–59.

Nicoloff, Philip. 1961. *Emerson on Race and History.* New York: Columbia University Press.
Nietzsche, Friedrich. 1966. *Beyond Good and Evil.* New York: Random House.
———. 1974. *The Gay Science.* New York: Random House.
Packer, Barbara, ed. 1982. *Emerson's Fall: A New Interpretation of the Major Essays.* New York: Continuum.
Patterson, Orlando. 1982. *Slavery and Social Death.* Cambridge, MA: Harvard University Press.
Paul, Ari. 2005. "Colombia's Agony, Coca-Cola's Responsibility, and America's Solidarity." August 31. https://www.opendemocracy.net/democracy-protest/colombia_2790.jsp.
Pinsky, Robert. 1990. *The Want Bone.* New York: Farrar, Straus and Giroux.
Reagan, Tom. 1985. *The Case for Animal Rights.* New York: Blackwell Publishing.
Riepe, Dale. 1967. "Emerson and Indian Philosophy." *Journal of the History of Ideas* 28, no. 1: 115–122.
Rilke, Ranier Maria. 1955. *Sämtliche Werke 2.* Frankfurt am Main, Germany: Insel Verlag.
———. 1996. *Uncollected Poems: Bilingual Edition.* Translated by Edward Snow. New York: North Point Press, Farrar, Strauss, and Giroux.
Rorty, Richard. 1979. *Philosophy and the Mirror of Nature.* Princeton, NJ: Princeton University Press.
———. 1982. *The Consequences of Pragmatism.* Minneapolis: University of Minnesota Press.
———. 1989. *Contingency, Irony, and Solidarity.* Cambridge: Cambridge University Press.
Rossi, William. 2000. "Emerson, Nature, and Natural Science." In *A Historical Guide to Ralph Waldo Emerson,* edited by Joel Myerson, 101–150. Oxford: Oxford University Press.
Saito, Naoko. 2005. *The Gleam of Light: Moral Perfectionism and Education in Dewey and Emerson.* New York: Fordham University Press. 2005
Salter, Chuck. 2005. "Job Title of the Future: Corporate Ethicist." *Fast Times.* December 1. http://www.fastcompany.com/blog/chuck_salter/dash-salt/job-title-future-corporate-ethicist.
Scott, Charles. 1990. *The Question of Ethics: Nietzsche, Foucault, Heidegger.* Bloomington: Indiana University Press.
———. 2002. *The Lives of Things.* Bloomington: Indiana University Press.
———. 2007. *Living with Indifference.* Bloomington: Indiana University Press.
Shah, Anup. 2014. "Foreign Aid Development Assistance." *Global Issues.* Modified September 28. http://www.globalissues.org/article/35/foreign-aid-development-asssistance.
Singer, Peter. 2002. *Animal Liberation.* New York: Harper Collins.
Slaughter, Mathew J. n.d. "How U.S. Multinational Companies Strengthen the U.S. Economy." Business Council and United States Council for International Business. 2010. http://www.uscib.org/docs/foundation_multinationals_update.pdf.
Smith, John. 1992. *America's Philosophical Vision.* Chicago: University of Chicago Press.
Strawson, Galen. 2004. "Against Narrativity." *Ratio* 17, no 4.: 428–452.
Stuhr, John. 1998. "Sidetracking American Philosophy." *Transactions* 34, no. 4: 841–860.
———. 2003. *Pragmatism, Postmodernism, and the Future of Philosophy.* New York: Routledge.
Taylor, Charles. 1989. *Sources of the Self: The Making of Modern Identity.* New York: Cambridge University Press.
Taylor, Paul C. 2013. *Race: A Philosophical Introduction.* Malden, MA: Polity.
Thiher, Allen. 2009. *Understanding Robert Musil.* Columbia: University of South Carolina Press.
Thoreau, Henry David. 1971. *The Writings of Henry David Thoreau: Walden.* Edited by J. Lyndon Shanley. Princeton, NJ: Princeton University Press.
Urbas, Joseph. 2013. "Bi-Polar Emerson: Nominalist and Realist." *Pluralist* 8, no. 2 (Summer): 78–105.

U.S. Department of Defense. n.d. "DoD Personnel, Workforce Reports & Publications." https://www.dmdc.osd.mil/appj/dwp/dwp_reports.jsp (accessed July 15, 2015).
Van Cromphout, Gustaaf. 1999. *Emerson's Ethics*. Columbia: University of Missouri Press.
Van Leer, David. 1986. *Emerson's Epistemology*. New York: Cambridge University Press.
Walls, Laura Dassow. 2003. *Emerson's Life in Science: The Culture of Truth*. Ithaca, NY: Cornell University Press.
West, Cornel. 1989. *American Evasion of Philosophy*. Madison: University of Wisconsin Press.
———. 1993. *Race Matters*. Boston: Beacon Press.
West, Cornel, and Christa Buschendorf. 2014. *Black Prophetic Fire*. Boston: Beacon Press.
Whitman, Walt. 1982. *Poetry and Prose*. New York: Literary Classics of the United States.
Wright, Charles. 1998. *Appalachia*. New York: Farrar, Straus, and Giroux.
Zahavi, Dan. 2000. *Exploring the Self*. Amsterdam: John Benjamin's Publishing Company.
———. 2005. *Subjectivity and Selfhood*. Cambridge, MA: MIT University Press.

INDEX

Addams, Jane, 53
"An Address on the Emancipation of the Negroes in the British West Indies," 91–93, 101
Adorno, Theodor, 15–16
America, 40–44, 47–48, 58n7, 60n25; as empire, 48–51, 58n13
"American Civilization," 108n9
"The American Scholar," 54, 94
"Anniversary of the West Indian Emancipation," 92
Aristotle, 112, 116, 123, 126, 129n4
"Art," 22–23, 39n14
asceticism, 8–9, 130n19
Ashbery, John, 26–27

Badiou, Alain, 121–123
"Behavior," 2, 167n2
Benjamin, Walter, 44
Buell, Lawrence, 35, 38n4, 108n11, 169n25

Cavell, Stanley, 5, 169n24, 170n33; on "Fate," 94–95, 107n5, 107–108n7; on metaethics, 113; on Emerson and Wittgenstein, 33–34
Celan, Paul, 3–4
"Circles," 7, 26, 31, 38n5, 106, 166
Conduct of Life, 3–4
"Culture," 28–29, 155

Damasio, Antonio, 75–76
Derrida, Jacques, 118–119
Descartes, René, 40, 57n1
Dewey, John, 46–47, 55, 124, 129n2, 131n24
dialogical self-theory, 82–83
DiMaggio, Giancarlo, 43, 86n4
"The Divinity School Address," 136
Du Bois, W.E.B., 53, 108n14

Emerson, Ralph Waldo: affirmative task of philosophy, 136–139; Emerson as poet, 134–136; of Fugitive Slave Law, 94; genius, 96, 169n19; Hafiz, 28; history, 141; inferential reasoning and philosophy, 162–165; language, 91–92; language in poetry, 24, 27; metamorphosis, 141, 168n18; mysticism, 147–148; nature, 22–26, 137–141, 168n13; philosophy, 159–161, 167n9, 170n30; philosophy of fluxuation, 149–153; Plato, 24, 29–30, 170–171n34; poetry, 20–25, 27, 38n3; poetry as a science, 29–31; poets, 26–31; prudence, 142–143; quotation, 63–64, 144, 168n18; race, 88–90, 104–107, 108n13; race and the philosophy of history, 90–92, 98–104; race as temperament, 89, 94–98, 100; skepticism, 136–137; slavery, 91–95, 99–100; temperament, 38n2 (*see also* "Race"); thought, 138–139, 14; transfiguration of philosophy, 154–162
empire, 48–51, 52–53, 58n13
English Traits, 144
Essays: First Series, 139, 142, 152–153, 159
Essays: Second Series, 139, 152
ethics, 110–111, 129–130n14, 129n8; forms of life and, 115–116; metaethics, 112–115; as praxis, 111–114, 130n21; third person inquiries and, 123–127
ethos, 11–12, 117–118
"Experience," 4, 12, 20, 22, 27–28, 66, 60n24, 79, 96, 104–105, 153, 156–157, 168n16

"Fate," 94–96, 98–99, 103–104, 107n6
Foucault, Michael, 41–43, 124

the good life, 111–112, 114–115
Gougeon, Len, 107n4, 108n13

181

Habermas, Jürgen, 113, 130n21
Hass, Robert, 62–63
Hegel, G.W.F., 57n1, 114–115, 127–128, 129n11, 145
Heidegger, Martin, 132, 146–147, 169n21; *Being and Time*, 3, 17, 68–69, 147
Heraclitus, 23
Hermans, Hubert, 86n4
"Heroism," 151
history, 73, 114–115, 141–142. *See also* Ralph Waldo Emerson
"History," 141–142
Hume, David, 66–67, 126

"Inspiration," 164
"Intellect," 135

Johnson, Denis, 13–17
Johnson, Mark, xiii, 86n4

Kant, Immanuel, 8–9, 41–43, 170n30

Letters and Social Aims, 168n17
Levinas, Emmanuel, 119–121, 130n17–19
Lysaker, Paul, xii, 86n4, 86n7

"Manners," 135
McKenna, Erin, 59n20
"Men of Thought," 160, 170n31
metaphysics, 38n4, 96–97, 141–145, 168n12
"The Method of Nature," 22, 168n12
"Montaigne," 169n22
moral, 13–14; non-moral, 14–17

naturalism, 6, 69–72
Natural Method of Mental Philosophy, 138–141, 164–165, 168n12
nature, 137–138
"Nature," 137, 143–144, 147–148
Nietzsche, Friedrich, 63–66
"Nominalist and Realist," 31, 134, 150
normativity, 117–118

"The Oversoul," 66, 145

Parnassus, 27
"Persian Poetry," 28
phenomenology, 83–84; of ethical life, 110–111, 114–115

philosophy, 2–3, 44–46, 132; American, 51–55, 57n2, 60n2; and poetic expression, 145–149
Pinsky, Robert, 24–28
"The Poet," 20–21, 23–24, 26–35, 38n3, 39n13, 88, 143–144, 145, 149
poetry, 35–37, 143–149, 153–156. *See also* Ralph Waldo Emerson
"Poetry and English Poetry," 3, 38n6, 39n13
"Poetry and Imagination," 29, 37n1, 38n12, 39n12
"Politics," 107n3, 171n35
Pratt, Scott, 59–60n20
praxis, 46–47; ethical, 111–112, 123–128, 130n21
"Prudence," 142–143, 168n15

"Quotation and Originality," 63

"Race," 89–98, 107n6
racialism, Emerson's, 100–104
Representative Men, 138, 161, 107n3, 168n18
Rilke, Rainer Maria, 15, 169n21
Rorty, Richard, 31–33, 44–45, 170n28

Scott, Charles, 8–12
self, 1–2, 7–8; as multiplicity, 61–66; philosophical psychology and, 68–72, 82–85
self-culture, 91–93
self-experience, 66–68, 77–82; positionality of, 72–76; purposiveness of, 74–78
"Self-Possession," 164
"Self-Reliance," 5–6, 151, 163, 86n2
"The Senses of the Soul," 148
Society and Solitude, 27
subjectivity, 69–72

Taylor, Charles, 6–8, 13
theodicy, 102, 164–165
Thoreau, Henry David, 18, 63, 89, 168n17
throwness, 68–69, 169n21

"Uses of Great Men," 156, 161

West, Cornel, 55, 88–89, 104, 154
Whitman, Walt, 28–29
Wittgenstein, Ludwig, 34, 132
Wright, Charles, 35–37
writing, 92–93, 155, 162, 170n33

Zahavi, Don, 83–84

JOHN T. LYSAKER is Professor of Philosophy at Emory University. He is author of *Emerson and Self-Culture* (IUP).

www.ingramcontent.com/pod-product-compliance
Lightning Source LLC
Chambersburg PA
CBHW021734220426
43662CB00008B/854